LYRIC AND

DRAMATIC POEMS

LYRIC AND DRAMATIC POEMS

OF JOHN G. NEIHARDT

UNIVERSITY OF NEBRASKA PRESS · LINCOLN

Prefatory Note to the Bison Book Edition

The present collection brings together most of my lyric poetry that appeared originally in three separate volumes (*A Bundle of Myrrh, Man Song, The Stranger at the Gate*), and two dramatic poems (*Eight Hundred Rubles, Agrippina*), formerly published together under the title *Two Mothers.*

All of these poems were written before 1912, when, at the age of thirty-one, I began work on my *Cycle of the West.*

Any reader who may take a serious interest in this collection should note that the three volumes of lyrics chronologically presented here constitute what may be called a spiritually progressive sequence, beginning with the experiences of groping youth and rising to the self-fulfillment of parenthood. When the poems were being written, there was, of course, no thought of such a sequence—only of the precious, passionate stuff of life as it was being lived. The progression was in the living.

In addition to the foregoing, there are miscellaneous poems that carry the spiritual progression onward to the loss of the sense of self in cosmic awareness.

It should be observed that the two poems of social revolt, "The Red Wind Comes" and "Cry of the People," were written and published some years before the Russian Revolution and are not, therefore, to be regarded as expressions of contemporary opinion. They expressed a young poet's response to the social injustice of his time, when a good man would work a hard, ten-hour day for a dollar or less, if he could only find work to do. There was no lack of bitter personal experience back of those wrathful outcries! We idealistic youngsters who were "radicals" then could not foresee the tremendous, peaceful social revolution that has taken place in our country since those days and is still in progress in the good American fashion.

But, in view of what has been, and is, happening throughout the world, was there not a definite prophetic note in those poems? Surely the "Red Wind" is blowing out of the East across the world. Surely the "Cry of the People" is heard more and more around our troubled planet.

JOHN G. NEIHARDT

Columbia, Missouri
1965

CONTENTS

A BUNDLE OF MYRRH (1907)

		PAGE
I.	Lines in Late March	1
II.	The Witless Musician	2
III.	The Sound My Spirit Calls You . .	4
IV.	At Parting	6
V.	Longing	7
VI.	Should We Forget	9
VII.	Come Back	10
VIII.	In Autumn	11
IX.	The Subtle Spirit	13
X.	Chaser of Dim Vast Figures . . .	14
XI.	The Temple of the Great-Outdoors .	16
XII.	There Was a Voice	19
XIII.	When I Am Dead	21
XIV.	In Dejection	22
XV.	A Fancy	24
XVI.	Retrospect	25
XVII.	Recognition	27
XVIII.	Confession	29
XIX.	Weary	30
XX.	If This Be Sin	31
XXI.	Let Down Your Hair	32
XXII.	The Lyric Night	33
XXIII.	Titan-Woman	34
XXIV.	The Morning Girl	36

CONTENTS

		PAGE
XXV.	The City of Dust	38
XXVI.	The Fool's Mother	40
XXVII.	Let Me Live Out My Years	41
XXVIII.	Prayer of an Alien Soul	42
XXIX.	The Ancient Story	45
XXX.	The Last Altar	47
XXXI.	Resurrection	49

A VISION OF WOMAN (1909)

	PAGE
A Vision of Woman	53
Woman-Wine	60
Eros	63
Gæa, Mother Gæa!	65
Nuptial Song	69

THE STRANGER AT THE GATE (1912)

		PAGE
I.	The Weavers	75
II.	Ballad of a Poet's Child	78
III.	The News	81
IV.	In the Night	82
V.	Break of Day	85
VI.	Song to the Sun	88
VII.	End of Summer	90
VIII.	Hymn Before Birth	92
IX.	Triumph	94
X.	Child's Heritage	95
XI.	Lullaby	97

CONTENTS
THE POET'S TOWN (1908-12)

	PAGE
The Poet's Town	101
The Poet's Advice	110
Hark the Music	113
April The Maiden	114
Easter	115
April Theology	117
Morning-Glories	119
Invitations	121
And the Little Wind—	122
On First Seeing the Ocean	124
Prairie Storm Rune	126
Prayer for Pain	131
Battle-Cry	133
The Lyric	135
Lonesome in Town	136
The Memory	137
What the Mother-Soul Says	138
At Sunrise	139
Money	141
Song of the Turbine Wheel	142
The Red Wind Comes	144
Cry of the People	147
Czolgosz	148
O Lyric Master!	149
Katharsis (1914)	151
The Farmer's Thanksgiving	153
The Voice of Nemesis	155
Echo Song	157
Fountain Song	159

CONTENTS

PAGE

Outward 160
The Ghostly Brother 162
When I Have Gone Weird Ways 165
L'Envoi 167

TWO MOTHERS

Eight Hundred Rubles (1913) 173
Agrippina (1911) 195

LYRIC AND

DRAMATIC POEMS

A BUNDLE OF MYRRH

(1907)

"Who is she that looketh forth as the morning,
Fair as the moon,
Clear as the sun,
And terrible as an army with banners?"

PRELUDE

I would sing as the Wind;
As the autumn Wind, big with rain and sad with prenatal dread.
I would sing as the Storm;
As the Storm whipped by the lightning and strong with giant despair.
I would sing as the Snow;
Wailing and hissing and writhing in the merciless grasp of the Blizzard.
I would sing as the Prairie;
As the Prairie droning in the heat, satisfied, drowsy and mystical.
For I am a part of the Prairie,
Kin to the Wind and the Lightning.
I love as the Prairie might love;
As the Storm would hate, I hate.
I feel the despair of the Storm,
Rejoice with the joy of the River.
Even as these would sing in their differing moods, I sing!

A BUNDLE OF MYRRH

I

LINES IN LATE MARCH

I WHISTLE; why not?
Have I not seen the first strips of green winding up the
    sloughs?
Have I not heard the meadow-lark?
I have looked into soft blue skies and have been uplifted!

Where are the doubts and the dark ideas I entertained?
What have I caught from the maple-buds that changes
    me?
Or was it the meadow-lark—or the blue sky—or the
    strips of green,
The green that winds up the sloughs?

I sought the dark and found much of it.
Is there in truth much darkness?
Have the meadow-larks lied to me?
Have the green grass and the blue sky testified falsely?

I want to trust the sky and the grass!
I want to believe the songs I hear from the fenceposts!
Why should a maple-bud mislead me?

II

THE WITLESS MUSICIAN

SHE is my violin!
As the violinist lays his ear to his instrument
That he may catch the low vibrations of the deeper
    strings,
So I lay my ear to her breast.
I hear her blood singing and I am shaken with ecstasy;
For am I not the musician?

She is my harp—I play upon her.
I touch her, and she trembles as a harp with the first
    chord of a revery.
I lay my hands upon her with that divine thrill in my
    finger-tips,
That reverent nervousness of the fingers,
Which a harpist feels when he reaches for a ravishing
    chord,
Elusive chord from among the labyrinthine strings.
I am a musician for the first time!
I have found an instrument to play upon!
She is my violin—she is my harp!

A song slept in her blood.
None had found it—and it slept.
Lo! I—even I who am so poor in power,
Who was a pauper in conception of harmony,
I have awakened by chance the slumbering song!

I am lost in the spaciousness of it;
I am only a part of the song which I have awakened
    mysteriously.

Lo, I, the witless musician!
I have wrought even as Masters of Melody,
Even as Masters of Song!

III

THE SOUND MY SPIRIT CALLS YOU

I WOULD I knew some slow soft sound to call you:
Some slow soft syllable that would linger on the lip
As loath to pass, because of its own sweetness.

I cannot shape the sound—tho' I have heard it;
Heard it in the night-wind and the rush of the rain;
Heard it in the dull monotony of the dozing noon;
Heard it among the leaves when Winds were fagged at
     nightfall!

Kind as the shade, this sound:
Kind as the dull blue shade that blade-like cuts
A kingdom of coolness from the cruel Noon:
Soft as the kiss of the Stream to the drooping Leaf;
Sad as the pale Sun's smile over the Blizzard's bier;
Deep and resonant as distant thunder after a day of heat;
Mystic as the dream of the illimitable Prairie under the
     August glare;
Mysterious as the blue haze in which the turbid River
     dwindles to a creek!

I cannot speak the language of the Hills.
I am unskilled to sing the notes of the June Southwind.
The Noon croons not with such a tongue as mine.

Yet—even tho' I be dead, this sound shall call you for
       me!
In the still blue nights—listen, and you shall hear it!
In the burst of the storm it shall be as a whisper to you!
The Morning shall sing it for you and the Sunset paint
       its meaning,
Even upon a background of burning gold, and from the
       palette of the Rainbow!

I would that my tongue could shape this sound my spirit
       calls you.
It would be as a rose-leaf becoming vocal;
As a honeycomb talking of sweetness!
And it would pass slowly and gloriously as a sunset passes;
Gloriously and lingeringly it would die away,
To be like fragrance remembered.

IV

AT PARTING

No more from light to light, from gloom to gloom,
Shall you grow up about me, making bloom
Each individual moment like a rose.
From morning to the quiet evening's close,
From dusk unto the coming of the sun,
I feel the hours grow empty one by one.

And yet in spite of our diverging ways,
You have a place in all my nights and days.
The lonely dusk, enchanted by the moon,
Shall sing you to me with a quiet tune.
When skies grow soft and blue in after days,
Then shall I feel your pure, calm, searching gaze.
And ever when the Green World wakes in dew,
It shall be fragrant with the soul of you.
So Night shall be my servant, and the Day
Shall conjure back that which has passed away;
That ever luring and elusive thing—
A song that I conceived, but could not sing;
A dream I dreamed but, waking, could not live;
Sweet wine for which my goblet was a sieve!

V

LONGING

O HOLD no more the prize of wealth before me,
Nor hope of praise;
Nor talk of things men toil for, to deplore me
My dream-filled days!

Give me a fastness distant from the city,
The human sea
Which I would hate, were not I forced to pity,
Because akin to me.

There in the wilds with only you to love me
And none to hate,
I could feel Something good and strong above me,
More kind than Fate.

The Wind would take my hand and lead me kindly
Through the wild;
And teach me to believe in beauty blindly,
Like a child.

I could forget the aches of hope and failing,
That with slow fires consume
This futile flesh that goes on groping, wailing
Toward the gloom.

Far from the bitter grin of human faces
I could sing,
Robed in the vast and lonesome purple spaces
Like a king.

VI

SHOULD WE FORGET

I WONDER if the skies would be so blue,
Or grass so kindly green as 'twas of old,
Or would there be such freshness in the dew
When purple mornings blossom into gold:
I wonder would the sudden song of birds,
Thrilling the storm-hushed forest dripping wet
After a June shower, be as idle words,
Should we forget.

I wonder if we'd feel the charm of night
Divinely lonesome with the changing moons;
Or could we prize the intermittent light
Burning the zenith with its transient noons.
I wonder if the twilight could avail
To charm us, as of old when suns had set,
If all these many dream-sweet days should fail—
And we forget.

VII

COME BACK

Come back and bring the summer in your eyes,
The peace of evening in your quiet ways;
Come back and lead again to Paradise
The errant days!

Of old I saw the sunlight on the corn,
The wind-blown ripple running on the wheat;
But now the ways are shabby and forlorn
That knew your feet.

Forget the words meant only by my lips!
Could you not understand
The silent language of my finger-tips
When last you took my hand?

VIII

IN AUTUMN

DREAR, dull autumnal rain,
Skies washed to gray;
Winds sighing like an unfleshed ancient pain;
Uncanny day!

A time for tears and musings on the past,
For vain regret;
A time to dream of joys that could not last
But mock us yet.

A time to dream of winter and to mourn;
To hear sad tunes;
To yearn unto the far and shadowed bourne
Of perished Junes.

Yet not for me this drear autumnal mood,
This winter fear;
I view from no dull mental solitude
The aging year.

For me—the memory of sun-shot days,
Nights kind and warm;
Moons purpling the weird star-enchanted haze;
The April storm.

The rain's drone on the roof, the wind's lament
Among the trees;
These make me hear through days of warm content
The hum of bees.

Because I see with eyes that saw your face
As none had seen;
And hear with ears that heard you—every place
Is summer-green.

And I shall hear the robin through the fall
And in the snow;
Because you live and breathe and love in all,
Wherever I may go.

IX

THE SUBTLE SPIRIT

I BUILT a temple for my spirit's home;
I filled it with myself—and it was fair.
From its dream-pavement to its dream-reared dome
No spirit but my own existed there.
About the walls I wrought with doting care
Huge fancies alien to the world of men,
Vague daubs and vast of youth and light and air.
Sublimely isolated in my spirit's den,
I lived and toiled and dreamed, and hoped—and then—
        and then—

Another spirit entered, subtle, slow,
Like summer coming when the winter flees,
With eyes that had the soft, warm, quiet glow
Of some calm evening of a day of ease:
And that was you! I felt, upon my knees,
A swift, mysterious spreading of the place!
My poor walls seemed to hold infinities
Too vast for peace! I fell upon my face
And worshipped you at last, the spirit of the place!

X

CHASER OF DIM VAST FIGURES

CHASER of dim vast figures in the mist,
Drawn by far cries, an alien to content,
Builder of burning worlds that passed in gloom,
Vain architect of great sky-spaces, filled
With unreal suns uncurtaining the day
That fell again in dismal night—'Twas I!

A pygmy in all else but daring dreams,
A grasper after monstrous shadow-shapes,
With stars for eyes and mass of cloud for cloak
And dreams for blood and winds of night for voice;
I sought, they fled; and wailing after—I!

And wailing after—I: for somewhere lurked
The form of Beauty that has never been;
A pagan goddess, vast of limb and thigh,
With burning hills for breasts, and for a face
Dim features dazzled with an inward sun;
A form of awful curves, voluptuous slope
Of neck and shoulders downward to the breasts;
Arms warm and languid as the soul of Love
And scintillant as rockets of the dawn!

And at her feet I dreamed to lay my head,
A pygmy worshipper, who could not reach

Unto the ankles mountain-high, where blazed
Circles of jewels like chained satellites,
To touch which with my finger-tips were death!

And I would guess sweet guesses—how her hair
Made sunlight upward where my eyes saw not;
How sweet the thunder of her beating heart
And terrible! I sought and found her not.

Yet everywhere I saw her with my soul:
Saw her in girlhood, strolling with the Spring;
And in the sultry summer sunsets saw
The glory of her searching woman-eyes,
That made me sing the songs that are despair.
And I have watched her hair trail down in flame
The vapor plains and mountains of the west!
Thus loving what was not, the dreamer—I!

And as I reached my eager arms to clasp
The prodigy that fled—*you* filled them full,
And in my hair I felt your fingers move,
And felt your woman's lips about my face,
And felt your cool cheek on my burning cheek.
So I have lost the wish to dream again.

XI

THE TEMPLE OF THE GREAT OUT-DOORS

Lo! I am the builder of a temple!
Even I, who groped so long for God
And laughed the broken laugh to find the darkness
    empty,
I am the builder of a temple!

The toiling shoulders of my dream heaved up the arch
And set the pillars of the Dawn,
The burning pillars of the Evening and the Dawn,
Under the star-sprent, sun-shot, moon-enchanted dome
    of blue!

And I, who knew no God,
Stood straight, unhumbled in my temple:
I did not fear the Mystery of the Darkness,
And I was only glad to feel the rush of sunlight in my
    blood!

I did not bend the knee.
I was unafraid, unashamed, careless and defiant.
I stood as in the centre of the universe and laughed!

And in my temple there were songs and organ tones,
And there was a silent Something holier than prayer.

I heard the winds and the streams and the sounds of many
    birds:
I heard the shouting of storms and the moaning of snows;
I heard my heart, and it was lifted up in song.
The Wind passing in a gust was as though an organ had
    been stricken by the hands of a capricious Master!

There was movement in the air, motion in the leaves,
    a stirring in the grass,
Even as of the reverent moving about of a congregation.
Yet I stood alone in my temple; I stood alone and was
    not afraid.

But once a Something glided into my temple
And I became afraid!
As the Moon-Woman of the Greeks the Something seemed,
Lithe and swift and pale,
A fitting human sheath for the keen chaste spirit of a
    sword!
And then it seemed my temple was too small.
The Presence filled it to the furthest nook!
There was no lonesomeness in any cranny!

I knelt—and was afraid!

I felt the Presence in the winds;
I heard it in the streams;
I saw it in the restless changing of the clouds!
I tried to be as I had been, unbending, not afraid—
    godless.

Subtle as the scent of the unseen swinging censer of the
    wild flowers
That Presence crept upon me!

I fled from the terrible sunlight that burned the dome
of my temple!
Childlike I hid my head in the darkness!
But I am not alone.

Where I have laughed defiantly into the blind emptiness,
Something moves!
I have placed my irreverent hand upon a Something in
the shadow!
I tremble lest the Thing shall illumine itself as the dawn;
I tremble lest at last I must see God—
See God and laugh no more.

XII

THERE WAS A VOICE

There was a Voice—
A Voice awful in the quiet!
As a deluge from the heavens it fell,
As a breath from the earth it arose—
A wild, compelling music;
Like the swift fingers of the Wind upon the harp-strings
      of the Rain;
Blind, groping, toiling roots, singing of predestined blos-
      soms;
Dying flowers chanting the glory of seed;
A sad, wise rune of growing,
Mysterious as birth,
Mystic as death;
Thin treble threads spun silverly out of Immensity;
Murmurous thunders, sullen with menace!
And all about me an Influence gathered,
A something motherly, cuddling me.
And I was a bud enfolded in sunlight,
A seed in a rain-warmed soil.
As a bud to the sun I responded,
As a seed in the damp, I expanded.
And a rustling of grasses went through me,
A shuddering murmur of wind-rumpled wheatfields.
And I knew this compassing, motherly, fatherly something

[19]

The thing I had groped for, striving to fashion and see it,
God of the trees and the grasses and men—
The tender, formless, vast unworshipped God!
And the Earth was a cradle rocked,
And I was an infant awakened,
Dazzled with star-mist and moon-shine.
When lo! a face leaned over me, smiling down,
Mothering me with gentle woman-eyes,
And in my cradle's purple canopy
Builded a shielding heaven!
                    It was you!
My sky is in your face, and all my dawns
Flush there, and all my evenings hallow it;
And it is awful with the drift of stars,
And mystic with the wandering of moons!
          Rain, rain upon me kisses, O my Sky!

XIII

WHEN I AM DEAD

WHEN I am dead, and nervous hands have thrust
My body downward into careless dust;
I think the grave cannot suffice to hold
My spirit 'prisoned in the sunless mould!
Some subtle memory of you shall be
A resurrection of the life of me.
Yea, I shall be, because I love you so,
The speechless spirit of all things that grow.
You shall not touch a flower but it shall be
Like a caress upon the cheek of me.
I shall be patient in the common grass
That I may feel your footfall when you pass.
I shall be kind as rain and pure as dew,
A loving spirit 'round the life of you.
When your soft cheeks by odorous winds are fanned,
'Twill be my kiss—and you must understand.
But when some sultry, storm-bleared sun has set,
I will be lightning if you dare forget!

XIV

IN DEJECTION

THIS thing I hold so closely in my arms,
Feeling its heart leap strongly at my kiss,
Its eyes closed gently like two cloud-veiled stars,
Its breath like some soft night wind on my neck;
What is it?   This soft thing I hold so closely?

Ah, head, like some pale flower asleep in shade,
Ah, breast, at which my passionate hands have thrilled,
O languid arms and white hands veined with blue,
A little while and these may be a lump
To make me shudder with a dismal dread!

O precious Thing of Flesh!
Let me exhaust the softness of your cheek
With one long desperate kiss, as one who drinks
The final maddening drop before the cup
Be shattered into dust!   O let me breathe
Your breath that I have made more quick and warm,

As one who drowns and takes the latest gasp!
The time may come when my fond touch shall fail
To cause your sigh, and my hot kiss be vain
To make your blue-veined temples throb as now.

I see your sunken eyes, your rose-like cheek
Burned black with agony!   And I shall be
So jealous of the ground that shall embrace you,
So jealous of the grass that grows above you,
So jealous of the silence that enfolds you.

XV

A FANCY

IF I should die, and some strong Voice should say,
Unto my soul lost in the vast black deep,
"Where wouldst thou take, O Soul, thy future way,
Wouldst still live on in pain, or fall asleep?"
It seems that I would answer: Let me creep
Into the roots of some rose she loves well;
Grow upward with the sap of June and steep
The petals with this love I cannot tell;
Breathe out these dreams in perfume that could speak
My longings for her, for which words are weak!
Thus grow one swift, soft summer day, then feel
The pang of plucking through my fibres reel!
I should not then go wailing after light;
I should not feel the terror of the night;
I should not weary of the endless rush
Of mad blind cycles through the awful hush.

XVI

RETROSPECT

WHEN first I looked upon your face
It seemed to me it was not new;
It seemed from some far-distant place
I but remembered you:
For some sweet subtle feeling told
That we two once had loved of old.

The clear-cut curve of lip and chin,
The low fond voice, the gentle way;
By these I knew that we had been
Fond lovers in our day:
It seemed I heard you singing still
To me by some Thessalian rill!

Perhaps I was a shepherd lad
And you a shepherd maid;
And O! what kisses sweet we had
The while our two flocks strayed—
Strayed off with distant bleat and bell
Along some lost Achæan dell.

Perhaps I was a bard and wrought
Some golden martial story,
How Helen loved, how Hector fought,

My harp a-thrill with glory:
Again you bring those mystic years,
I hear your praise, I feel your tears.

The golden God sat in my shell
And Venus breathed in you;
Did I not sing both wild and well?
Did I not warmly woo?
Perhaps we swooned to some sweet **wrong**
That thrilled us like a battle song!

O let us take the ancient way,
The way we knew of old
Ere Time flew o'er and made us gray,
Ere Death had made us cold:
Again the old sweet way begin!—
How can it lead us into sin?

XVII

RECOGNITION

WHAT far-hurled cry is this—what winged shout
That drives the winter of my spirit out
With trumpets and the cymballed joy of spring?
No more am I the shivering beggared thing
That dreamed of summer in a bed of snow!
Hark yonder how the scarlet trumpets blow
A glad, delirious riot of sweet sound!

O I have found
At last the one I lost so long ago
In Thessaly, where Peneus' waters flow!
For thou wert Lais, and of yore 'twas thus
That thou didst speak to me—Hippolochus!
And I have not forgot.

Still dreaming of the old impassioned spot,
I passed through many pangful births in Time,
Weaving in many tongues the aching rhyme
That groped about and cried for thee in vain!
Of many deaths I passed the gates of pain;
And down to many hells the bitter ways
I trod, still seeking for the ancient days.
Through many lands in many women's eyes
I longed to overtake thee with surprise.

O the long ages that I sought for thee!
Hast thou kept pure the ancient drink for me?
Who touched with careless lips my goblet's brim,
Daring to dream the vintage was for him?
Half jealous of those lips of dust am I!

O let us journey back to Thessaly,
And from these echoes build the olden song!
Hast thou forgotten, through these ages long,
The tinkle of the sheep-bells and the shrill
Glad oaten reeds of shepherds on the hill?
Our days of sultry passion and the nights
That flashed the dizzy lightning of delights?

At last I feel again thy finger-tips!
Be as a purple grape upon my lips,
Made sweet with dew of dreams, and wholly mine!
O let me drink the sweet forbidden wine
Crushed out with bruising kisses! Death is near,
And I shall lose thee once again, my dear!

The dust of ages chokes me! Quick! The wine!
Lift up the goblet of thy lips to mine!

The bony Terror! Hark his muffled drums!—
Let us be drunken when the Victor comes!

XVIII

CONFESSION

My love is like the snarl of haughty drums
And blare of trumpets, when a great one comes
Down some thronged breathless city thoroughfare:
And yours is like a song that fills the air
Of evening when the dew has made it sweet
And Peace walks through the dusk with quiet feet.

My love is like the visual shout of red
That threads the drowsing of a poppy bed
In summer, when the sun makes heavy heat:
And yours is like the white flower, cool and sweet,
That fills the shadow with a pleasant scent,
Unshrivelled by the sun and well content.

My dreams come robed in scarlet flame to me
And lead through gardens of strange phantasy
My wayward feet; where heavy odors cling
And birds of blood-red plumage nest and sing
Delirious loves, mad doubts and sacred trust,
The pathos and the joy of human dust.

[29]

XIX

WEARY

My brain is weary with the whirling day!
Snatch me away!
Away from cold, sane living, quiet breath!

I have not seen the proof of human laws:
Only the warm vast Cause
Shall lead me to your arms, your lips, your breast!
Teach me to wrest
The sweetness out of living unto death!

I only know I draw a fevered breath,
I only know my eyes are fagged and dim—
Fill up my soul with beauty to the brim!

I am so weary, and your mouth is red—
Pillow my head!

XX

IF THIS BE SIN

CAN this be sin?
This ecstasy of arms and eyes and lips,
This thrilling of caressing finger-tips,
This toying with incomparable hair?
(I close my dazzled eyes, you are so fair!)
This answer of caress to fond caress,
This exquisite maternal tenderness?
How could so much of beauty enter in,
If this be sin?

Can it be wrong?
This cry of flesh to flesh, so like a song?
This fusing of two atoms with a kiss,
Hurled to the black and pitiless abyss?

Can it be crime
That we should snatch one happy hour from Time—
Time that has naught but death for you and me?
(How soon, O Dearest, shall we cease to be!)
And could one frenzied hour of love or lust
Augment the final tragedy of dust?

Although we be two sinners burned with bliss,
Kiss me again, that warm round woman's kiss!
Close up the gates of gold! I go not in—
If this be sin.

XXI

LET DOWN YOUR HAIR

Unbind your hair, and let its masses be
Soft midnight on the weary eyes of me.
I faint before the dazzle of your breast;
Make shadow with your hair that I may rest,
And I will cool my fevered temples there:
Let down your hair.

Ah—so! It falls like night upon a day
Too bright for peace. It is a cruel way
That leads to this, alas, which is but pain.
I am athirst—your tresses fall like rain;
Ah, wrap me close and bind me captive there
Amid your hair!

How much my soul has given that my flesh
Might lie a thrall in this enchanted mesh!
Something I grope for that I used to hold;
Something it was bought dearly—cheaply sold;
Something divine was strangled unaware
Here in your hair!

But no—I will not grieve—will not complain.
Let your hair fall upon me like night rain
And shut me from myself, and make me blind!
How can I deem this bondage aught but kind?
And yet—I cannot sleep for some dumb care
Here in your hair.

XXII

THE LYRIC NIGHT

O GIRL, if you could die before the dawn
Makes shoddy this the garment of our dream,
Above your shapely form of chiselled ice
I could weep tears of gladness, seeing how
The bitter freeze of death had chastened you!

But Day will come a-knocking at the blinds,
Flooding the secret nooks of this delight.
The night lamp's glow, conniving at our joy,
Shall struggle vainly with the virile Dawn,
Sending a loathsome odor from its grease;
And all the gaud and tinsel of this dream,
That now seems gold, shall be a mockery!

O I could smile upon you here in death,
For Death is chaste and wise and very kind;
But my soul aches that it must see you walk
To-morrow in the vulgar gaze of Day,
Lifelike, yet dead—so dead to what you were.
Kiss me again before the stars snuff out!
Once more before the lyric night be lost
Amid the prosy droning of the day!

XXIII

TITAN-WOMAN

O GREAT kind Night,
Calm Titan-Woman Night!
Broad-bosomed, motherly, a comforter of men!
Reach out thy arms for me
And in thy jewelled hair
Hide thou my face and blind my aching eyes!

I hate the strumpet smile
Of Day! No peace hath she.
Draw thou me closer to thy veilèd face!
For thou art womanlike,
A lover and a mother,
And thou canst wrap me close and make me dream,
As one not cursed with light.
I shall forget my flesh,
This flesh that burns and aches
And fevers into hideous, shameless deeds!

And in the sweet blind hours
I shall seek out thy lips,
I shall dream sweetly of thy Titan form;
The languid majesty
Of smooth colossal limbs
At ease upon the hemisphere for couch!

[34]

And of thy veiled face
Sweet fancies I shall fashion;
Half lover-like I seek thee, yearning toward thee!
For I am sick of light,
Mine eyes ache, I am weary.

O Woman, Titan-Woman!
Though lesser ones forsake me,
Yet thou wilt share my couch when I am weary.
Thy fingers! Ah, thy fingers!
They touch me! Lift me closer,
Extinguish me amid thy jewelled tresses!

Thou wert the first great mother,
Shalt be the last fair woman:
White breasts of flesh grow cold, soft flesh lips wither:
O First and Ultimate,
O Night, thou Titan-Woman,
Thou wilt not fail me when these fall to dust!

The moon upon thy forehead!
The stars amid thy black locks!
Extinguish me upon thy breast, amid thy tresses!

[35]

XXIV

THE MORNING GIRL

LISTEN! All the world is still;
One bleared hour and night is gone.
See the lonely moon-washed hill
Lift its head to catch the dawn!

In the east the eager light
Sets the curtained dusk a-sag;
And all the royal robe of Night
Frays cheaply—like a rag!

Once I felt a lifting joy
When I saw the day unfurl,
Watching, just a laughing boy,
For the Morning Girl.

Oft I met her in the dew
Face to face, her sapphire eyes
Burning on me through the blue
Of the morning skies.

Then her pure and dazzling breast
Made with joy my senses swoon,
As she burned from crest to crest
Upward to the noon.

[36]

Now no more I seek her shrine,
Seek no more her golden hair
Sparkling in the morning shine
And the purple air.

Comes no more the Morning Girl,
Glows not now her golden head,
When the clouds of dawn unfurl—
Purple, yellow, red.

Now the waning of the night
Means another day is near;
Just a haggard splotch of light,
A turning of the sphere!

Would that in the coming hour
I might be that boy who knew
Fragrant import of the flower,
Lyric impulse of the dew!

XXV

THE CITY OF DUST

BEHOLD me——a shadow!
The shadow of an ancient laughing thing!

Fallen columns disintegrated with time;
Sacred mounds insulted with the growth of scornful
      weeds;
Shattered arches haunted by the lizard and the snake:
This is my Babylon——the Babylon I built and feasted in!

O, but the wantonness of my Babylon!
The princely prodigality of my Babylon!
This was the throne—— I sat upon it.
I sat upon it and feasted mine ears with the haughty
      trumpets,
Mine eyes with the scarlet and purple.

And once in this long fallow garden a lily grew:
It was my lily——it grew for me.
Weeds grow there now——they grow for me.
They grow there now and flaunt their ragged coats in the
      sun——
Ruffians and shameless!
If I weep above my fallen lily, will it grow?

The lizard flees from me and the snake hisses,
And I am lonesome——lonesome in my Babylon.

How shall I pile up again the kingly walls?
I cry out: my voice is as the yell of a jackal—impotent.
The Wind dances with the Dust across my tessellated
        courtyards;
The Wind and the Dust—their music is a threnody.

How can I rebuild my Babylon?
How conjure back the magic of the olden time?
How can I rebuild my dust heaps into a city—
The City of My Ancient Dream?

XXVI

THE FOOL'S MOTHER

WHEN I—the fool—am dead,
There will be one to stand above my head,
Her wan lips yearning for my quiet lips
That stung her soul so oft with bitter cries.
And I shall feel forgiving finger-tips
And I shall hear her saying with her sighs:
"This fool I mothered sucked a bitter breast;
His life was fever and his soul was fire:
O burning fool, O restless fool at rest,
No other knew how high you could aspire,
No other knew how deep your soul could sink!"

And when these words above the fool are said,
The others ranged about the room shall think:
'The fool is dead.'

XXVII

LET ME LIVE OUT MY YEARS

LET me live out my years in heat of blood!
Let me die drunken with the dreamer's wine!
Let me not see this soul-house built of mud
Go toppling to the dust—a vacant shrine!

Let me go quickly like a candle light
Snuffed out just at the heyday of its glow!
Give me high noon—and let it then be night!
Thus would I go.

And grant me, when I face the grisly Thing,
One haughty cry to pierce the gray Perhaps!
O let me be a tune-swept fiddlestring
That feels the Master Melody—*and snaps!*

XXVIII

PRAYER OF AN ALIEN SOUL

O CENTER of the Scheme,
Star-Flinger, Beauty-Builder, Shaping Dream!
Now as the least in all thy space I stand
An alien in a strange and lonesome land.
I lift a little voice of pygmy pain;
I hurl it out—up—down—and shall I cry in vain?
Hear thou the prayer that struggles in this song—
Let me not linger long!

I crave the boon of dying into life!
Extend a pitying knife
And let these flesh-gyves part, let me be free!
Are we not kin?   Am I not part of thee?
Am I not as a ripple in a cranny of thy sea?
What part have I in sequent wretched eves,
Blear dawns, dull noons, the budding and the falling of
      the leaves?
Why must I drag about this chain of years,
Long rusted red with tears?
Why must I crawl when I have wings to fly?
Behold thy child—the winged one—it is I!
At times here in the dust
I lift my head, I strive to sing—I *must!*
The miracle of growing wraps me round!
Light!   Sound!

Form! Motion! Upward yearning! Outward reaching!
A universal praying, dumb beseeching!
I feel that I am more than flesh and futile,
A being ultra-carnal, super-brutal!
I understand these growing green beseechers,
These hopeful climbers and these earnest reachers!
I understand their yearnings every one,
How each tense fibre hungers for the sun!
I lay my hand upon the sturdy weed
Whose darkling purpose burst the prison-seed
And cleft the mud and took its light and dew,
Looked up, reached out, believed in life—*and grew!*
I know that we are kin;
That hope is virtue and that doubt is sin;
And o'er me comes a hungering for song:
I lift my voice—I falter. Ah, the long
Dumb years, the aching nights and days!
And yet I raise
My unavailing, immelodious cry.
Thine erstwhile singing child—behold!—'Tis I!
In this strange wretched prison of the soul
Shall I not lose my swiftness for the goal?
It seems I must
At length become too much the kin of dust.
Ah me, the fever born of hate and lust!
Ah me, the senseless unmelodic din!
Ah me, the soul-hope sick with fleshly sin!

And in my prison ancient dreams grow up
To fill with dust my cracked and thirst-betraying cup;
Dreams mantled in the purple of dead glory
That filled the æons out of reach of human story:

Not always have I worn these dusty rags!
The purpose of my being falters, lags,
And I am sick, sick, sick to live again.
Yet not because of this poor dust-born pain
Do I cry out and grope about for thee.
I hear the far cry of my destiny
Whose meaning sings beyond the furthest sun.
I faint in these red chains, and I would 'rise and run,
O Center of the Scheme,
Star-Flinger, Beauty-Builder, Shaping Dream!

XXIX

THE ANCIENT STORY

IT is the ancient story lived anew.
Dost thou remember how the mighty Jew
Spoke at the table of the Pharisee
And puzzled all who heard Him; tenderly
Forgiving her whose soul was red with sin
And seared with lust? How that she entered in
Where sat the Lord, and cast her down and wept?
How to His feet she crept
And washed them with her tears?

                Howe'er that be,
I have lived out this ancient tale with thee;
Only I am the sinner, thou the saint.
With heart bowed down and limbs grown strangely faint,
I creep unto thy feet; cleanse off with tears
The stains they got that followed all these years
The guilty paths I made, the cruel ways
That led unto a blood-red night of haze.
They were my paths, and this for thee sufficed!
I gaze into thine eyes and see the Christ,
Calm-eyed, great-souled, the Pitier! I see
How much and yet how little after me
Thine aching feet have followed! see how deep
I grovel from the height that thou dost keep,
A sinner, yet unsoiled.

Lift thou me there
Unto the heaven of thy face and hair
That shines for me far off as summer dawn.
The night is gone!
I feel the sunrise quicken in my blood!
My soul leaps clean from out its lair of mud!

With nard I do anoint thee; at thy feet
I burn this myrrh of bitter and of sweet.

Lift thou me there
Unto the heaven of thy face and hair,
And make my soul complete!

XXX

THE LAST ALTAR

EREWHILE beneath the lightning flare of passion
I saw huge visions flung across the gloom;
I built me altars after pagan fashion
And of my hours I made a hecatomb.

I wrought weird gods of night-stuff and of fancy;
I sought their hidden faces for my law:
My days and nights were filled with necromancy,
And an Olympian awe.

O many a night has seen my riot candles,
And heard the drunken revel of my feast,
Till Dawn walked up the blue with burning sandals
And made me curse the east!

For my faith was the faith of dusk and riot,
The faith of fevered blood and selfish lust;
Until I learned that love is cool and quiet
And not akin to dust.

For once, as in apocalyptic vision,
Above my smoking altars I could see
My god's face, veilless, ugly with derision—
The shameless, magnified, projected—*Me!*

And I have left my ancient fanes to crumble,
And I have hurled my false gods from the sky;
I wish to know the joy of being humble,
To build great Love an altar ere I die.

XXXI

RESURRECTION

THERE—close your eyes, poor eyes that wept for me!
Pillow your weary head upon my arm.
You need not clutch me so, I will not flee;
Here am I bound by no mere carnal charm.

At last I am not blind, for I can see
Through your mere flesh as only spirit can;
I feel at last the world-old tragedy,
The sacrifice of woman unto man.

In that far time when my first father sought
To cool the strange mad fever in his veins,
Seeing how fair the creature he had bought
With straining sinews and wild battle pains;

Then was this moment of your anguish sown,
And you have reaped but do not understand.
How frail and thin your blue-veined hands have grown,
How trustingly they clutch my guilty hand!

The story of the world is in your face;
I gaze upon it, hearing through dead years
The wailings of the women of the race,
The melancholy fall of many tears.

[49]

In many a Garden of Gethsemane,
Sweet with strange odors, redolent of bliss,
Again is played the human tragedy
With Judas waiting in the dark to kiss.

Not only upon Calvary has died
The patient tortured Christ misunderstood;
Over and over is He crucified
Wherever man besmirches womanhood.

I who have laughed too long at sacred things,
Who felt no god about me in the gloom,
Now hear a Something mystical that sings
Sweeter than love, yet terrible as doom.

In your frail face I see a glory grow
That smites me, guilty, like a burning rod!
I kneel before you, suppliant, and know
That your thin hands can lead me unto God!

A VISION OF WOMAN
(1909)

A VISION OF WOMAN

I LOVE you. Do you smile? And well you may:
You who have heard the beast in many men
Mouth glibly that old spirit phrase so oft.
It is a word you scoff at here, I know.
And yet—when one dreams sleepless all the night,
Somehow a sense of the enduring things,
Creeps in upon him, till the old beast sleeps,
And spirits wise with time possess the hush.

It seems a life has passed since yestereve;
'Twas then I met you—just a night ago:
How little can a clock-gong measure dreams!

You sat beneath the tawdry glare of gas
Among the weary painted woman-flowers,
Exhaling sickly scents; while to the tune
Of shrill barbaric fiddles, squawking horns,
And that piano the mulatto played,
(Nay, smitten by the devil's dancing feet!)
The haggard creatures wreathed the dizzy dance.

Sin errant rides for heavens built of mist;
But once, O once it lead me to the goal!
I saw you—virgin-eyed and sunny haired,
With cheeks whereon the country's kiss remained,
And round you, somehow, the effluvium
Of green things smiling upward in the day.

Gazing upon you, over me there came
The drone of cornfields in the warm damp night;
Far, far away I saw the wheat a-shimmer;
The smell of fresh-turned earth was everywhere!
And O your touch flung trooping through my blood
Such dream-wrought throngs of maiden violets!
So all my thirsty soul cried out to you,
The one green spot in all that arid place.

And yet—I did not love you then as now.
The smouldering ashes of old primal lusts
The strident fiddles wakened, and the wine.
And so I bought you—paid the stated price—
Washed out my scruples in a flood of wine.
Then all the smell of violets died out,
The visioned fields of happy growing things
Went stifling hot, oppressive with the breath
Of flowers that never blossomed in the day.
And then when I had borne you from the place
Of glare and noise, where painted lilies swayed
Unto the shrieking hell-wind of the fiddles,
You flung aside those garish strumpet garments
And stood before me!

                So would April look
If all the lure and wonder of that time
Could flesh itself in woman!   And I knew
'Twas thus of old the maiden Lais stood,
Fresh from the wholesome fields of Sicily,
Before Apelles quickened with his dream.
A ghost of spring crept back into the world
Haunting the hot, autumnal hollow of it.
It seemed the time when maples ooze their sap,

When humid winds of promise sing all night
Beneath the stars that run aghast through mist:
When rivers wake and burst their shrouds of ice
To boom down swollen channels. Cherry bows
Flung to the winds their odorous living snows,
And apple blossoms drifted in the breeze,
Pink as the buds that tipped your spotless breasts.
Up through the spring-sweet vistas of the dream
Old Greece came back with all her purple bays,
Her ships of venture and her fighting men,
Her sculptors and her painters and her bards,
Her temples and her ever-living gods,
Her women whom to name must be to sing.
I touched you—and 'twas Helen that I touched;
And in my blood young Paris lived again;
And all the grief and gloom of Ilium,
Her wailing wives enslaved to foreign lords,
Her stricken warriors and her gutted fanes,
Her song-built towers falling in the smoke,
And all the anguish of her tragic Queen,
Seemed naught for one round burning kiss from you!

You thought it was the wine; ah, so it was—
The wine of woman fraught with life and death,
The wine of beauty and the wine of doom.
You laughed; and Greece with all her purple bays,
Her gladness and her weeping went to dust;
While through the panting hollow of the world
A hot storm grumbled up. And we alone
In some tremendous lightning-riven night!

But when the quiet came, and down the dark
The awful music of our youth died out,

And in the gloomy hollow lived no sound
Except the sullen thunder of our hearts,
Your languid kissing mouth seemed like a wound
Wet with the blood of something I had killed!
And while you stroked my dampened hair, and lisped
Delirious nothings, over me there came
The sad still singing of the things that are.
Close nestled in the hollow of my arm,
You slept like any weary little girl,
Unconscious of the ancient weight you bore.
But I lay wakeful with the ghostly years.

Above the glooming surf of yesterdays
The faces of all women that have been
Bloomed beacon-like, and lit with ghastly glare
The wreck-strewn coasts of the eternal sea!
Faces of patient woe and wise with grief,
Faces from which my mother gazed at me,
Faces that were one face with that of Christ!
And some with haggard unforgetting eyes
Haunted far sea-rims, gray with ships of mist;
And some were drawn and white above the slain,
With sick lips mumbling kisses of farewell;
And in them all the wistful mother-light.
Once more for me the Carthaginian pyre
Built day amid the dusk of sordid things;
And that sad Queen whom all the world shall love
Because one man forsook her, far away
Followed with tearless tragic eyes the sail
That bellied skyward in a wind of Fate.
And through the night the wail of Hecuba
Brought back the Thracian sorrow, made it mine:
While in the aching hush that followed it

Red drop by drop I heard the Virgin's blood.
Fair Phryne came and bared her breast to me
With ancient sorrow pleading in her gaze,
And on her painted cheeks my sister's tears.
And one with ashen face and tiger eyes
Held huddled close the remnant of her brood.
One, pale above a loom, with nervous hands
Wove and unwove the shroud of each day's hope—
The web of Woman's weaving. Hand in hand,
The Roman wife, the subtle Queen of Nile,
Walked down the night—one woman at the last.
And haloed round with an eternal spring,
Rode she with whom all men have sinned; her face
Foreshadowed with the doom that was to be:
And aged with more than years, unqueened, and yet
Ten times the former queen, I heard her sob
Amid the cloistral gloom at Almesbury.
And O, I saw upon a mystic sea
A rose-souled lily fleshed into a girl,
Tall as a fighting man and terrible
With all the keen clean beauty of a sword,
That one who took the luring mystic cup
And drank of it, and thirsted evermore.
From myriad graves they came, till night was day
Lit with the radiance of them. Queens and slaves;
Sweet maidens with the life-dawn in their eyes;
Mothers with babes at breast, and painted harlots;
Unsung forgotten daughters of the ground,
Dumb under burdens, with dull questioning eyes
That stared uncomprehending upon Fate.
All lifted up imploring arms to me
And over them a wind of music went,
The crooning of the mothers of the Race.

The vision passed.   Out in the quiet night
Across the huddled roofs the clock-gong tolled.
I raised the blind.   The tremulous woman-star,
Like a great tear moon-smitten, watched the town,
And thin soft whispers prophesied the dawn.

Bathed in the glamorous beauty of the stars
You lay asleep——a chiselled Parian dream,
A spotless vase of sleeping sacred fire,
A still white awe!   No vandal hand had filched
The meaning from the breasts that might not know
The sad sweet thrill of nurture.   With cool lips
That yearned with primal worshippings, I kissed them;
And, though you slept, the tender mother arm,
Wise with old memories, sought the restless babe.

God makes you mothers spite of milkless breasts!
He only knows how sterile gardens dream
Of bloom flung riot: how through arid night
The wooing rain comes kissing like a ghost,
Unfruitful kisses!

                    O that you might know
The cleansing wonder quickening in your blood,
The sweet dream fleshing with the passing moons,
The wild red pang, the first thin strangled cry
From world to world, the great white after-peace!

But O I saw you sitting in the sun
Before a green-girt cottage with your babes;
And grapes hung purple in the afternoon,
And there were bees abroad and smell of fruit;
And up the shimmering hillside went the man——

Stamped with the kinship of the giving Earth,
The old Antæan wisdom in his heart—
Glad in the flowing furrow turned for you.

See! faint upon the melancholy roofs
The gray light, like the aching backward creep
Of some familiar sorrow!

                    O the grapes
That never sun shall purple!

                    It is day.

WOMAN-WINE

I

Once again I see it, touch it,
Fatal cup with many a name;
Make it mine and madly clutch it,
Drink its blasting draught of flame!

Cup of grief and cup of woe,
Cup of ancient woman-wine:
Victor in my overthrow—
It is mine!

Awful burning lips of Thais,
Kiss me back Persepolis!
Break my heart—I'm Menelaus!
Make me Paris with a kiss!

Smiling Thing with painted heart,
Canker at the soul of Peace,
Thou hast wakened by thine art
All the wanton flutes of Greece!

Lest I kill thee in my fury
Let the heaped white wonders speak:
Awe me as the ancient jury—
Phryne, make me weak!

Asker, Taker, Devil-Woman,
Hiss the hellish wish again!
Death fleshed out to mask as human,
Dancer for the heads of men!

Honied Wooer, Victor-Slayer,
Sing me drowsy, take my sword!
I am paid, O sweet Betrayer
Awful as a battle-horde!

Ancient wine of gloom and glory
Wets thy warm, red, wooing lips:
All the scarlet Queens of Story
Touch me through thy finger-tips.

II

Nay! In gentler, sweeter fashion
How thy warm soul blossoms up!
Martyr to the deathless Passion,
Quaffer of the Iseult-cup!

Thou wert heart-sick Sappho, burning
Downward to the mourning sea.
Thou didst soothe the Master, yearning
For the hills of Galilee.

Thou the hopeful heart of sorrow
Singing through the gloom of years;
Light of every black to-morrow,
Wise with yesterdays of tears.

[61]

Thou the doomed eternal Maiden,
Wailing by the windless sea.
Thou art Mary, sorrow-laden—
Pray for me!

Pale night-weeper at the cross,
Death for thee hath not sufficed;
Trusting through the gloom of loss,
Thou didst view the risen Christ.

Burden-bearer, Beauty-maker,
Sacred Fountain of my life;
Mighty Giver, meagre Taker—
Mother, Sister, Wife!

O, at last, my heart's Desire,
Build the dream that shall endure!
Fair white Urn of Sacred Fire,
Burn me pure!

Cup of sweet felicity,
Cup of ancient woman-wine!
Vanquished in my victory—
It is mine!

EROS

LURED as the Earth lures Summer,
Wooing as Sunlight the Seed—
I am the mystical Comer,
I am the Will and the Deed!

Over and over forever
The glad sad story is told;
Fleeing, escaping me never,
I am your Shower of Gold.

Subtle as April creeping
Flower-shod out of the South,
I am the dream of your sleeping,
Fever am I at your mouth.

I am the sap-lift singing
The hope of a last glad birth:
I am the May-Fog clinging—
You are the Earth!

And mine are the pangful kisses
That waken the Dream in the Dust;
Bringer of aching blisses,
Cruel I seem as Lust.

I come like a wind of disaster,
Flinging the whips of the rain;

O, I am a pitiless Master—
I am glorified Pain.

This is the Story of stories—
(The Rain and the Seed and the Sod)—
Awful with glooms and glories,
These are the rites of the god!

But O, when the storm and its riot
Sleeps in the after-hush,
I am the dawn-filled quiet—
I am the thrush.

I am the sun to cherish,
I am the dew to feed
You with your blooms that perish,
Martyrs unto the seed.

Ancient and ending never,
This is the Law and the Plan.
O, you are the Woman forever—
I am the Man!

GÆA, MOTHER GÆA!

Gæa, Mother Gæa, now at last,
Wearied with too much seeking, here I cast
My soul, my heart, my body down on thee!
Dust of thy dust, canst thou not mother me?

Not as an infant weeping do I come;
These tears are tears of battle; like a drum
Struck by wild fighting hands my temples throb;
Sob of the breathless swordsman is my sob,
Cry of the charging spearman is my cry!

O Mother, not as one who craves to die
I fall upon thee panting. Fierce as hate,
Strong as a tiger fighting for his mate,
Soul-thewed and eager for yet one more fray—
O Gæa, Mother Gæa, thus I pray!

Have I not battled well?
My sword has ripped the gloom from many a hell
To let the sweet day kiss my anguished brow!
O, I have begged no favors until now;
Have asked no pity, though I bit the dust;

For always in my blood the battle-lust
Flung awful sword-songs down my days and nights.
But now at last of all my golden fights
The greatest fight is on me—and I pray.

[65]

O let my prayer enfold thee as the day,
Crush down upon thee as the murky night,
Rush over thee a thunder-gust, alight
With swift electric blades! Nay, let it be
As rain flung down upon the breast of thee!
With something of the old Uranian fire
I kiss upon thee all my deep desire.

If ever in the silence round about,
Thy scarlet blossoms smote me as a shout;
If ever I have loved thee, pressed my face
Close to thy bosom in a lonesome place
And breathed thy breath with more than lover's breath-
        ing;
If ever in the spring, thy great trees, seething
With hopeful juices, felt my worship-kiss—
Grant thou the prayer that struggles out of this,
My first blood-cry for succor in a fight!

Alone I shouldered up the crushing night,
Alone I flung about me halls of day,
Unmated went I fighting on my way,
Lured on by some far-distant final good,
Unwarmed by grudging fires of bitter wood,
Feeding my hunger with my tiger heart.
Mother of things that yearn and grow, thou art!
The Titan brood sucked battle from thy paps!
O Mother mine, sweet-breasted with warm saps,
Once more Antæus touches thee for strength!
My victories assail me! Now at length
My lawless isolation dies away!
For Mother, giving Mother, like the day

Flung down from midnight, she who was to be
Floods all thë brooding thunder-glooms of me!
And in the noon-glow that her face hath wrought,
Stands forth the one great foe I have not fought—
The close-ranked cohorts of my selfish heart.

Suckler of virile fighting things thou art!
Breathe in me something of the tireless sea;
The urge of mighty rivers breathe in me!
Cloak me with purple like thy haughty peaks;
O arm me as a wind-flung cloud that wreaks
Hell-furies down the midnight battle-murk!
Fit me to do this utmost warrior's work—
To face myself and conquer!

                              Mother dear,
Thou seemest a woman in this silence here;
And 'tis thy daughter who hath come to me
With all the wise, sad mother-heart of thee,
Thy luring wonder and immensity!
For in her face strong sweet earth-passions brood:
I feel them as in some wild solitude
The love-sweet panting summer's yearning-pain.

Teach me the passion of the wooing rain!
Teach me to fold her like a summer day—
To kiss her in the great good giant way,
As Uranus amid the cosmic dawn!

Now all the mad spring revelling is gone,
And comes the fruiting summer! Let me be
Deep-rooted in thy goodness as a tree,

Strong in the storms with skyward blossomings!
Teach me the virile trust of growing things,
The wisdom of slow fruiting in the sun!

I would be joyous as the winds that run
Light footed on the wheatfields.   O for her,
I would be gentle as the winds that stir
The forest in the noon hush.   Lift me up!
Fill all my soul with kindness as a cup
With cool and bubbling waters!   Mother dear,
Gæa, great Gæa, 'tis thy son—O hear!

NUPTIAL-SONG

Lo! the Field that slumbered,
Sowed and winter-sealed;
Thralled and dream-encumbered!
O the maiden Field!
Never Thunder roused her,
Rain or yearning Fire;
Never Sun espoused her,
Virile with desire.

Yet betimes a vague thrill
Running in a thaw,
Hinted at the World-Will
And the Lyric Law;
Made her guess at splendor
Bursting out of pain;
Feel the clutching tender
Fingers of the grain.

Now an end of dreaming!
Lo! the lover comes—
Flame-wrought banners gleaming,
Haughty thunder drums;
Joy- and sorrow-laden,
Eager, wondershod!
Sacrifice the Maiden
On the altar of the god!

Though he come with terror,
Though he woo with pain,

Love is never error,
Kisses never vain.
Victress in her capture,
Let the Maiden know
All the aching rapture,
All the singing woe!

Hark! the regal Thunder!
(O the huddled Field!)
'Tis the Night of Wonder—
Let the Maiden yield!
O the quiet after
All the singing pain!
O the rippling laughter
Of the nursing grain!

Older and yet younger,
Sadder, and yet blessed,
With a baby-hunger
Tugging at her breast,
She shall feel the Great Law—
Love, and you shall grow.
Give her to the wild Awe,
Let the Maiden know!

Sweeter than all other
Songs of lip or lyre—
Every Maid a Mother,
Every Man a Sire:
Joy beneath the pain warm,
God amidst the plan;
Field unto the Rainstorm,
Maid unto the Man!

THE STRANGER AT THE GATE

A Lyric Sequence Celebrating the
Mystery of Birth

(1912)

To Enid

THE STRANGER AT THE GATE

I

THE WEAVERS

SUNS flash, stars drift,
Comes and goes the moon;
Ever through the wide miles
Corn-fields croon
Patiently, hopefully,
A low, slow tune.

Lovingly, longingly,
Labors without rest
Every happy cornstalk,
Weaving at her breast
Such a cozy cradle
For the coming guest.

In the flowing pastures,
Where the cattle feed,
Such a hidden love-storm,
Dying into seed—
Blue grass, slough grass,
Wild flower, weed!

Mark the downy flower-coats
In the hollyhocks!

Hark, the cooing Wheat-Soul
Weaving for her flocks!
Croon-time, June-time,
Moon of baby frocks!

Rocking by the window,
Wrapt in visionings,
Lo, the gentle mother
Sews and sings,
Shaping to a low song
Wee, soft things!

Patiently, hopefully,
Early, late,
How the wizard fingers
Weave with Fate
For the naked youngling
Crying at the Gate!

Sound, sight, day, night
Fade, flee thence;
Vanished is the brief, hard
World of sense.
Hark! Is it the plump grape
Crooning from the fence?

Droning of the surf where
Far seas boom?
Chanting of the weird stars
Big with doom?
Humming of the god-flung
Shuttles of a loom?

O'er the brooding Summer
A green hush clings,
Save the sound of weaving
Wee, soft things:
Everywhere a mother
Weaves and sings.

II

BALLAD OF A POET'S CHILD

YEARLY thrilled the plum tree
With the mother-mood;
Every June the rose stock
Bore her wonder-child:
Every year the wheatlands
Reared a golden brood:
World of praying Rachels,
Heard and reconciled!

"Poet," said the plum tree's
Singing white and green,
"What avails your mooning,
Can you fashion plums?"
"Dreamer," crooned the wheatland's
Rippling vocal sheen,
"See my golden children
Marching as with drums!"

"By a god begotten,"
Hymned the sunning vine,
"In my lyric children
Purple music flows!"
"Singer," breathed the rose bush,
"Are they not divine?

Have you any daughters
Mighty as a rose?"

Happy, happy mothers!
Cruel, cruel words!
Mine are ghostly children,
Haunting all the ways;
Latent in the plum bloom,
Calling through the birds,
Romping with the wheat brood
In their shadow plays!

Gotten out of star-glint,
Mothered of the Moon;
Nurtured with the rose scent,
Wild, elusive throng!
Something of the vine's dream
Crept into a tune;
Something of the wheat-drone
Echoed in a song.

Once again the white fires
Smoked among the plums;
Once again the world-joy
Burst the crimson bud;
Golden bannered wheat broods
Marched to fairy drums;
Once again the vineyard
Felt the Bacchic blood.

"Lo, he comes—the dreamer—"
Crooned the whitened boughs,
"Quick with vernal love-fires—

O, at last he knows!
See the bursting plum bloom
There above his brows!"
"Boaster!" breathed the rose bush,
" 'Tis a budding rose!"

Droned the glinting acres,
"In his soul, mayhap,
Something like a wheat-dream
Quickens into shape!"
Sang the sunning vineyard,
"Lo, the lyric sap
Sets his heart a-throbbing
Like a purple grape!"

Mother of the wheatlands,
Mother of the plums,
Mother of the vineyard—
All that loves and grows—
Such a living glory
To the dreamer comes,
Mystic as a wheat-song,
Mighty as a rose!

Star-glint, moon-glow,
Gathered in a mesh!
Spring-hope, white fire
By a kiss beguiled!
Something of the world-joy
Dreaming into flesh!
Bird-song, vine-thrill
Quickened to a child!

III

THE NEWS

LITTLE Breezes, lurking in the green-roofed covers,
Where the dappled gloaming keeps the cool night dews,
Up, and waft the wonder of it unto countless lovers!
Set the tiger-lily bells a-tolling out the news!

Down the eager rivers make the glory of the story roll;
Waken joyful shivers in the green gold hush;
Set it to the warble of the early morning oriole;
Fill it with the tender, kissing rapture of a thrush!

Take a little sorrow from the night rain pattering,
Drowning in a black flood stars and moon;
Take a little terror from the zigzag, shattering,
Blue sword-flash of a storm-struck noon!

Breathing through the green-aisled orchard chapels,
Learn the holy music of the world-old dream;
Borrow from the still scarlet singing of the apples;
Weave it in the weird tale's gloom and gleam!

Hasten with the woven music, make the Summer lyrical,
Sweet as with the odors of a southeast rain:
Set the corn a-chatter o'er the glad, impending miracle—
A little Stranger whimpers at the Gate of Pain!

IV

IN THE NIGHT

OVER the steep cloud-crags
The marching Day went down—
Bickering spears and flags,
Slant in a wind of Doom!
Blear in the huddled shadows
Glimmer the lights of the town;
Black pools mottle the meadows,
Swamped in a purple gloom.

Is it the night wind sobbing
Over the wheat in head?
Is it the world-heart throbbing,
Sad with the coming years?
Is it the lifeward creeping
Ghosts of the myriad dead,
Livid with wounds and weeping
Wild, uncleansing tears?

'Twas not a lone loon calling
There in the darkling sedge,
Still as the prone moon's falling
Where in the gloom it slinks!
Hark to the low intoning
There at the hushed grove's edge—

Is it the pitiless, moaning
Voice of the timeless Sphinx?

Woven of dust and quiet,
Winged with the dim starlight,
Hideous dream-sounds riot,
Couple and breed and grow;
Big with the dread to-morrow,
Flooding the hollow night
With more than a Thracian sorrow,
More than a Theban woe!

Dupe of a lying pleasure,
Dying slave of desire!
Dreading the swift erasure,
The swoop of the grisly Jinn,
Lo, you have trammelled with dust
A spark of the slumbering Fire,
Given it nerves for lust
And feet for the shards of sin!

Woe to the dreamer waking,
When the Dream shall stalk before him,
With terrible thirsts for slaking
And hungers mad to be fed!
O, he shall sicken of giving,
Cursing the mother that bore him—
Earth, so lean for the living,
Earth, so fat with the dead!

Cease, O sounds that smother!
Peace, mysterious Flouter!
Lo, where the sacred mother

Sleeps in her starry bed,
Dreams of the blessèd Comer,
A white awe flung about her,
Wrapped in the hopeful Summer,
The starlight round her head!

V

BREAK OF DAY

SILENT are the green looms
And the weavers sleep,
Nestled in the piled glooms,
Deep on deep.

Gaunt, grim trees stand,
Etched on space,
Like a mirrored woodland
On a purple vase.

Faithful in the dun hour,
Like a praying priest,
Eagerly the sunflower
Scans the East.

Corn rows, far hurled,
Mist-enthralled,
Vanish in a star world,
Sapphire-walled.

Leaning out of dim space
Over field and town,
Some hushed mother face
Peers, bends down;

Veiled in gleam-blurs,
Starry locked,
Brooding o'er the dreamers
Dawnward rocked.

Is a spirit walking?
On a sudden seem
All the sleepers talking
In a broken dream!

All along the corn rows,
O'er the glinting dews,
Hark!   A muffled horn blows
Some wild news!

Listen!   From a plum-close,
Like a troubled soul,
Tremulous a voice goes—
'Tis the oriole!

Star-lorn, staring,
The East goes white!
Is a Terror faring
Up the steep of night?

Boldly, gladly,
Through the paling hush,
Wildly, madly,
Cries a thrush!

Tumbled are the piled glooms
And the weavers stir:

Once again the wild looms
Drone and whir.

Glowing through the gray rack
Breaks the Day—
Like a burning haystack
Twenty farms away!

VI

SONG TO THE SUN

TREADER of the blue steeps and the hollows under,
Day-Flinger, Hope-Singer, crowned with awful hair;
Battle Lord with burning sword to cleave the gloom
      asunder,
Plunger through the eyries of the eagles of the Thunder,
Stroller up the flame-arched air!

All-Beholder, very swift and tireless your pace is:
Now you snuff the guttered moon above the gray abyss,
Moaning with the sagging tide in shipless ocean spaces;
Now you gladden windless hollows thronged with daisy
      faces;
Now the corn salutes the Morn that sought Persepolis.

Searcher of the ocean and the islands and the straits,
The mountains and the rivers and the deserts and the
      dunes,
Saw you any little spirit foundling of the Fates,
Groping at the world-wall for the narrow gates
Guarded by the nine big moons?

Numberless and endlessly the living spirit tide rolls,
Like a serried ocean on a pleasant island hurled!
Sun-lured, rain-wooed, color-haunted wild souls

Trooping with the love-thralled, mother-seeking child
        souls,
Throng upon the good green world!

Surely you have seen it in your wide sky-going—
An eager little comrade of the spirits of the wheat;
All the hymning forests and the melody of growing,
All the ocean thunderings and all the rivers flowing,
Silenced by the music of its feet!

VII

END OF SUMMER

PURPLE o'er the tree tops
Wild grapes sprawl;
In the golden silence
Few birds call;
Heavy-laden Summer
Ripens into Fall.

Weary with the seed pods
Droop the hollyhocks;
Up and down the wide miles,
Corn in shocks;
Silent is the Wheat Mother,
And her merry flocks

Go no more a-marching
Unto fairy drums.
Hark! Is it the footfall
Of the One who comes?
Silence—save the dropping
Of the purple plums!

Patient, stricken Summer
Feels the Odic Fires,
Awful in her ripe domes,

Mystic in her spires.
In a holy sadness
Fruit the Spring desires.

Last of all the awe-moons,
Three times three,
Glimmers down the sun-track
Slenderly—
Omen of the Wonder
Soon to be.

Does the darkness listen
For a shout of Doom?
Hist! Was it a thin voice
Crying from a womb?
Silence—save a dry leaf's
Whisper down the gloom.

VIII

HYMN BEFORE BIRTH

Soon shall you come as the dawn from the dumb abysm
of night,
Traveller birthward, Hastener earthward out of the
gloom!
Soon shall you rest on a soft white breast from the
measureless mid-world flight;
Waken in fear at the miracle, light, in the pain-hushed
room.

Lovingly fondled, fearfully guarded by hands that are
tender,
Frail shall you seem as a dream that must fail in the
swirl of the morrow:
O, but the vast, immemorial past of ineffable splendor,
Forfeited soon in the pangful surrender to Sense and to
Sorrow!

Who shall unravel your tangle of travel, uncurtain your
history?
Have you not run with the sun-gladdened feet of a thaw?
Lurked as a thrill in the will of the primal sea-mystery,
The drift of the cloud and the lift of the moon for a law?

Lost is the tale of the gulfs you have crossed and the
  veils you have lifted:
In many a tongue have been wrung from you outcries
  of pain:
You have leaped with the lightning from thunder-heads,
  hurricane-rifted,
And breathed in the whispering rain!

Latent in juices the April sun looses from capture,
Have you not blown in the lily and grown in the weed?
Burned with the flame of the vernal erotical rapture,
And yearned with the passion for seed?

Poured on the deeps from the steeps of the sky as a chalice,
Flung through the loom that is shuttled by tempests at
  play,
Myriad the forms you have taken for hovel or palace—
Broken and cast them away!

You who shall cling to a love that is fearful and pities,
Titans of flame were your comrades to blight and con-
  sume!
Have you not roared over song-hallowed, sword-stricken
  cities,
And fled in the smoke of their doom?

For, ancient and new, you are flame, you are dust, you
  are spirit and dew,
Swirled into flesh, and the winds of the world are your
  breath!
The song of a thrush in the hush of the dawn is not
  younger than you—
And yet you are older than death!

IX

TRIUMPH

SEE how the blue-girt hills are spread
With regal cloth of gold;
How, panoplied in haughty red,
The frosted maples stand;
The golden-rod, with torch alight,
Makes glory up the wold—
As though a monarch's bannered might
Were marching up the land!

Now should ecstatic bugles fret
The hush, and drums should roll;
The shawms of all the breezes set
The scarlet leaves a-dance!
And now should flash in vatic rhyme
The battles of the Soul—
To welcome to the realm of Time
The Vanquisher of Chance!

For, though there rolls no gilded car
That spurns the shaken earth,
And shout no captains, flinging far
The law to parlous spears;
With throbbing hearts for smitten drums,
Up through the Gates of Birth—
The Victor comes! The Victor comes!
To claim the ripened years!

X

THE CHILD'S HERITAGE

O, THERE are those, a sordid clan,
With pride in gaud and faith in gold,
Who prize the sacred soul of man
For what his hands have sold.

And these shall deem thee humbly bred:
They shall not hear, they shall not see
The kings among the lordly dead
Who walk and talk with thee!

A tattered cloak may be thy dole
And thine the roof that Jesus had:
The broidered garment of the soul
Shall keep thee purple-clad!

The blood of men hath dyed its brede,
And it was wrought by holy seers
With sombre dream and golden deed
And pearled with women's tears.

With Eld thy chain of days is one:
The seas are still Homeric seas;
Thy sky shall glow with Pindar's sun,
The stars of Socrates!

Unaged the ancient tide shall surge,
The old Spring burn along the bough:
The new and old for thee converge
In one eternal Now!

I give thy feet the hopeful sod,
Thy mouth, the priceless boon of breath;
The glory of the search for God
Be thine in life and death!

Unto thy flesh, the soothing dust;
Thy soul, the gift of being free:
The torch my fathers gave in trust,
Thy father gives to thee!

XI

LULLABY

SUN-FLOOD, moon-gleam
Ebb and flow;
Twinkle-footed star flocks
Come and go;
Eager little Stranger,
Sleep and grow!

Yearning in the moon-lift
Surge the seas;
Southering, the sun-lured
Gray goose flees:
Eager with the same urge,
You and these!

Canopied in splendor—
Red, gold, blue—
With the tender Autumn
Cooing through;
O, the mighty cradle
Rocking you!

THE POET'S TOWN

(1908-12)

THE POET'S TOWN

I

'MID glad green miles of tillage
And fields where cattle graze,
A prosy little village,
You drowse away the days.

And yet—a wakeful glory
Clings round you as you doze;
One living lyric story
Makes music of your prose.

Here once, returning never,
The feet of Song have trod;
And flashed—O, once forever!—
The singing Flame of God.

II

These were his fields Elysian:
With mystic eyes he saw
The sowers planting vision,
The reapers gleaning awe.

Serfs to a sordid duty,
He saw them with his heart,

Priests of the Ultimate Beauty,
Feeding the flame of art.

The weird, untempled Makers
Pulsed in the things he saw;
The wheat through its virile acres
Billowed the Song of Law.

The epic roll of the furrow
Flung from the writing plow,
The dactyl phrase of the green-rowed maize
Measured the music of Now.

III

Sipper of ancient flagons,
Often the lonesome boy
Saw in the farmer's wagons
The chariots hurled at Troy.

Trundling in dust and thunder
They rumbled up and down,
Laden with princely plunder,
Loot of the tragic Town.

And once when the rich man's daughter
Smiled on the boy at play,
Sword-storms, giddy with slaughter,
Swept back the ancient day!

War steeds shrieked in the quiet,
Far and hoarse were the cries;

[102]

And O, through the din and the riot,
The music of Helen's eyes!

Stabbed with the olden Sorrow,
He slunk away from the play,
For the Past and the vast To-morrow
Were wedded in his To-day.

IV

Rich with the dreamer's pillage,
An idle and worthless lad,
Least in a prosy village,
And prince in Allahabad;

Lover of golden apples,
Munching a daily crust;
Haunter of dream-built chapels,
Worshipping in the dust;

Dull to the worldly duty,
Less to the town he grew,
And more to the God of Beauty
Than even the grocer knew!

V

Corn for the buyers, and cattle—
But what could the dreamer sell?
Echoes of cloudy battle?
Music from heaven and hell?

Spices and bales of plunder,
Argosied over the sea?
Tapestry woven of wonder.
And myrrh from Araby?

None of your dream-stuffs, Fellow,
Looter of Samarkand!
Gold is heavy and yellow,
And value is weighed in the hand!

VI

And yet, when the years had humbled
The kings in the Realm of the Boy,
Song-built bastions crumbled,
Ash-heaps smothering Troy;

Thirsting for shattered flagons,
Quaffing a brackish cup,
With all of his chariots, wagons—
He never could quite grow up.

The debt to the ogre, To-morrow,
He never could comprehend:
Why should the borrowers borrow?
Why should the lenders lend?

Never an oak tree borrowed,
But took for its needs—and gave.
Never an oak tree sorrowed;
Debt was the mark of the slave.

Grass in the priceless weather
Sucked from the paps of the Earth,
And hills that were lean it fleshed with its green—
O, what is a lesson worth?

But still did the buyers barter
And the sellers squint at the scales;
And price was the stake of the martyr,
And cost was the lock of the jails.

VII

Windflowers herald the Maytide,
Rendering worth for worth;
Ragweeds gladden the wayside,
Biting the dugs of the Earth;

Violets, scattering glories,
Feed from the dewy gem:
But poets are fed by the living and dead—
And what is the gift from them?

VIII

Never a stalk of the Summer
Dreams of its mission and doom:
Only to hasten the Comer—
Martyrdom unto the Bloom.

Ever the Mighty Chooser
Plucks when the fruit is ripe,
Scorning the mass and letting it pass,
Keen for the cryptic type.

[105]

Greece in her growing season
Troubled the lands and seas,
Plotted and fought and suffered and wrought—
Building a Sophocles!

Only a faultless temple
Stands for the vassal's groan;
The harlot's strife and the faith of the wife
Blend in a shapen stone.

Ne'er do the stern gods cherish
The hope of the million lives;
Always the Fact shall perish
And only the Truth survives.

Gardens of roses wither,
Shaping the perfect rose;
And the poet's song shall live for the long,
Dumb, aching years of prose.

IX

King of a Realm of Magic,
He was the fool of the town,
Hiding the ache of the tragic
Under the grin of the clown.

Worn with the vain endeavor
To fit in the sordid plan;
Doomed to be poet forever,
He longed to be only a man.

To be freed from the god's enthralling,
Back with the reeds of the stream;
Deaf to the Vision calling,
And dead to the lash of the Dream.

X

But still did the Mighty Makers
Stir in the common sod;
The corn through its awful acres
Trembled and thrilled with God!

More than a man was the sower
Lured by a man's desire,
For a triune Bride walked close at his side—
Dew and Dust and Fire!

More than a man was the plowman,
Shouting his gee and haw;
For a something dim kept pace with him,
And ever the poet saw;

Till the winds of the cosmic struggle
Made of his flesh a flute,
To echo the tune of a whirlwind rune
Unto the million mute.

XI

Son of the Mother of mothers,
The womb and the tomb of Life,
With Fire and Air for brothers
And a clinging Dream for a wife;

Ever the soul of the dreamer
Strove with its mortal mesh,
And the lean flame grew till it fretted through
The last thin links of flesh.

O, rending the veil asunder,
He fled to mingle again
With the dread Orestean thunder,
The Lear of the driven rain!

XII

Once in a cycle the comet
Doubles its lonesome track.
Enriched with the tears of a thousand years,
Æschylus wanders back.

Ever inweaving, returning,
The near grows out of the far;
And Homer shall sing once more in a swing
Of the austere Polar Star.

Then what of the lonesome dreamer
With the lean blue flame in his breast?
And who was your clown for a day, O Town,
The strange, unbidden guest?

XIII

'Mid glad green miles of tillage
And fields where cattle graze,
A prosy little village,
You drowse away the days.

[108]

And yet—a wakeful glory
Clings round you as you doze;
One living, lyric story
Makes music of your prose!

THE POET'S ADVICE

I

YOU wish to be a poet, Little Man?
More verses limping 'neath their big intent?
Well—one must be a poet if one can!
But do you know the way the others went?

Who buys of gods must pay a heavy fee.
The world loves not its dreamers overmuch:
And he who longs to drink at Castaly,
Must hobble there upon a broken crutch.

One sins by being different, it seems;
At least so in our human commonweal.
Who goes to market with his minted dreams,
Must buy and bear the Cross of the Ideal.

Lo, tall amid the forest, blackened, grim,
The lightning-riven pine!—God-kissed was he.
How all the little beeches jeer at him,
Safe in their snug arrays of greenery!

And who shall call the little beeches mad?
Not I, who know how big are little acts.
Want what you have, and cherish, O my Lad,
The downright, foursquare, geometric facts!

II

But—O, the ancient glory in your eyes!
How bursts a dazzling wonder all around!
Wild tempests of ineffable surprise—
All color, dream and sound!

You lip the awful flagons of old time,
And mystic apples lure you to the bite!
Blown down the dizzy winds of woven rhyme,
Dead women come and woo you in the night!

You tread the myrtle woods past time and place,
Where shadows flit and ghostly echoes croon;
And through the boughs some fatal storied face
Breathes muted music like a Summer moon!

I know the secret altars where you kneel.
I know what lips fling fever in your kiss.
That sorry little drab to whom you steal
Is Queen Semiramis!

The Bacchanalia of the sap now reigns!
Priapic fires burn yonder bough with blooms!
Lo, goat-songs warbled from the vineyard fanes!
Lo, Venus-nipples in the apple-glooms!

Ah, who is older than the vernal surge,
And who is wiser than the sap a-thrill?
Forever, he who feels the lyric urge
Shall do its will!

Your rhymes?—Some nimbler footed have been worse.
What broken trumpet echoes from the van
Where march the cohorts of Immortal Verse!
Well—one must be a poet if one can.

HARK THE MUSIC

HARK, the music calling!
From the earth it grows,
From the sky 'tis falling,
In the wind it blows!

Silver-noted star-gleams
Through the moony glooms;
Golden-noted sunbeams
Wooing cherry blooms!

Flying-fingered Winds smite
Throbbing strings of rain;
Through the misty midnight
Moans the Growing Pain!

Cradle-buds are shaken
By a hand they know:
Brother, Sister, waken—
'Tis the time to grow!

APRIL THE MAIDEN

LONGINGS to grow and be vaster,
Sap songs under the blue;
Hints of the Mighty Master
Making his dream come true.

Gaunt limbs winter-scarred, tragic,
Blind seeds under the mold,
Planning new marvels of magic
In scarlet and green and gold!

O passionate, panting, love-laden,
She is coming, she sings in the South—
The World's Bride—April the Maiden—
With the ghost of a rose for a mouth!

EASTER

ONCE more the northbound Wonder
Brings back the goose and crane,
Prophetic Sons of Thunder,
Apostles of the Rain.

In many a battling river
The broken gorges boom;
Behold, the Mighty Giver
Emerges from the tomb!

Now robins chant the story
Of how the wintry sward
Is litten with the glory
Of the Angel of the Lord.

His countenance is lightning
And still His robe is snow,
As when the dawn was brightening
Two thousand years ago.

O who can be a stranger
To what has come to pass?
The Pity of the Manger
Is mighty in the grass!

[115]

Undaunted by Decembers,
The sap is faithful yet.
The giving Earth remembers,
And only men forget.

APRIL THEOLOGY

O to be breathing and hearing and feeling and seeing!
O the ineffably glorious privilege of being!
All of the World's lovely girlhood, unfleshed and made
      spirit,
Broods out in the sunlight this morning—I see it, I hear
      it!

So read me no text, O my Brothers, and preach me no
      creeds;
I am busy beholding the glory of God in His deeds!
See! Everywhere buds coming out, blossoms flaming,
      bees humming!
Glad athletic growers up-reaching, things striving,
      becoming!

O, I know in my heart, in the sun-quickened, blossom-
      ing soul of me,
This something called self is a part, but the world is the
      whole of me!
I am one with these growers, these singers, these earnest
      becomers—
Co-heirs of the summer to be and past æons of summers!

I kneel not nor grovel; no prayer with my lips shall I
      fashion.
Close-knit in the fabric of things, fused with one common
      passion—

To go on and become something greater—we growers
    are one;
None more in the world than a bird and none less than
    the sun;
But all woven into the glad indivisible Scheme,
God fashioning out in the Finite a part of His dream!

Out here where the world-love is flowing, unfettered,
    unpriced,
I feel all the depth of the man-soul and girl-heart of
    Christ!
'Mid this riot of pink and white flame in this miracle
    weather,
Soul to soul, merged in one, God and I dream the vast
    dream together.
We are one in the doing of things that are done and to be;
I am part of my God as a raindrop is part of the sea!

What! House me my God? Take me in where no
    blossoms are blowing?
Roof me in from the blue, wall me in from the green
    and the wonder of growing?
Parcel out what is already mine, like a vender of staples?
*See! Yonder my God burns revealed in the sap-drunken
    maples!*

MORNING-GLORIES

DISTANT as a dream's flight
Lay an eerie plain,
Where the weary moonlight
Swooned into a moan;
Wailing after dead seed,
Came the ghost of rain;
There was I a wild weed
Growing all alone.

Like a doubted story
Came the thought of day;
God and all his glory
Lingered otherwhere,
Busy with the dawn-thrill
Many dreams away.
Could a little weed's will
Fling so far a prayer?

O, the sudden wonder!
(Is a prayer so fleet?)
From the desert under,
Morning-glories grew!
Twined me, bound me
With caressing feet!
Wove song round me—
Pink, white, blue!

As a fog is rifted
By the eager breeze,
Darkness broke and lifted,
Tossing like a sea!
Lo, the dawn was flowering
Through the maple trees!
O, and you were showering
Kisses over me!

INVITATIONS

I

O COME with me and through my gardens run,
And we shall pluck strange flowers that love the sun,
Of which the sap is blood, the petals flame,
The sweet, forbidden blossoms of no name!
O splendid are my gardens walled with night,
Dim-torched with stars and secret for delight;
And winds breathe there the lure of smitten strings,
Vocal of the immensity of things!
Come, Wailer out of Nothing, nowhere hurled,
Frustrate the bitter purpose of the World!
Thou shalt drink deep of all delights that be—
So come with me!

II

I have a secret garden where sacred lilies lift
White faces kind with pardon, to hear my shrift.
And all blood-riot falters before those faces there;
Bowed down at quiet altars, my hours are monks at
            prayer.
There through my spirit kneeling the silence thrills and
            sings
The cosmic brother feeling of growing, hopeful things:
Old soothing Earth a mother; a sire the shielding Blue;
The Sun a mighty brother—and God is in the dew.
O Garden hushed and splendid with lily, star and tree!
There all vain dreams are ended—so come with me!

AND THE LITTLE WIND—

SAID a rose amid the June night to a little wind there
      walking
(And the whisper of the moonlight was no fainter than
      its talking) :
"It is plainly providential," so remarked the garden Tory,
"That the ultimate essential is the gentle rose's glory.
Let the sordid delvers cavil!   Through the world-fog
      sinking seaward
And the planetary travail God was slowly groping me-
      ward.
Weary ages of designing, æons of creative throes
Spent the Master in refining sullen chaos to a rose!
Shall He robe His chosen meanly?   Look upon me; am
      I splendid?"
Here she stood erect and queenly, curled a lip and ended.
And the little wind there walking, not desirous of
      dissension,
In a gust of cryptic talking freely granted the contention.

Like the murmur of a far stream or a zephyr in the sedges,
Scarcely louder than the star-gleam raining silver on the
      hedges,
Came a whisper from the humus where the roots were
      toiling blindly:
"They enslave us, they entomb us!   Is it just and is it
      kindly?
Ours, forever ours, to nourish—O, the drear, eternal
      duty!—

That the idle rose may flourish in aristocratic beauty.
Not for us the wooing, tender moon emerges from the
far night;
Not for us the morning splendor 'and the witchery of
starlight;
Not for us the dulcet cantion of the rain to throbbing
lutes;
And there's no cerulean mansion for the roots."
Now the little wind, demurely sympathetic, cogitated,
And declared the matter surely ought to be investigated.

"Fie!" observed the fair patrician, "on their silly martyr
poses!
Not content with their condition, always wanting to be
roses!"
Whereupon a theophanic, superlunar phosphorescence
Flung the haughty into panic, awed the humble to
quiescence.
'Twas the Vintner of the June-wine on his world-wide,
endless vagrance;
And he spoke the tongue of moonshine in the dialect of
fragrance:
"Brother, Sister, softly, softly!   Glooming, gleaming
though the way be,
Who is low and who is lofty in the scheme of what you
may be?
Pride and plaint are irreligious.   Root and blossom, lo!
you plod
Upward to some far, prodigious Rose of God!"
And the little wind, though slyly sleeping out the time
of talking,
Woke to praise the sermon highly, and continued with
his walking.

ON FIRST SEEING THE OCEAN

AND *this* is the dreamed-of wonder!
   This—at last—is the sea!
Billows of liquid thunder—
   Vocal immensity!
But where is the thrill of glory
   Born of a great surprise?
This is the old, old story;
   These are the ancient skies.

Child of the prairie expanses,
   Often the soul of me
Hungered for long sea-glances;
   And here—at last—is the sea.
Yon goes a sea-gull flying;
   There is a sinking mast;
This is the ocean crying!
   This is the rune of the Vast!

But out in my mother country,
   Ever since I was born,
This is the song my brother Winds
   Sang in the fields of corn.
And there, in the purple midnights
   Sullen and still with heat,
This is the selfsame drone that ran
   Over the heading wheat.

Ere Time, the mystical motion,
　　Mothered and cradled thee,
This was the song, O Ocean,
　　That saddened the soul of me.
And I long to be as the steamer
　　That dwindles, dissolves, in the Blue;
For mine is the soul of the dreamer—
　　And nothing to me is new.

PRAIRIE STORM RUNE

I

THE wild bee sips at the heat-drugged lips
Of the passionless lily a-nod;
The sunflowers stare through the hush at the glare
Of the face of their tutelar god, and the hair
Of the gossamer glints in the listless air.

Ragged and grim on the parched hill-rim,
The cottonwoods sulk in gray:
The guiding word of the plowman is heard
A dream-thralled mile away—half blurred,
Wounding the calm as a blunted sword.

Prophecy's minister, dolorous, sinister,
Hark to the rain crow! Incredible story!
For the clouds of fleece like banners in peace
Pine for the winds of glory. Cease,
Chanter of storm in the ancient peace!

The sick land lies as a man ere he dies,
Loosing his grip in a hush profound;
Save when the hidden insects scream
In jets of watery sound that seem
Taunts of thirst in a fever dream.

II

What mean yon cries where the flat world dies
In hazy rotundity—
Tumult a-swoon, silence a-croon,
Lapped in profundity—bane or boon
Or only the drone of a fever rune?

No bird sings—but a grasshopper's wings
Snap in the meadow.
On the rim of the hill the cottonwoods spill
Stagnant puddles of shadow; and still—
The air is quick with a subtle thrill!

A cool fresh puff!   The meadows are rough,
The cottonwoods whiten and whisper together!
The plowman at gaze, knee-deep in the maize,
Judges the weather.   A plow horse neighs,
Faint and clear as a horn of the fays.

Haunting the distance with taunting insistence,
Fiery portents and mumblings of wonder!
In gardens of gloom, walled steep with doom,
Strange blue buds burst in thunder, and bloom
Dizzily, vividly, gaudily, lividly—
Death-flowers sown in a cannon-gloom!

III

Lo, on a height hewn sheer out of night,
Where Mystery labors,
Through the Hadean heath from an awe beneath,
A sprouting of sabres lean from the sheath!

And bursting the husk of the travailing dusk,
The world-old crop of the dragon's teeth!

Banners of battle-might, spear-glint and sword-light
Over the dream-vague, frowning battalions!
Hark, the hoarse trumpets bray!   Sensing the coming fray,
Wraith-ridden, thunder-hoofed stallions neigh
Terror into the glooming day!

A death-hush falls.   The shadow sprawls
Sick in the failing noon.
The sun flies shorn, aghast, forlorn,
Like a spectral moon surprised at morn.
Deathly green is the meadow-sheen,
Ghastly green the corn.

IV

Hark—at last—the burst of the blast—
The roar of the charge and howls of defiance!
The cottonwoods, grim on the bleared hill-rim,
Grapple with giants weird and dim—
Titan torses, galloping horses—
Gods and demons and seraphim!

Bloody light from the sword-slashed night—
Shuddering darkness after!
Terrible feet trample the wheat!
Olympian laughter overhead!
Over the roofs rumble the hoofs,
Over the graves of the dead!

And yet—somewhere through the crystal air
A golden rain is swelling the oats,
And wild doves croon to the splendid noon
Of love too big for their throats; and there
Never the beat of terrible feet—
Somehow, somewhere.

Stark in the rain like a face of the slain .
The gray land stares in the fitful light.
Is it a glimmer of some vague story—
The corn's green might, the wheatfield's shimmer,
The sunflower's glory?

V

The war wind fails.   A gray cloud trails
Over the sodden plain.
Swift and bright, the arrowy light
Smites the rear of the Rain in flight!
And lo, on high, spanning the sky,
The arch of a Victor's might!

Nothing is heard . . . Hark!—a bird
Calls from a green-gloomed, dripping cover!
Surely wrath rode not in the blast,
But some inscrutable Lover passed,
Aflame with the lust of the Dew for the Dust,
Out of the Vast into the Vast.

The wild bee slips from the housing lips
Of the lily a-nod.

Odors sweet in the humid heat!
A glimmer of God athwart the wheat!
Aglow with prayer, the sunflowers stare
At the face of their Paraclete.

PRAYER FOR PAIN

I DO not pray for peace nor ease,
Nor truce from sorrow:
No suppliant on servile knees
Begs here against to-morrow!

Lean flame against lean flame we flash,
O Fates that meet me fair;
Blue steel against blue steel we clash—
Lay on, and I shall dare!

But Thou of deeps the awful Deep,
Thou breather in the clay,
Grant this my only prayer—O keep
My soul from turning gray!

For until now, whatever wrought
Against my sweet desires,
My days were smitten harps strung taut,
My nights were slumbrous lyres.

And howsoe'er the hard blow rang
Upon my battered shield,
Some lark-like, soaring spirit sang
Above my battle-field;

And through my soul of stormy night
The zigzag blue flame ran.

I asked no odds—I fought my fight—
Events against a man.

But now—at last—the gray mist chokes
And numbs me. *Leave me pain!*
O let me feel the biting strokes
That I may fight again!

BATTLE-CRY

MORE than half beaten, but fearless,
Facing the storm and the night;
Breathless and reeling, but tearless,
Here in the lull of the fight,
I who bow not but before Thee,
God of the fighting clan,
Lifting my fists I implore Thee,
Give me the heart of a man!

What though I live with the winners
Or perish with those who fall?
Only the cowards are sinners,
Fighting the fight is all.
Strong is my foe—he advances!
Snapt is my blade, O Lord!
See the proud banners and lances!
O spare me this stub of a sword!

Give me no pity, nor spare me;
Calm not the wrath of my foe.
See where he beckons to dare me!
Bleeding, half beaten—I go.
Not for the glory of winning,
Not for the fear of the night;
Shunning the battle is sinning—
O spare me the heart to fight!

[133]

Red is the mist about me;
Deep is the wound in my side;
"Coward" thou criest to flout me?
O terrible Foe, thou hast lied!
Here with my battle before me,
God of the fighting clan,
Grant that the woman who bore me
Suffered to suckle a man!

THE LYRIC

GIVE the good gaunt horse the rein,
Sting him with the steel!
Set his nervous thews a-strain,
Let him feel the winner's pain,
Master-hand and -heel!
Fling him, hurl him at the wire
Though he sob and bleed!
Play upon him as a lyre—
Speed is music set on fire—
O, the mighty steed!

Hurl the lyric swift and true
Like a shaft of Doom!
Like the lightning's blade of blue
Letting all the heavens through,
And shuddering back to gloom!
Like the sudden river-thaw,
Like a sabred throng,
Give it fury clothed in awe—
Speed is half the lyric law—
O, the mighty song!

LONESOME IN TOWN

THE long day wanes, the fog shuts down,
The eave-trough spouts and sputters;
The rain sighs through the huddled town
And mumbles in the gutters.

The emptied thoroughfares become
Long streams of eerie light;
They issue from the mist and, dumb,
Flow onward out of sight.

A crowded street-car grumbles past,
Its snapping trolley glows;
Again where yon pale light is cast
The hackman's horses doze.

In vain the bargain windows wink,
The passers-by are few:
The grim walls stretch away and shrink
In dull electric blue.

A stranger hurries down the street,
Hat dripping, face aglow:
O happy feet, O homing feet,
I know where mine would go!

For there, far over hills and dells
The cows come up the lane,
With steaming flanks and fog-dulled bells
That tinkle in the rain.

THE MEMORY

LONG since the ruined town we fled,
   And dust heaps mark the spot
Where you and I clasped hands and said,
   "My friend, forget me not."

The shout of War was loud at heel,
   The foeman pressed behind;
Then you and I turned round with steel
   To meet the Future—blind!

I do not know what foes we fought
   Nor when we gained release;
I only know with pain we bought
   The ultra-stellar peace.

I touch your hand—old sorrows wake,
   Like smoke the long night lifts;
And O, the faint far bugles make
   Weird music through the rifts!

WHAT THE MOTHER-SOUL SAYS

SLEEP, Little Stem, with the mother-dream
That I shall shape for you.
The sun is soft on the silvery stream,
And the wind shall bring you a tune for the dream.
Dream of the bud that awakes in you.
Dream——and it shall be true!

The years have toiled and the seasons died
To make you a time to be,
And a tearful spirit has prophesied
Of you in the summer sea:
For you are a part of the great warm Vast
From the worm at your root to the Sun above you;
And it softly croons "At last, at last,
We shall breathe of your flower and love you!"

AT SUNRISE

'TWIXT midnight and the dawn a weirdness falls;
In hush of wonder, night-winds softlier blow:
A far cock hails the wane of night—and lo!
An eerie dream-horn through the silence calls.
Through the thin air faint drones of meaning go;
Capricious gusts wake drowsily and run
Across the dusky fields to prophesy the sun.

I, wakened by the spirit of the time,
Slough off the drowse, as soul doth flesh at last;
Over the window-sill myself I cast;
With feet of awe that seem not mine, I climb
The hill moon-washed and silent. All is past—
The bitter longing and the dull delay,
The fever that is wrought of dream and clay.

Grown strangely big and cognizant, I stand
No more a thing of hours and sordid miles,
No more the slave of sought-for afterwhiles:
I seem to hear and half way understand
The wash of æther upon stellar isles!
Entempled 'twixt the sky and summit there
I know what makes men rear their domes of prayer.

Dawn-blanched the slinking moon to westward dips:
Across enchanted hills from some far farm
A dog bays out its sense of vague alarm.

I hear a sigh as though from Titan lips,
    Yearning for speech, yet fettered with a charm;
Speech which, it seems, if I could only hear,
Would make death seem less cold and life less dear.

If this could last, it seems that I might lay
    My hand on God and understand the Scheme;
    But breaking in upon my groping dream
Now blares the scarlet music of the Day.
    Drenched with the dew and shivering, I seem
A wailer in a bitter scheme of mud,
A hope half strangled in a stream of blood!

And yet—the birds are singing to the sun!
    With clank of harness and a whistled lay
    The plowman goes afield, as glad he may,
While I am wishing that the day were done!
    What is it that the wild bees strive to say?
Would I could hear with some sixth, subtler sense
The meadow-lark at worship on the fence!

MONEY

A SON of Adam dug beside the way.
"Why Brother, do you dig?" I stopped to ask.
Standing at stoop and pausing in his task,
From dreary eyes he wiped the sweat away.
"I work for money." "What is money, pray?"
"A foolish question, this you come to ask!"
Yet in that gray and worry-haunted mask
At hide-and-seek I saw my query play.

"It is the graven symbol of your ache,"
I said, "—the minted meaning of your blood;
And he who works not, robs you when he buys!
You are the vassal of a thing you make!"
I left him staring hard upon the mud,
The glimmer of a portent in his eyes.

SONG OF THE TURBINE WHEEL

HEARKEN the bluster and brag of the Mill!
The heart of the Mill am I,
Doomed to toil in the dark until
The springs of the world run dry;
With never a ray of sun to cheer
And never a star for lamp!
It cries its song in the great World's ear—
I toil in the dark and damp.

And ever the storm-clouds cast their showers
And the brook laughs loud in the sun,
To goad me on through the dizzy hours
That the will of the Mill be done!
And that is why I groan at work;
For deep down under the flood I lurk
Where the icy midnight lingers;
While *tinkle, tinkle* the waters play
Through starless night and sunless day—
All with their crystal fingers.

O, the waters have such a rollicking way
And they taunt me in my pain;
" 'Tis thou alone art sad," they say,
"Thy rusty whine is vain;
For the grass is green and the skies are blue
And a fisherman whistled, as we came through,
A careless merry tune;

And a bevy of boys were out with their noise
In our flood made warm with June!"

And, bound as I am where the darkness lingers,
I half forgive their careless way,
Such soothing, tinkling tunes they play—
All with their icy fingers.

THE RED WIND COMES!

Too long mere words have thralled us. Let us think!
O ponder, are we "free and equal" yet?
That July bombast, writ with blood for ink,
Is blurred with floods of unavailing sweat!

An empty sound we won from Royal George!
Yea, till a greater fight be fought and won,
A sentimental show was Valley Forge,
A mawkish, tawdry farce was Lexington!

No longer blindfold Justice reigns; but leers
A barefaced, venal strumpet in her stead!
The stolen harvests of a hundred years
Are lighter than a stolen loaf of bread!

O pious Nation, holding God in awe,
Where sacred human rights are duly priced!
Where men are beggared in the name of Law,
Where alms are given in the name of Christ!

The Country of the Free?—O wretched lie!
The Country of the Brave?—Yea, let it be!
One more good fight, O Brothers, ere we die,
And this shall be the Country of the Free!

What! Are we cowards? Are we doting fools?
Who built the cities, fructified the lands?

We make and use, but do we own the tools?
Who robbed us of the product of our hands?

A tiger-hearted Tyrant crowned with Law,
Whose flesh is custom and whose soul is greed!
Ubiquitous, a nothing clothed in awe,
We sweat for him and bleed!

Daft Freedom sings the glory of his reign;
Religion is a pander of his lust:
Surviving tyrants, he eludes the vain,
Tyrannicidal thrust.

Yea, and *we* serve this Insult to our God!
Gnawing our crusts, we render Cæsar toll!
We labor with the back beneath his rod,
His shackles on the soul!

He is a System—wrought for human hogs!
So long as we shall hug a hoary Lie,
And gulp the vocal swill of demagogues,
The Fat shall rule the sty!

Behold potential plenty for us all!
Behold the pauper and the plutocrat!
Behold the signs prophetic of thy fall,
O Dynast of the Fat!

Lo, even now the haunting, spectral scrawl!
Lo, even now the beat of hidden wings!
The ghosts of millions throng thy banquet-hall,
O guiltiest and last of all the kings!

[145]

Beware the Furies stirring in the gloom!
They mutter from the mines, the mills, the slums!
No lie shall stay or mitigate thy doom—
The Red Wind comes!

CRY OF THE PEOPLE

TREMBLE before thy chattels,
Lords of the scheme of things!
Fighters of all earth's battles,
Ours is the might of kings!
Guided by seers and sages,
The world's heart-beat for a drum,
Snapping the chains of ages,
Out of the night we come!

Lend us no ear that pities!
Offer no almoner's hand!
Alms for the builders of cities!
When will you understand?
Down with your pride of birth
And your golden gods of trade!
A man is worth to his mother, Earth,
All that a man has made!

We are the workers and makers!
We are no longer dumb!
Tremble, O Shirkers and Takers!
Sweeping the earth—we come!
Ranked in the world-wide dawn,
Marching into the day!
The night is gone and the sword is drawn
And the scabbard is thrown away!

[147]

CZOLGOSZ

WITH fire of Heaven he withers like a leaf.
He killed; we kill, and deem it over now,
Nor see, as once beside a punished thief,
What woe hangs ripe upon a sapless bough.

This futile Brutus struck at Cæsar's life;
He killed a husband and the People's friend.
Our Cæsar has not flesh to feel the knife;
Still Cæsar lives—and this is not the end!

Hark to the human groans from mire and muck
Where still the streams of sunless millions flow!
He missed the tyrant's heart at which he struck,
Nor do we kill the thing that struck the blow!

The pistol ball wounds not the vaporous mark,
Nor can the dagger pick our prison lock!
Strike Night!—you stab some brother in the dark;
And Henry Fourth survives poor Ravaillac!

O LYRIC MASTER!

OUT of thy pregnant silence, brooding and latent so long,
Burst on the world, O Master, sing us the great man-song!
Have we not piled up cities, gutted the iron hills,
Schooled with our dream the lightning and steam, giving
      them thoughts and wills?
We are the poets of matter. Latent in steel and stone,
Latent in engines and cities and ships, see how our songs
      have grown!
Long have we hammered and chiselled, hewn and hoisted,
    until
Lo, 'neath the wondering noon of the world, the visible
    Epic of Will!
Breathless we halt in our labor; shout us a song to cheer;
Something that's swift as a sabre, keen for the mark as a
      spear;
Full of the echoes of battle—souls crying up from the
      dust.
Hungry we cried to our singers—our singers have flung
      us a crust!
Choked with the smoke of the battle, staggering, weary
      with blows,
We cried for a flagon of music—they gave us the dew of
      a rose!
Gewgaw goblets they gave us, jewelled and crystalline,
But filled with the tears of a weakling. Better a gourd—
      and wine!

O immanent Lyric Master, thou who hast felt us build,
Moulding the mud with our sweat and blood into a thing
    we willed;
Soon shall thy brooding be over, the dream shall be
    ripened——and then,
Thunderous out of thy silence, hurl us the Song of Men!

KATHARSIS

(1914)

I

WHO pray for calm, abhorring flood and fire,
Would shun the purging and espouse the blight.
Lo, in the marshland where the tempest's might
Has raged not, how life's meaner forms aspire!
How breeds and skitters in the fetid mire
Spawn reminiscent of the primal light!
What saturnalias of the parasite
Where corpse-lights ape the elemental fire!

Disaster, riding on a thunder-smoke,
Serpents of flame upon his forehead set,
Hurls the black legions of cyclonic strife!
We trace his progress by the shattered oak,
Bewail the wasted centuries—and yet,
The land shall know a more dynamic life.

II

They hasten to the ancient bath again,
And shall emerge unto a saner peace.
Lo, how they made a fetich of caprice,
And worshipped with aberrant brush and pen!
What false dawns summoned by the crowing hen!

How toiled the lean to batten the obese!
What straying from the sanity of Greece
While yet her seers and bards were fighting-men!

A canting generation, smug in greed,
With neurasthenic shudders, suavely wroth,
Bemoans the ruin of Icarian wings!
Lo, latent in its luxury, the Mede;
Potential in bland cruelties, the Goth—
Stern teachers of the fundamental things!

THE FARMER'S THANKSGIVING

(1914)

NOT ours to marshal, rank on rank,
   The might a Kaiser wields;
Not ours the harvest of the Frank
   On rifle-pitted fields:
But we have fought, and we have won
   As never wins the sword;
And now that our good war is done,
   We humbly thank the Lord.

Prepare the feast and let us sing
   Of how the foe we slew;
How on a bleak frontier of Spring
   We ran our trenches true;
How, trudging through the harrow smoke,
   Went forth our army leaders;
And how the golden volleys broke
   From batteries of seeders.

The King Most High was our ally.
   What drilling and recruiting!
How thronged the glades and hills with blades!
   What eagerness for shooting!
And when, midmost the June campaign,
   Old Drought swooped in to plunder,

How charged the lancers of the rain!
  What cannonade of thunder!

Well may we boast; our wheaten host
  Outnumbered all the Russians;
Our pluméd corn might laugh to scorn
  The Uhlans of the Prussians!
They seek a ghastly triumph now;
  Our victories are kinder.
God bless the good old twelve-inch plow
  And automatic binder!

Lo, where like stacked triumphant arms
  The corn shocks dot yon rise!
Let golden bombs on all the farms
  Now burst in pumpkin pies!
And let us sing, for we have won
  As never wins the sword;
And now that our good fight is done,
  Be praises to the Lord!

THE VOICE OF NEMESIS

You knew me of old and feared me,
Dreading my face revealed;
Temples and altars you reared me,
Wooed me with shuddering names;
Masking your fear in meekness,
You pæaned the doom I wield,
Wrought me a robe of your weakness,
A crown of your woven shames.

Image of all earth's error,
Big as the bulk of its guilt,
Lo, I darkled with terror,
A demon of spite and grudge;
You made me a vessel of fury
Brimmed with the blood you spilt;
With devils of hell for jury,
You throned me a pitiless judge.

For ever the wage of sorrow
Paid for the lawless deed;
Never the gray to-morrow
Paused for a pious price;
Never by prayer and psalter
Perished the guilty seed;
Vain was the wail at the altar,
The smoke of the sacrifice.

[155]

I come like a crash of thunder;
I come as a slow-toothed dread;
With fire and sword to plunder
Or only with lust and sloth.
By star or sun I creep or run,
And lo, my will was sped
By the might of the Mede, the hate of the Hun,
The bleak northwind of the Goth!

Yet, older than malice and cunning,
The love and the hate of your creed,
I smile in the blossom sunning,
I am hurricane lightning-shod!
Revealed in a myriad dresses,
I am master or slave at need.
You grope for my face with your guesses,
And kneel to your guess for a god.

I am one in the fall of the pebble,
The call of the sea to the stream,
The wrath of the starving rebel,
The plunge of the vernal thaw:
The yearning of things to be level,
The stir of the deed in the dream;
I am these—I am angel and devil—
I am Law!

ECHO SONG

Lo, a wandering echo I,
Flung afar, confused, forlorn;
Yearning with a broken cry,
Yet of mighty music born!

Echo from a Wonder-Horn
That sends the music flying far,
Blaring through the scarlet morn,
Tinkling in the spangled star!

Where in all the songs that are
May the echo cease to be,
Filling out a wondrous bar,
Blending with a melody?

Like a ghost there lives in me,
Frustrate in my monotone,
Something chanted by a Sea,
Something out of vastness blown.

Lost, reiterant, alone,
I grow weary, seeking long,
Out of master-music blown,
Homesick for the Mother-Song.

Yet—what though the way be long?
Hark the music flying far!

Trumpets from the scarlet morn,
Lyrics from the evening star!

Kin to all the songs that are,
Of a mighty singing born,
Sun and I and Sea and Star,
Echoes from a Wonder-Horn.

FOUNTAIN SONG

I AM the sprite of the fountain,
Sprung from the gloom am I,
Out of the womb of the Mountain,
Big with the kiss of the Sky!
I am the Fugitive Glory,
Singing the strong soul's story.
Twinkling, tinkling, glad to be
Out of the prison of Earth set free;
Dancing, mad with the cosmic tune,
Laughing under the stars and moon—
Back to the Ocean soon!

Back to the Sky and back to the Sea—
O I was a prisoner long!
But the love of the Vast was strong in me,
Straining the leash of song.
What of the hush and what of the chain?
Seek me soon in the rush of the rain,
The hope of the grass, the faith of the stream,
And ocean dreaming the infinite dream!
Kin of the wave and cloud am I,
And the world grows green as I pass by—
Back to the Sea and Sky!

OUTWARD

WHITHER away, O Sailor, say?
Under the night, under the day,
Yearning sail and flying spray,
Out of the black into the blue,
Where are the great Winds bearing you?

Never port shall lift for me
Into the sky, out of the sea!
Into the blue or into the black,
Onward, outward, never back!
Something mighty and weird and dim
Calls me under the ocean rim!

Sailor under sun and moon,
'Tis the ocean's fatal rune.
Under yon far rim of sky
Twice ten thousand others lie.
Love is sweet and home is fair,
And your mother calls you there.

Onward, outward I must go
Where the mighty currents flow.
Home is anywhere for me
On this purple-tented sea.
Star and Wind and Sun my brothers,
Ocean one of many mothers.

[160]

Onward under sun and star
Where the weird adventures are!
Never port shall lift for me—
I am Wind and Sky and Sea!

THE GHOSTLY BROTHER

BROTHER, Brother, calling me
Like a distant surfy sea,
Like a wind that moans and grieves
All night long about the eaves;
Let me rest a little span;
Long I've followed, followed fast;
Now I wish to be a man,
Disconnected from the Vast!
Let me stop a little while,
Feel this snug world's pulses beat,
Glory in a baby's smile,
Hear it prattle, round my feet;
Eat and sleep and love and live,
Thankful ever for the dawn;
Wanting what the world can give—
With the cosmic curtains drawn!

Brother, Brother, break the gyves!
Burst the prison, Son of Power!
Product of forgotten lives,
Seedling of the final flower!
What to you are nights and days,
Drifting snow or rainy flaw,
Love or hate or blame or praise—
Heir unto the Outer Awe?

I am breathless from the flight
Through the speed-cleft, awful night!
Panting, let me rest awhile
In this pleasant æther-isle.
Here, content with transient things,
How the witless dweller sings,
Rears his brood and steers his plow,
Nursing at the breasts of Now!
Here the meanest, yea, the slave
Claims the heirloom of a grave!
O, this little world is blest—
Brother, Brother, let me rest!

    I am you and you are I!
    When the world is cherished most,
    You shall hear my haunting cry,
    See me rising like a ghost.
    I am all that you have been,
    Are not now, but soon shall be!
    Thralled awhile by dust and din—
    Brother, Brother, follow me!

'Tis a lonesome, endless quest;
I am weary; I would rest.
Though I seek to fly from you,
Like a shadow, you pursue.
Do I conquer? You are there,
Claiming half the victor's share.
When the night-shades fray and lift,
'Tis your veiled face lights the rift.
In the sighing of the rain,
Your voice goads me like a pain.
Happy in a narrow trust,

Let me serve the lesser will
One brief hour—and then, to dust!
O, the dead are very still!

Brother, Brother, follow hence!
Ours the wild, unflagging speed!
Through the outer walls of sense,
Follow, follow where I lead!
Love and hate and grief and fear—
'Tis the geocentric dream!
Only shadows linger here,
Cast by the eternal Gleam!
Follow, follow, follow fast!—
Somewhere out of Time and Place,
You shall lift the veil at last,
You shall look upon my face;
Look upon my face and die,
Solver of the Mystery!
I am you and you are I—
Brother, Brother, follow me!

WHEN I HAVE GONE WEIRD WAYS

WHEN I have finished with this episode,
Left the hard up-hill road,
And gone weird ways to seek another load,
O Friend, regret me not, nor weep for me—
Child of Infinity!

Nor dig a grave, nor rear for me a tomb,
To say with lying writ: "Here in the gloom
He who loved bigness takes a narrow room,
Content to pillow here his weary head—
For he is dead."

But give my body to the funeral pyre,
And bid the laughing fire,
Eager and strong and swift as my desire,
Scatter my subtle essence into Space—
Free me of Time and Place.

Sweep up the bitter ashes from the hearth!
Fling back the dust I borrowed from the Earth
Unto the chemic broil of Death and Birth—
The vast Alembic of the cryptic Scheme,
Warm with the Master-Dream!

And thus, O little House that sheltered me,
Dissolve again in wind and rain, to be
Part of the cosmic weird Economy:
And O, how oft with new life shalt thou lift
Out of the atom-drift!

L'ENVOI

SEEK not for me within a tomb;
You shall not find me in the clay!
I pierce a little wall of gloom
To mingle with the Day!

I brothered with the things that pass,
Poor giddy Joy and puckered Grief;
I go to brother with the Grass
And with the sunning Leaf.

Not Death can sheathe me in a shroud;
A joy-sword whetted keen with pain,
I join the armies of the Cloud,
The Lightning and the Rain.

O subtle in the sap athrill,
Athletic in the glad uplift,
A portion of the Cosmic Will,
I pierce the planet-drift.

My God and I shall interknit
As rain and Ocean, breath and Air;
And O, the luring thought of it
Is prayer!

TWO MOTHERS

TO
ALICE AND MONA

EIGHT HUNDRED RUBLES

(1913)

GIRL'S SONG

NOBLE KREIDER

The heart's an o - pen inn,   And
And with their wounds of care   And

from the four winds fare......   Va - grants blind with
with their scars of   sin......   All these shall en - ter

care,   Waifs that limp with sin;
in   To find a   wel - come there;   And

a tempo

Ghosts of what has been,.... Wraiths of what may
he who gives with pray-er Shall be the rich-er

be:.... But One shall bring the sa-cred gift And
host:.. For sure-ly un-to him shall come The

which...... is He?
Ho - - ly Ghost.

The last stanza same as second except in second " 'Tis he " at close of stanza
take "he" on C for end.

TWO MOTHERS

EIGHT HUNDRED RUBLES

The combined living room and kitchen of a peasant house. Before an open fire, where supper is in preparation, stoops a girl of about sixteen. It is evening and dusk is growing. Vines hang outside and the light of a rising moon comes through the window.

GIRL

(Singing)

2   The heart's an open inn,
    And from the four winds fare
    Vagrants blind with care,
    Waifs that limp with sin;
    Ghosts of what has been,
    Wraiths of what may be:
    But One shall bring the sacred gift—
    And which is He?

    And with their wounds of care
    And with their scars of sin,
    All these shall enter in
    To find a welcome there;
    And he who gives with prayer
    Shall be the richer host;

[177]

For surely unto him shall come
The Holy Ghost.

(*Ceases singing and stares into the fire*)

What if he'd vanish like a dream one keeps
No more than starshine when the morning breaks!
I'll look again.

(*Arises, goes softly to the open window and looks
out into the garden*)

How peacefully he sleeps!

The red rose shields him from the moon that makes
The garden like a witch-tale whispered low.
He came a stranger, yet he is not strange;
For O, how often I have dreamed it so,
Until a sudden, shivering gust of change
Went over things, making the cow-sheds flare
On fire with splendor while one might count three,
And riding swiftly down the populous air,
Prince-like he came for me.
There were no banners when he really came,
No clatter of brave steel chafing in the sheath,
No trumpets blown to hoarseness with his fame.
Silently trudging over the dusky heath,
Clad in a weave of twilight, shod with dew,
Weary he came and hungry to the door.
The lifting latch made music, and I knew
My prince was dream no more.

(*Sings low*)

O weary heart and sore,
O yearning eyes that blur,
A hand that drips with myrrh
Is knocking at the door!
The waiting time is o'er,
Be glad, look up and see
How splendid is a dream come true—
'Tis he! 'Tis he!

(*During the latter part of the song, the back door
opens and the father and mother enter, stooped
beneath heavy packs*)

MOTHER

What's this, eh? Howling like a dog in heat,
Snout to the moon! And not a bite to eat,
And the pot scorching like the devil's pit!
Bestir yourself there, will you! Here you sit
Tra-la-ing while the supper goes to rack,
And your old father like to break his back,
Tramping from market!

FATHER

Tut, tut! Girls must sing,

And one burned supper is a little thing
In seventy creeping years.

MOTHER

Ah, there it goes!

[179]

My hunger makes no difference, I suppose!
Tra-la, tut tut, and I can slave and slave
Until my nose seems sniffing for a grave,
I'm bent so——and it's little that you care!

GIRL

(*Who has arisen from window and regards her
mother as in a dream*)

Hush, Mother dear, you'll wake him!

MOTHER

Wake him?   Where?
Who sleeps that should not wake?   Are you be-
witched?
Hush me again, and you'll be soundly switched!
As though I were a work brute to be dumb!
I'll talk my fill!

GIRL

O Mother, he has come——

MOTHER

(*Her body straightening slightly from its habitual
stoop*)

Eh?   Who might come that I should care to know
Since Ivan left?——He's dead.

[180]

FATHER

Aye, years ago,

And stubborn grieving is a foolish sin.

MOTHER

(*With the old weary voice*)

One's head runs empty and the ghosts get in
When one is old and stooped.

(*Peevishly to the girl*)

Bestir yourself!

Lay plates and light the candles on the shelf.
No corpse lies here that it should be so dark.

(*Girl, moving as in a trance, lights candles with
a brand from the fireplace. Often she glances
expectantly at the window. The place is fully
illumined*)

What ails the hussy?

FATHER

'Tis a crazy lark

Sings in her head all day. Don't be too rough.
Come twenty winters, 'twill be still enough,
God knows!

MOTHER

(*At the fireplace*)

I heard no lark sing at her age.
They put me in the field to earn a wage
And be some use in the world.

(*To girl*)

What! Dawdling yet?

I'll lark you in a way you won't forget,
Come forty winters! Speak! What do you mean?

GIRL

(*Still staring at the window and speaking dreamily as to herself*)

Up from the valley creeps the loving green
Until the loneliest hill-top is a bride.

MOTHER

The girl's gone daft!

FATHER

'Tis vapors. Let her bide.

She's weaving bride-veils with a woof of the moon,
And every wind's a husband. All too soon
She'll stitch at grave-clothes in a stuff more stern.

GIRL

(*Arousing suddenly*)
I'm sorry that I let the supper burn—
'Tis all so sweet, I scarce know what I do—
He came——

MOTHER

Who came?

GIRL

A stranger that I knew;
And he was weary, so I took him in
And gave him supper, thinking 'twere a sin
That anyone should want and be denied.
And while he ate, the place seemed glorified,
As though it were the Saviour sitting there!
It could not be the sunset bound his hair
Briefly with golden haloes—made his eyes
Such depths to gaze in with a dumb surprise
While one blinked thrice!—Then suddenly it passed,
And he was some old friend returned at last
After long years.

MOTHER

A pretty tale, indeed!
And so it was our supper went to feed
A sneaking ne'er-do-well, a shiftless scamp!

[183]

GIRL

O Mother, wasn't Jesus Christ a tramp?

MOTHER

Hush, will you! hush! 'Tis plain the Devil's here!
To think my only child should live to jeer
At holy things!

FATHER

          Come, don't abuse the maid.
They say He was a carpenter by trade,
Yet no one ever saw the house He built.

MOTHER

So! Shield the minx! Make nothing of her guilt,
And let the Devil get her—as he will!
I'll hold my tongue and work, and eat my fill
From what the beggars leave, for all you care!
Quick! Where's this scoundrel?

GIRL

          'Sh! He's sleeping there
Out in the garden.

(*Shows a gold piece*)

          Mother, see, he paid
So much more than he owed us, I'm afraid.
We lose in taking, profit what we give.

[184]

MOTHER

(*Taking the coin*)

What! Gold? A clever bargain, as I live!
It's five times what the fowls brought!—Not so bad!
And yet—I'll wager 'tis not all he had—
Eh?

GIRL

No—eight hundred rubles in a sack!

MOTHER

Eight—hundred—rubles! Yet the times are slack,
And coins don't spawn like fishes, Goodness knows!
I'll warrant he's some thief that comes and goes
About the country with a ready smile
And that soft speech that is the Devil's guile,
Nosing out hoards that reek with honest sweat!
Ha, ha—there's little here that he can get.

(*Goes to window softly, peers out, then closes the
casement*)

Eight—hundred—rubles—

GIRL

Mother, had you heard
How loving kindness spoke in every word,
You could not doubt him. O, his eyes were mild,
And there were heavens in them when he smiled!

MOTHER

Satan can outsmile God.

GIRL

                              No, no, I'm sure
He brought some gift of good that shall endure
And be a blessing to us!

MOTHER

                              So indeed!
Eight—hundred—rubles—with the power to breed
Litters of copecks till one need not work!
Eight hundred hundred backaches somehow lurk
In that snug wallet.

   (*To the father*)

                    What's the thing to do?

FATHER

It would be pleasant with a pot of brew
To talk until the windows glimmer pale.
'Tis good to harken to a traveller's tale
Of things far off where almost no one goes.

MOTHER

As well to parley with a wind that blows
Across fat fields, yet has no grain to share.

Rubles are rubles, and a tale is air.
I'll have the rubles!

GIRL

(*Aghast*)

Mother!   Mother dear!
What if 'twere Ivan sleeping far from here,
And some one else should do this sinful deed!

MOTHER

Had they not taken my son, I should not need
Eight hundred rubles now!   The world's made
      wrong,
And I'll not live to vex it very long.
Who work should take their wages where they can.
It should have been my boy come back a man,
With this same goodly hoard to bring us cheer.
Now let some other mother peer and peer
At her own window through a blurring pane,
And see the world go out in salty rain,
And start at every gust that shakes the door!
What does a green girl know?   You never bore
A son that you should prate of wrong and right!
I tell you, I have wakened in the night,
Feeling his milk-teeth sharp upon my breast,
And for one aching moment I was blest,
Until I minded that 'twas years ago
These flattened paps went milkless—and I know!

[187]

GIRL

O Mother! 'twould be sin!

MOTHER

         Sin?   What is that—
When all the world prowls like a hungry cat,
Mousing the little that could make us glad?

FATHER

Don't be forever grieving for the lad.
'Twas hard, but there are troubles worse than death.
Let's eat and think it over.

MOTHER

         Save your breath,
Or share your empty prate with one another!
One moment makes a father, but a mother
Is made by endless moments, load on load.

  (*Pause: then to girl*)

I left a bundle three bends down the road.
Go fetch it.

GIRL

  (*Pleadingly*)

         Mother, promise not to do
This awful thing you think.

[188]

MOTHER

(*Seizing a stick from the fireplace*)

I'll promise you,
And pay in welts—you simpering hussy!

(*The girl flees through back door. After a pause
the woman turns to the man*)

—Well?
Eight hundred rubles, and no tale to tell—
The fresh earth strewn with leaves—is that the plan?

FATHER

(*Startled*)

Eh?—That?—You mean—You would not kill a
man?
Not that!

MOTHER

Eight—hundred—rubles.

FATHER

It is much.
Old folk might hobble far with less for crutch—
But murder!—Rubles spent are rubles still—
Blood squandered—'tis a fearsome thing to kill!

[189]

I know what rubles cost—they all come hard,
But life's the dearer.

MOTHER

                    Kill a hog for lard,
A thief for gold—one reason and one knife!
I tell you, gold is costlier than life!
What price shall we have brought when we are gone?
When Ivan died, the heartless world went on
Breeding more sons that men might still be cheap.
And who but I had any tears to weep?
I mind 'twas April when the tale was brought
That he'd been lost at sea.   I thought and thought
About the way all things were mad to breed—
One big hot itch to suckle or bear seed—
And my boy dead!
                    Life costly?—Cheap as mud!
You want the rubles, sicken at the blood,
You grey old limping coward!

FATHER

                    Come now, Mother!
I'd kill to live as lief as any other.
You women don't weigh matters like a man.
I like the gold—'tis true—but not the plan.
Why not put pebbles where the rubles were,
Then send him forth?

MOTHER

                    And set the place a-whir
With a wind of tongues!   I tell you, we must kill!
No tale dies harder than a tale of ill.
Once buried, he will tell none.

[190]

FATHER

> Let me think—
I'll go down to the tavern for a drink
To whet my wits—belike the dread will pass.

(*He goes out through the back door, shaking his head in perplexity*)

MOTHER

(*Alone*)

He'll find a coward's courage in his glass—
Enough to dig a hole when he comes back.

(*She goes to shelf and snuffs the candles. The moon shines brightly through the window and the firelight glows. She takes a knife from a table drawer, feels the edge; goes to the window and peers out; turns about, uneasily scanning the room, then moves toward the side door, muttering*)

Eight hundred shining rubles in a sack!

(*She goes out softly and closes the door. A cry is heard as of one in a nightmare. After a considerable interval the mother reenters with a small bag which she is opening with nervous fingers. The moonlight falls upon her. Now and then she endeavors to shake something from*)

her hands, which she finally wipes on her apron,
muttering the while)

When folks get rich they find their fingers dirty.

(She counts the coins in silence for a while, then
aloud)

Eight and twenty—nine and twenty—thirty—

(Clutching a handful of gold, she suddenly stops
counting and stares at the back door. There
is the sound of rapidly approaching footsteps.
The door flies open and the old man enters
excitedly)

FATHER

Mother! Mother! Wake him! Wake him—
  quick!
'Tis Ivan with an old-time, merry trick—
They told me at the tavern—'tis our son!

(Rushes toward the side door)

Ivan! Ivan!

(Stops abruptly, aghast at the look of the woman.
The coins jangle on the floor)

God! What have you done!

(As the curtain falls, the singing voice of the returning girl is heard nearer and nearer)

GIRL

(Outside)

O weary heart and sore,
O yearning eyes that blur,
A hand that drips with myrrh
Is knocking at the door!
   The waiting time is o'er,
Be glad, look up and see
How splendid is a dream come true—
'Tis he! 'tis he!

AGRIPPINA
(1911)

AGRIPPINA

(The courtyard of the Imperial villa at Baiae. A moonlit night in late March. Occupying the left half of background is seen a portion of the villa. A short, broad flight of steps leads through the arched doorway to a pillared hall beyond, vague, but seeming vast in the uncertain lights that flicker in the draught. To the right of the doorway is a broad open window at the height of a man's head from the courtyard. An urn stands near window in the shadow to the right. From within harp music is heard threading the buzzing merriment of a banquet that is being given to celebrate Nero's reconciliation with his mother. To the right of stage a glimpse of the moonlit sea is caught through trees.

Enter from left walking toward the sea, Anicetus and the Captain of a galley.)

CAPTAIN

(Pointing toward sea.)

Yon lies the galley weltering in the moon,
A fair ship!— like a lady in a swoon
Of languid passion.   Never fairer craft
Flung the green rustle of her skirts abaft
And wooed the dwindling leagues!

ANICETUS

A boat's a boat!
And were she thrice the fairest keel afloat
Tonight she founders, sinks—make sure of that!

CAPTAIN

And all to drown one lean imperial cat
With claws and teeth too sharp despite the purr!
Ah, scan the graceful woman-lines of her!
Fit for the male Wind's love is she—alas!
Scuttled and buried in a sea of glass
By her own master! It will cost me pain.
Better a night of lightning-riven rain
With hell-hounds baying in the driven gloom!

ANICETUS

The will of Nero is her wind of doom—
Woe to the seaman who defies that gale!
Go now—make ready that we may not fail
To crown the wish of Caesar with the deed.

CAPTAIN

Aye, Master!

(*Exit Captain toward sea.*)

ANICETUS

And no brazen wound shall bleed
Red scandal over Rome; the nosing mob

Shall sniff no poison.   Just a gulping sob
And some few bubbles breaking on the swell—
Then, good night, Agrippina, rest you well!
And may the gods revamp the silly fish
With guts of brass for coping with that dish!

(*A muffled outburst of laughter in banquet hall.*
Anicetus turns toward window.   Uproar dies
out.)

They're drinking deep—the banquet's at its height
And all therein are kings and queens tonight.

(*Goes to urn, mounts it and peers in at window.*)

A merry crew!   Quite drunk, quite drunk I fear,
My noble Romans!—Burrus' eyes are blear!
One goblet hence, good Burrus, you will howl!
E'en Seneca sits staring like an owl
And strives to pilot in some heavy sea
That wisdom-laden boat, his head.   Ah me,
Creperius Gallus, you are floundering deep
In red Falernian bogs, so you shall sleep
Quite soundly while your mistress takes the dip!
Fair Acerronia thinks the place a ship
And greenly sickens in the dizzy roll!
There broods Poppaea, certain of her goal,
Her veil a sea-fog clutching at the moon,
A portent to wise sailors!   Very soon
The sea shall wake in hunger and be fed!
She smiles!—the glimmer on a thunderhead
That vomits ruin!—What has made her smile?
Ah, Nero's wine is sugared well with guile!

So—kiss your mother—gently fondle her—
Pet the old she-cat till she mew and purr
Unto the tender hand that strokes her back:
So shall there be no sniffing at the sack!
Would that her eyes, like his, with wine were dim!
Gods! What a tragic actor died in him
To make a comic Caesar!

                                   I surmise

By the too rheumy nature of your eyes,
Divine imperial Nero, and their sunk
Lugubrious aspect—pardon!but you're drunk,
Drunk as a lackey when the master's out!
O kingly tears that down that regal snout
Pour salty love upon a mother's breast!
So shall her timid doubts be lulled to rest!

(*Bustle within as of many rising to their feet.*)

They rise!   The prologue's ended—now the play!

(*He gets down from urn and goes off toward sea.*)

HERALDS

(*Crying within.*)

Make way for Caesar! Ho! Make way! Make way!

(*The musicians within strike up a martial strain.
After a few moments, within the hall appear Nero
and Agrippina, arm in arm, approaching the flight
of steps.   Nero is robed in a tunic of the color
of amethyst, with a winged harp embroidered on*

*the front. He is crowned with a laurel wreath,
now askew in his disordered hair. Agrippina
wears a robe of maroon without decoration. Nero
endeavors to preserve the semblance of supporting
his mother, but in fact is supported by her, while
he caresses her with considerable extravagance.
They pause half way down the steps, and the
music within changes to a low melancholy air.)*

AGRIPPINA

(*Lifting her face to the moon seaward.*)
How fair a moon to crown our happy revel!

NERO

(*Gazing blankly at the moon.*)

Eh? Veil the hussy!

AGRIPPINA

Son, son!

NERO

She's a devil!

AGRIPPINA

(*Placing a loving arm closer about Nero.*)

Just such a night 't was, Lucius—you remember?—
When Claudius' spirit like a smouldering ember
Struggled 'twixt flame and ash—do you forget?

[201]

NERO

Ha ha—'t was snuffed—ho ho!

AGRIPPINA

(*Stroking his hair.*)

                   'T was then I set
The imperial circlet here; 't was then I cloaked
My boy with world-robes!

NERO

(*Still staring at moon and pointing unsteadily.*)

                Have that vixen choked!
Her staring makes me stagger—where's her veil?

AGRIPPINA

It all comes back like an enchanted tale—
The moon set and the sun rose—

NERO

                  Dead and gone—
The sun set and the moon rose—

AGRIPPINA

                    Nay, at dawn
The blear flame died, the new flame blossomed up.

NERO

Did someone drop a poison in my cup?
The windless sea crawls moaning—

(*They move slowly down stairs, Nero clinging to his mother.*)

AGRIPPINA

Son of mine,
Cast off the evil humors of the wine!
I am so happy and was so forlorn!
Ah, not another night since you were born
Has flung such purple through me!   Son—at last
The haggard hours that parted us are past;
I've wept my tears and have no more to shed!
I live—I live—I live!   And I was dead.

NERO

(*Clinging closer.*)

Dead—dead—what ails the sea?—'tis going red— ·

(*Laughter in banquet hall.*)

Who's laughing?—Mother—drive them from the
    place!
Who gave the moon Poppaea's dizzy face
To scare the sea?

AGRIPPINA

Your message gave me life!
Ah, Lucius, not for us to mar with strife
A world so made for loving!

Lucius dear,
I was too harsh, perhaps; the fault is here.

(*Places hand on heart.*)

NERO

(*Staring into his mother's eyes.*)

Too harsh perhaps——

AGRIPPINA

Yea, so we mothers err:
Too long we see our babies as they were,
And last of all the world confess them tall.
They stride so far——we shudder lest they fall——
They toddle yet.

And she who bears a son
Shall be two women ever after; one
The fountain of a seaward cooing stream,
And one the shrouded virgin of a dream
Whom no man wooes, whose heart, a muted lyre,
Pines with a wild but unconfessed desire
For him who——never understands, my son!
I'll be all fountain——kill that other one!

[204]

NERO

That other one—

AGRIPPINA

O, like a wind of Spring
Wooing the sere grave of a buried thing,
Your summons came! Such happy tendrils creep
Out of me, in that old ache rooted deep,
To blossom sunward greener for the sorrow.
And, O my Emperor, if on the morrow
Your heart could soften toward that gentle one,
That frail white lily pining for the sun,
Octavia, your patient little wife!
Smile, smile upon that flower and give it life!
Make of my Lucius emperor in truth,
Not Passion's bondman!
                                    'T is the way of youth
To drive wild stallions with too slack a rein
Toward fleeing goals no fleetness can attain!
O splendid speed that fails for lack of fear!
The grip of iron makes the charioteer!
The lyric fury heeds the master beat
And is the freer for its shackled feet!
You who are Law shall be more free than others
By seeming less so, Lucius.

NERO

                                    Best of mothers,
Tomorrow—yes, tomorrow—Mother, stay!
You must not go so far, so far away!

Only to Bauli.

>(*They have reached the extreme right of stage. The
>guests now begin to come out of banquet hall,
>scattering a rippling laughter. Nero is aroused
>by the merry sound, looks back, gathers himself
>together with a start.*)

NERO

Ah! The moon is bright!

The sea is still! We'll banquet every night,
Will we not, Mother?

Certain cares of state

Weigh heavily—'tis awful to be great—
Nay, terrible at times! Can I be ill?
It seemed the sea moaned—yet 'tis very still!
Mother, my Mother—kiss me! Let us go
Down to the galley—so.

>(*They pass out toward the sea, Nero caressing his
>mother. The guests now throng down the steps
>into the courtyard. They are in various states of
>intoxication. Many are dressed to represent
>mythological figures: Fauns and Satyrs; Bacchus
>crowned with grape leaves, wearing a leopard
>skin on his shoulders; six Bacchantes; Psyche
>with wings; Luna in a spangled tunic with silver
>horns in her hair; Mercury with winged sandals
>and the caduceus; Neptune in an emerald robe,
>crowned and bearing the trident; Iris, rainbow-*

clad; Silenus.   Some are dressed in brilliant orien-
tal garments.   There are Senators in broad bor-
dered togas with half moons embroidered on their
sandals; Pages dressed as Cupids and infant Bacchi;
Officers of the Praetorian Guard in military uni-
form.   Turbaned, half nude Numidian slaves,
with bronze rings in their ears, come trotting in
with litters, attended by torch-bearers.   Some of
the guests depart in the litters.   The music con-
tinues in banquet hall.)

NEPTUNE

(Staggering against Luna.)

Who'd be a sailor when great Neptune staggers
Dashed in the Moon's face!——Calm me, gentle Luna,
And silver me with kisses!

LUNA

(Fleeing from his outstretched arms, but regarding
him invitingly over her shoulder.)

                                    Fie, you wine-skin!
A hiccough's not a tempest!   Lo, I glide,
Treading a myriad stars!

(Neptune follows with a rolling gait.)

A SATYR

(Looking after them as they disappear.)

Roll, eager Tide!
Methinks ere long the wooing moon shall fall!

(*Those near laugh.*)

FIRST SENATOR

(*To Second Senator.*)

Was Nero acting, think you?

SECOND SENATOR

Not at all.
'Twas staged, no doubt, but——

FIRST SENATOR

Softly, lest they hear!

SECOND SENATOR

The mimic is in mimicry sincere—
The rôle absorbed the actor. So he wept.

(*They pass on, talking low.*)

A PRAETORIAN OFFICER

(*To Psyche leaning on his arm.*)

Was it a vision, Psyche? Have I slept?
By the pink-nippled Cyprian, I swear

[208]

Our Caesar knows a woman! Gods! That hair!
Spun from the bowels of Ophir!

PSYCHE

Who's so fair?

PRAETORIAN

Poppaea!

PSYCHE

She?—A Circe, queen of hogs;
A cross-road Hecate, bayed at by the dogs!
A morbid Itch—

PRAETORIAN

Sh!

PSYCHE

—strutting in a cloak
Of what she has not, virtue!

PRAETORIAN

Ha! You joke!
All cloaks are ruses, fashioned to reveal
What all possess, pretending to conceal—
Who'd love a Psyche else?

[209]

(They pass on.)

IRIS

(To a Satyr who supports her.)

A clever wile
Her veil is!   Ah, we women must beguile
The stupid male by seeming to withhold
What's dross, displayed, but, guarded well, is gold!
Faugh!   Hunger sells it and the carter buys!

SATYR

Consume me with the lightning of her eyes!
She's Aphrodite!

IRIS

Helen!

SATYR

Helen, then!
A peep behind that veil, and once again
The sword-flung music of the fighting men,
Voluptuous ruin and wild battle joy,
The swooning ache and rapture that was Troy!
Delirious doom!

IRIS

(Laughing.)

[210]

O Sorcery of Night!
We're all one woman in the morning light!

SATYR

(*Laughing.*)

You're jealous!

IRIS

No, I rend the veil in twain!

(*They mingle with the throng.*)

SILENUS

(*To a Naval Officer.*)

The wind veers and the moon seems on the wane!
What bodes it—reinstatement for the Queen?

NAVAL OFFICER

No seaman knows the wind and moon you mean;
Yet land were safer when those signs concur!

(*They pass on.*)

MERCURY

(*To a Bacchante.*)

[211]

'T would rouse compassion in a toad, and stir
A wild boar's heart with pity!

BACCHANTE

(*Placing a warning hand on his mouth.*)

Hush! Beware!

MERCURY

Could you not feel the hidden gorgon stare
The venom of her laughter dripping slow?

(*The musicians from within, having followed the
departing throng from the banquet hall, and having stationed themselves on the steps, now strike
up a wild Bacchic air.*)

BACCHUS

(*Swinging into the dance.*)

Bacchantes, wreathe the dance!

BACCHANTES

(*From various parts of the throng.*)

Io, Bacche! Io!

(*Pirouetting to the music, they assemble, circling
about Bacchus, joining hands and singing. When*

[212]

the song is finished, the circle breaks, the dancers wheel, facing outward. Bacchus endeavors to kiss a Bacchante who regards him with head thrown back. The dance music becomes more abandoned, and the Bacchante flees, pursued by Bacchus, who reels as he dances. All the other Bacchantes follow, weaving in and out between pursuer and pursued. The throng laughingly makes way for them. At length the pursued Bacchante flings off in a mad whirl toward the grove in the background, followed by Bacchus and the Bacchantes. Fauns and Satyrs now take up the dance and join in the pursuit. The throng follows eagerly, enjoying the spectacle. All disappear among the trees. Laughter in the distance, growing dimmer. The musicians withdraw into the villa and disappear, their music dying out. The lights go out in the banquet hall. The stage is now lit by the moon alone, save for the draughty lamps within the pillared hall.. After a period of silence, re-enter Nero, walking backward from the direction of the sea toward which he gazes.)

NERO

Dimmer—dimmer—dimmer—
A shadow melting in a moony shimmer
Down the bleak seaways dwindling to that shore
Where no heaved anchor drips forevermore
Nor winds breathe music in the homing sail:
But over sunless hill and fruitless vale,
Gaunt spectres drag the age-long discontent

And ponder what this brief, bright moment meant—
The loving—and the dreaming—and the laughter.
Ah, ships that vanish take what never after
Returning ships may carry.

                    Dawn shall flare,
Make bloom the terraced gardens of the air
For all the world but Lucius.　He shall see
The haunted hollow of Infinity
Gray in the twilight of a heart's eclipse.
With our own wishes woven into whips
The jealous gods chastise us!—I'm alone!
About the transient brilliance of my throne
The giddy moths flit briefly in the glow;
But when at last that light shall flicker low,
A taper guttering in a gust of doom,
What hand shall grope for Nero's in the gloom,
What fond eyes shed the fellows of his tears?
She bore her heart these many troublous years
Before me, like a shield.　And she is dead.
Her hand 'twas set the crown upon my head;
Her heart's blood dyed the kingly robe for me.
The seaweed crowns her, and the bitter sea
Enshrouds with realmless purple!

                    Round and round,
Swirled in the endless nightmare of the drowned,
Her fond soul gropes for something vaguely dear
That lures, eludes forever.　Shapes that leer,
Distorted Neros of a tortured sleep,
Cry *"Mother, come to Baiae."*　Deep on deep
The green death folds her and she can not come.
Vague, gaping mouths that hunger and are dumb
Mumble the tired heart so ripe with woe,
Where night is but a black wind breathing low

And daylight filters like a ghostly rain!
O Mother! Mother! Mother!—

>   (*With arms extended, he stares seaward a moment,
>   then covers his face, turns, and walks slowly to-
>   ward entrance of villa.*)

>   Vain, 'tis vain!
How shall one move an ocean with regret?

>   (*He has reached the steps and pauses.*)

Ah, one hope lives in all this bleakness yet.
Song!—Mighty Song the hurt of life assuages!
This fateful night shall fill the vaulted ages
With starry grief, and men unborn shall sing
The mournful measure of the Ancient King!
I'll write an ode!

>   (*He stands for a moment, glorified with the
>   thought.*)

>   Great heart of Nero, strung
Harplike, endure till this last song be sung,
Then break—then break—

>   (*Turns and mounts the steps.*)

>   O Fate, to be a bard!
The way is hard, the way is very hard!

>   (*A dim outburst of laughter from the revellers in
>   the distance.*)

II

*(The same night. Nero's private chamber in his
villa at Baiae. Nero is discovered asleep in his
state robes on a couch, where he has evidently
thrown himself down, overcome by the stupor in-
cident to the feast of the night. Beside the couch
is a writing stand, bearing writing materials.
A few lights burn dimly. Nero groans, cries
out, and, as though terrified by a nightmare, sits
up, trembling and staring upon some projected
vision of his sleep. He is yet only half awake.)*

NERO

O—O—begone, blear thing!—She is not dead!
You are not she—my mother!—Ghastly head—
Trunkless—and oozing green gore like the sea,
Wind-stabbed! Begone! Go—do not look at me—
I will not be so tortured!—Eyes burned out
With scorious hell-spew!—Locks that grope about
To clutch and strangle!

*(He has got up from the couch and now struggles
with something at his throat, still staring at the
thing.)*

Off! Off!

*(In an outburst of terrified tenderness extends his
arms as toward a woman.)*

[216]

                              Mother—Mother—come.
Into these arms—speak to me—be not dumb!
Stare not so wildly—kiss me as of old!
Be flesh again—warm flesh! O green and cold
As the deep grave they gave you!

                                        'Twas not I!
Mother, 'twas not my will that you should die—
'Twas hers!—I hate her! Mother, pity me!
O, is it you?—Sole goddess of the sea
I will proclaim you! Pity! I will pour
The hot blood of your foes on every shore,
A huge libation! Hers shall be the first!
I swear it! May my waking be accursed,
My sleep a-swarm with furies if I err!

    (*He has advanced a short distance toward what he
    sees, but now shrinks back burying his face in
    his robe.*)

Go!—Spare me!—Guards! Guards!

    (*Three soldiers, who have been standing guard with-
    out the chamber, rush in and stand at attention.*)

                                   Seize and shackle her!

There 'tis!—eh?

    (*He stares blankly, rubs his eyes.*)

                    It is gone!
                    [217]

(Blinks at soldiers, and cries petulantly.)

What do you here?

FIRST SOLDIER

Great Caesar summoned us.

NERO

(Glancing nervously about.)

The night is drear—
Make lights! I will not have these shadow things
Crawling about me! Poisoners of kings
Fatten on shadows! Quick there, dog-eyed scamp,
Lean offal-sniffer! Kindle every lamp!

(Soldier tremblingly takes a lamp and lights a num-
ber of others with its flame. Stage is flooded
with light.)

By the bronze beard I swear there shall be lights
Enough hereafter, though I purge the nights
With conflagrating cities, till the crash
Of Rome's last tower beat up the smouldering ash
Of Rome's last city!
So—I breathe again!
Some cunning, faneless god who hated men
Devised this curse of darkness! What's the hour?

SECOND SOLDIER

The third watch wanes.

NERO

        Too late! Too late! The power
Of Nero Caesar can not stay the sun!
The stars have marched against me—it is done!
And all Rome's legions could not rout this swarm
Of venom-footed moments!

                     —She was warm
One little lost eternity ago.

   (With awakening resolution.)

'Twas not my deed! I did not wish it so!
Some demon, aping Caesar, gave the word
While Lucius Aenobarbus' eyes were blurred
With too much beauty!

                  O, it shall be done!
Ere these unmothered eyes behold the sun,
She shall have vengeance, and that gift is mine!

   (To First Soldier.)

Rouse the Praetorians! Bid a triple line
Be flung about the palace!

   (To Second Soldier.)

                    Send me wine—
Strong wine to nerve a resolution!

   (To Third Soldier.)

                       You—
Summon Poppaea!

(The soldiers go out.)
                              This deed I mean to do
Unties the snarl, but broken is the thread.
Would that the haughty blood these hands will shed
Might warm my mother! that the breath I crush—
So—*(clutching air)* from that throat of sorceries, might
     rush
Into the breast that loved and nurtured me!
The heart of Nero shivers in the sea,
And Rome is lorn of pity!
                              Could the world
And all its crawling spawn this night be hurled
Into one woman's form, with eyes to shed
Rivers of scalding woe, her towering head
Jeweled with realms aflare, with locks of smoke,
Huge nerves to suffer, and a neck to choke—
That woman were Poppaea! I would rear
About the timeless sea, my mother's bier,
A sky-roofed desolation groined with awe,
Where, nightly drifting in the stream of law,
The vestal stars should tend their fires, and weep
To hear upon the melancholy deep
That shipless wind, her ghost, amid the hush!
Alas! I have but one white throat to crush
With these world-hungry fingers!

> *(From behind Nero, enter Page—a little boy—bear-*
> *ing a goblet of wine on a salver. Nero turns,*
> *startled.)*
>   Ah!—You!—You!

PAGE

I bring wine, mighty Caesar.

[220]

(*Nero passes his hand across his face, and the ex-pression of fright leaves.*)

NERO

So you do—

I saw—the boy Brittanicus!—One sees—
Things—does one not?—such eerie nights as these?

PAGE

(*With eager boyish earnestness.*)
With woozy heads?

NERO

(*Irritably.*)

The wine!

(*The Page, startled, presents the salver, from which
Nero takes the goblet with unsteady hand. Page
is in the act of fleeing.*)

Stay!

(*Page stops trembling.*)

Never dare
Again to look like—anyone! Beware!
(*Page's head shakes a timid negative. Nero stares
into goblet and muses.*)

[221]

Blood's red too.   Ah, a woman is the grape
Ripe for the vintage, from whose flesh agape
Glad feet tonight shall stamp the hated ooze!
It boils!——See!——like some witch's pot that brews
Venomous ichor!——Nay——some angry ghost
Hurls bloody breakers on a bleeding coast!——
'Tis poisoned!——Out, Locusta's brat!
   (*Hurls goblet at Page, who flees precipitately.*)

                                    'Twas she!
The hand that flung my mother to the sea
Now pours me death!
                      Alas, great Hercules
Too long has plied the distaff at the knees
Of Omphale, spinning a thread of woe!
Was ever king of story driven so
By unrelenting Fate?   Lo, round on round
The slow coils grip and croke——a mother drowned,
Her wrathful spirit rising from the dead——
A gentle wife outcast, discredited,
With sighs to wake the dread Eumenides!
Some thunder-hearted, vaster Sophocles,
His aeon-beating blood the stellar stream,
Has flung on me the mantle of his dream,
And Nero grapples Fate!   O wondrous play!
With smoking brand aloft, the haggard Day
Gropes for the world!   Pursued by subtle foes,
Superbly tragic 'mid a storm of woes,
The fury-hunted Caesar takes the cue!
One time-outstaring deed remains to do,
Then let the pit howl——Caesar sings no more!
Go ask the battered wreckage on the shore
Who sought his mother in a sudden sleep,

To be with her forever on the deep
A twin ship-hating tempest!

(*Enter Anicetus excitedly.*)

ANICETUS

Lost! We're lost!
The Roman ship yaws rockward tempest-tossed
And Nero is but Lucius in the wreck!

NERO

Croak on! Each croak's a dagger in that neck,
You vulture with the hideous dripping beak,
The clutching tearing talons that now reek
With what dear sacred veins!

ANICETUS

O Caesar, hear!
So keen the news I bear you, that I fear
To loose it like the arrow it must be.
I know not why such wrath you heap on me;
I know what peril deepens 'round my lord;
How, riven by the lightning of the sword,
The doom-voiced blackness labors 'round his head!

NERO

Say what I know, that my poor mother's dead—
So shall your life be briefer!

[223]

ANICETUS

Would 't were so!

NERO

(*A light coming into his face.*)
She lives?

ANICETUS

Yea, lives—and lives to overthrow!

NERO

Not perished?

ANICETUS

—And her living is our death!

NERO

She moves and breathes?

ANICETUS

—And potent is her breath
To blow rebellion up!

NERO

(*Rubbing his eyes.*)
                                        Still do I sleep?
Is this a taunting dream that I may weep
More bitterly?   Or some new foul intrigue?

[224]

ANICETUS

'Tis bitter fact to her who swam a league,
And bitter fact to Nero shall it be!
At Bauli now, still dripping from the sea,
She crouches snarling!

NERO

(*In an outburst of joy.*)
                                    O, you shall not die,
My best-loved Anicetus!   Though you lie,
Sweeter these words are than profoundest truth!
They breathe the fresh, white morning of my youth
Upon the lampless night that smothered me!
O more than human Sea
That spared my mother that her son might live!
What bounty can I give?
I—Caesar—falter beggared at this gift
Of living words that lift
My mother from the regions of the dead!
Ah—I shall set a crown upon your head,
Snip you a kingdom from Rome's flowing robe!
I'll temple you in splendors!   Yea, I'll probe
Your secret heart to know what wishes pant
In wingless yearning there, that I may grant!
    (*Pause, while Anicetus regards Nero with gloomy
      face.*)
What sight thus makes your face a pool of gloom?

ANICETUS

The ghost of Nero crying from his tomb!

[225]

NERO

(*Startled.*)
Eh?—Nero's ghost—mine?

ANICETUS

                    Even so I said.
The doomed to perish are already dead
Who woo not Fate with swift unerring deeds!
That breathless moment when the tigress bleeds
Is ours to strike in, ere the tigress spring!
What could it boot your servant to be king
While any moment may the trumpets cry,
Hailing the certain hour when we shall die—
Caesar, the deaf, and his untrusted slave?
Peer deep, peer deep into this yawning grave
And tell me who shall fill it!—Wind and fire,
Harnessed with thrice the ghost of her dead sire,
Your mother is tonight! She knows, she knows
How galleys founder when no tempest blows
And moonlight slumbers on a glassy deep!
The beast our wound has wakened shall not sleep
Till it be gorged with slaughter, or be slain!
Lull not your heart, O Caesar! It is vain
To dream this cub-lorn tigress will not turn.
Lo, flaring through the dawn I see her burn,
A torch of revolution! Hear her raise
The legions with a voice of other days,
Worded with pangs to fret their ancient scars!
And every sword-wound of her father's wars
Will shriek aloud with pity!

NERO

(*During Anicetus' speech he has shown growing fear.*)

Listen!—There!
You heard it?—Did you hear a trumpet blare?

ANICETUS

'Tis but the shadow of a sound to be
One rushing hour away!

NERO

(*In panic.*)

Where shall I flee?—
I, the sad poet whom she made a king!
At last we flesh the ghost of what we sing—
We bards!—I sang Orestes.
(*His face softens with a gentler thought.*)

Ah—I'll go
To my poor heartsick mother.   Tears shall flow,
The tears of Lucius, not imperial tears.
I'll heap on her the vast, too vast arrears
Of filial love.   The Senate shall proclaim
My mother regnant with me—write her name
Beside Augustus with the demigods!
Yea, lictors shall attend her with the rods,
And massed Praetorians tramp the rabble down
Whene'er her chariot flashes through the town!
One should be kind to mothers.

ANICETUS

Yea, and be

Kind to the senseless fury of the sea,
Fondle the tempest in a rotten boat!

NERO

What would you, Anicetus?

ANICETUS

Cut her throat!
(*Nero gasps and shrinks from Anicetus.*)

NERO

No, no!——her ghost!——one can not stab so deep——
One can not kill these tortures spawned of sleep!
No, no——one can not kill them with a sword!

ANICETUS

Faugh! One good thrust——the rest is air, my lord!
(*Enter Page timorously. Nero turns upon him.*)

PAGE

(*Frightened.*)
Spare me, good Caesar!——Agerinus——

[228]

NERO

Go!

Bid Agerinus enter!
(*Page flees. Nero to Anicetus menacingly.*)
We shall know
What breath from what damned throat tonight shall
hiss!
(*Enter Agerinus, bowing low.*)

AGERINUS

My mistress sends fond greetings and a kiss
To her most noble son, and bids me say,
She rests and would not see him until day.
The royal galley, through unhappy chance,
Struck rock and foundered; but no circumstance
So meagre might deprive a son so dear
Of his beloved mother! Have no fear,
The long swim leaves her weary, but quite well.
She knows what tender love her son would tell
And yearns for dawn to bring him to her side.

NERO

(*To Anicetus.*)
So! Spell your doom from that! You lied! You
lied!
I'll lance that hateful fester in your throat!
Yea, we shall prove who rides the rotten boat
And supplicates the tempest!
(*With a rapid motion, Nero draws Agerinus' sword*

[229]

*from its sheath.. Anicetus shrinks back. Nero
cries to Agerinus.)*

Wait to see
The loving message you bear back from me!
*(Nero brandishing the sword, makes at Anicetus. As
he is about to deliver the stroke, enter Poppaea
from behind.. She has evidently been quite
leisurely about her toilet, being dressed gorgeously,
and wearing her accustomed half-veil. Her man-
ner is stately and composed. She approaches
slowly. Nero stops suddenly in the act to strike
Anicetus, and stares upon the beautiful apparition.
Anger leaves his face, which changes as though
he had seen a great light.)*

POPPAEA

(Languidly.)
My Nero longed for me?
*(Nero with his free hand brushes his eyes in per-
plexity.)*

NERO

I—can not—tell—
What—'twas—I wished—I wished—

POPPAEA

(Haughtily.)
Ah, very well.
*(She walks slowly on across the stage. Nero stares
blankly after her. The sword drops from his*

[230]

*hand. As Poppaea disappears, he rouses suddenly
as from a stupor.)*

NERO

Ho! Guards!
(Three soldiers enter. Nero points to Agerinus.)
          There—seize that wretch who came to kill
Imperial Caesar!
(Agerinus is seized. Nero turns to Anicetus.)
                              Hasten! Do your will!
*(Nero turns, and with an eager expression on his face,
goes doddering after Poppaea.)*

III

*(The same night. Agrippina's private chamber in
her villa at Bauli near Baiae. There is one lamp
in the room. At the center back is a broad door
closed with heavy hangings. At the right is an
open window through which the moonlight falls.
Agrippina is discovered lying on a couch. One
maid, Nina, is in attendance and is arranging
Agrippina's hair.)*

AGRIPPINA

He was so tender—what should kindness mean?
(The maid seems not to hear.)
I spoke!—you heard me speak?

NINA

                              I heard, my Queen.

AGRIPPINA

And deemed my voice some ghostly summer wind
Fit for autumnal hushes?   He was kind!
Was ever breath in utterance better spent?

NINA

Your slave could scarcely fancy whom you meant,
There are so many tender to the great.

AGRIPPINA

When all the world is one sky-circled state,
Pray, who shall fill it as the sun the sky?
The mother of that mighty one am I—
And he caressed me!
                                    I shall feel no pain
Forever now.   So, drenched with winter rain,
The friendless marshland knows the boyish South
And shivers into color!
                                    On the mouth
He kissed me, as before that other came—
That Helen of the stews, that corpse aflame
With lust for life, that—
                                    Ah, he maidened me!
What dying wind could sway so tall a tree
With such proud music?   I shall be again
That darkling whirlwind down the fields of men,
That dart unloosed, barbed keenly for his sake,
That living sword for him to wield or break,
But never sheathe!

(Lifts herself on elbow.)

                            O Nina, let me be
Robed as the queen I am in verity!
Robed as a victrix home from splendid wars,
Whom, 'mid the rumble of spoil-laden cars
Trundled by harnessed kings, the trumpets hail!
Let quiet garments be for those who fail,
Mourning a world ill-lost with meek surrenders!
I would flare bright 'mid Death's unhuman splendors,
Dazzle the moony hollows of the dead!
Ah no—
    (Arising and going to window.)
        I shall not die yet.
    (Parts the curtains and gazes out.)

NINA

                          'Tis the dread
Still clinging from the clutches of the sea,
That living, writhing horror! Ugh! O'er me
Almost I feel the liquid terror crawl!
Through glassy worlds of tortured sleep to fall,
Where winds blow not, nor mornings ever blush,
But green, cold, ghastly light-wraiths wander—

AGRIPPINA

    (Turning from window with nervous anger.)
                                  Hush!
    (Turns again to window; after pause, continues
      musingly.)
She battles in a surf of spectral fire.
No—like some queen upon a funeral pyre,

[233]

Gasping, she withers in a fever swoon.
Had she a son too?

NINA

(*Approaching the window.*)

Who, O Queen?

AGRIPPINA

The moon!
See, she is strangled in a noose of pearl!
What tell-tale scars she has!

—Look yonder, girl—
Your eyes are younger—by the winding sea
Where Baiae glooms and blanches; it may be
Old eyes betray not, but some horsemen take
The white road winding hither by the lake.

NINA

The way lies plain—I see no moving thing.

AGRIPPINA

Why thus is Agerinus loitering?
For he was ever true.
    (*Joyously.*)

Ah foolish head!
My heart knows how my son shall come instead,
My little Lucius! Even now he leaps
Into the saddle and the dull way creeps
Beneath the spurred impatience of his horse,

[234]

He longs so for me!
(*Pause—She scans the moonlit country.*)
                              Shrouded like a corse,
Hoarding a mother's secret, lies the sea;
And Capri, like a giant Niobe,
Outgazes Fate!
                         O sweet, too gentle lies
And kisses sword-like! Would the sun might rise
No more on Baiae! Would that earth might burst
Spewing blear doom upon this world accursed
With truth too big for hiding!
                              See! He sleeps
Beside her, and the shame-dimmed lamp-light creeps
Across her wine-stained mouth—so red—so red—
Like mother blood!—See! hissing round her head
Foul hate-fanged vipers that he calls her hair!
Ah no—beyond all speaking is she fair!
Sweet as a sword-wound in a gasping foe
Her mouth is; and too well, too well I know
Her face is dazzling as a funeral flame
Battened on queen's flesh!
    (*Turning angrily from window.*)
                              O the blatant shame!
The bungling drunkard's plot!—Tonight, tonight
I shall swoop down upon them by the light
Of naked steel! Faugh! Had it come to that?
Had Rome no sword, that like a drowning rat
The mother of a king should meet her end?
What Gallic legion would not call me friend?
Did they not love Germanicus, my sire?
O, I will rouse the cohorts, scattering fire
Till all Rome blaze rebellion!
    (*She has advanced to a place beside the couch, stands*
[235]

in a defiant attitude for a moment, then covers
her face with her hands and sinks to the couch.)

                 No, no, no—
It could not be, I would not have it so!
Not mine to burn the tower my hands have built!
And somewhere 'mid the shadows of his guilt
My son is good.

    (Lifts herself on elbow.)

              Look, Nina, toward the roofs
Of sleeping Baiae.   Say that eager hoofs
Beat a white dust-cloud moonward.

    (Nina goes to window and peers out.)

            NINA

                 Landward crawls
A sea fog; Capri's league-long shadow sprawls
Lengthening toward us—soon the moon will set.

         AGRIPPINA

No horsemen?

            NINA

    None, my Queen.

         AGRIPPINA

             —And yet—and yet—
He called me baby names.   Ah, ghosts that wept

Big tears down smiling faces, twined and crept
About my heart, and still I feel their tears.
They make me joyous.——After all these years,
The little boy my heart so often dirged
Shivered the man-husk, beardless, and emerged!
He kissed my breasts and hung upon my going!
Once more I felt the happy nurture flowing,
The silvery, tingling shivers of delight!
What though my end had come indeed tonight—
I was a mother!

                  ——Have you children?

          NINA

                        No,
My Queen.

          AGRIPPINA

       Yet you are winsome.

          NINA

                     Lovers go
Like wind, as lovers come; I am unwed.

          AGRIPPINA

How lonely shall you be among the dead
Where hearts remember, but are lorn of hope!
Poor girl! No dream of tiny hands that grope,
And coaxing, hunting little mouths shall throw
Brief glories 'round you!

Nina, I would go
Like any brazen bawd along the street,
Hailing the first stout carter I should meet,
Ere I would perish childless!   Though we nurse
The cooing thing that some day hurls the curse,
Forge from our hearts the matricidal sword,
The act of loving is its own reward.
We mothers need no pity!

'Twill be said,
When this brief war is done, and I am dead,
That I was wanton, shameless—be it so!
Unto the swarm of insect scribes I throw
The puffed-up purple carcass of my name
For them to feast on!   Pointed keen with shame,
How shall each busy little stylus bite
A thing that feels not!   I have fought my fight!
That mine were but the weapons of the foe,
Too well the ragged scars I bear can show.
O, I have triumphed, and am ripe to die!
About my going shall the trumpets cry
Forever and forever!

I can thread
The twilit under-regions of the dead
A radiant shadow with a heart that sings!
Before all women who have mothered kings
I shall lift up each livid spirit hand
Spotted with blood—and they shall understand
How small the price was!

NINA

Hark!

(*The tramp of soldiery and the clatter of arms are
heard from without.   Nina, panic-stricken, runs*

[238]

to window, peers out, shrinks back, and, turning,
flees by a side door.)

AGRIPPINA

                              Why do you flee?
Did I not say my son would come to me?
'Tis Nero—Nero Caesar, Lord of Rome!
My little boy grown tall is coming home!
  (She goes to window, peers out, shrinks back, then
    turns toward the door and sees three armed men
    standing there—Anicetus, the Captain of a Galley
    and a Centurion of the Navy. The men stare at
    her without moving.)
Why come you here?
  (Silence.)
                              To know my health?—Go tell
My son, your master, I am very well—
And happy—
  (The men make no reply. Agrippina straightens her
    body haughtily.)
                              —If like cowards in the night
You come to stab a woman—

ANICETUS

  (Drawing his sword and speaking to Captain.)
                              Snuff the light!
  (The men spring forward with drawn swords.
    Agrippina does not move. The light is stricken
    out.)

EPICS OF THE WEST

THE SONG OF THREE FRIENDS

(1919)

TO HILDA

Οἶον τὸ γλυκύμαλον ἐρεύθεται ἄκρῳ ἐπ᾽ ὕσδῳ
ἄκρον ἐπ᾽ ἀκροτάτῳ · λελάθοντο δὲ μαλοδρόπηες,
οὐ μὰν ἐκλελάθοντ᾽, αλλ᾽ οὐκ εδύναντ᾽ ἐπίκεσθαι.

THE SONG OF THREE
FRIENDS

I

ASHLEY'S HUNDRED

Who now reads clear the roster of that band?
Alas, Time scribbles with a careless hand
And often pinchbeck doings from that pen
Bite deep, where deeds and dooms of mighty men
Are blotted out beneath a sordid scrawl!

One hundred strong they flocked to Ashley's call
That spring of eighteen hundred twenty-two;
For tales of wealth, out-legending Peru,
Came wind-blown from Missouri's distant springs,
And that old sireny of unknown things
Bewitched them, and they could not linger more.
They heard the song the sea winds sang the shore
When earth was flat, and black ships dared the steep
Where bloomed the purple perils of the deep
In dragon haunted gardens. They were young.
Albeit some might feel the winter flung
Upon their heads, 'twas less like autumn's drift
Than backward April's unregarded sift
On stout oaks thrilling with the sap again.
And some had scarce attained the height of men,

Their lips unroughed, and gleaming in their eyes
The light of immemorial surprise
That life still kept the spaciousness of old
And, like the hoarded tales their grandsires told,
Might still run bravely.

        For a little span
Their life-fires flare like torches in the van
Of westward progress, ere the great wind 'woke
To snuff them. Many vanished like a smoke
The blue air drinks; and e'en of those who burned
Down to the socket, scarce a tithe returned
To share at last the ways of quiet men,
Or see the hearth-reek drifting once again
Across the roofs of old St. Louis town.

And now no more the mackinaws come down,
Their gunwales low with costly packs and bales,
A wind of wonder in their shabby sails,
Their homing oars flung rhythmic to the tide;
And nevermore the masted keelboats ride
Missouri's stubborn waters on the lone
Long zigzag journey to the Yellowstone.
Their hulks have found the harbor ways that know
The ships of all the Sagas, long ago—
A moony haven where no loud gale stirs.
The trappers and the singing *voyageurs*
Are comrades now of Jason and his crew,
Foregathered in that timeless rendezvous
Where come at last all seekers of the Fleece.

Not now of those who, dying, dropped in peace
A brimming cup of years the song shall be:
From Mississippi to the Western Sea,

From Britain's country to the Rio Grande
Their names are written deep across the land
In pass and trail and river, like a rune.

Pore long upon that roster by the moon
Of things remembered dimly. Tangled, blear
The writing runs; yet presently appear
Three names of men that, spoken, somehow seem
Incantatory trumpets of a dream
Obscurely blowing from the hinter-gloom.
Of these and that inexorable doom
That followed like a hound upon the scent,
Here runs the tale.

II

THE UP-STREAM MEN

When Major Henry went
Up river at the head of Ashley's band,
Already there were robins in the land.
Home-keeping men were following the plows
And through the smoke-thin greenery of boughs
The scattering wild-fire of the fruit bloom ran.

Behold them starting northward, if you can.
Dawn flares across the Mississippi's tide;
A tumult runs along the waterside
Where, scenting an event, St. Louis throngs.
Above the buzzling voices soar the songs
Of waiting boatmen—lilting *chansonettes*
Whereof the meaning laughs, the music frets,
Nigh weeping that such gladness can not stay.
In turn, the herded horses snort and neigh
Like panic bugles.   Up the gangplanks poured,
Go streams of trappers, rushing goods aboard
The snub-built keelboats, squat with seeming sloth—
Baled three-point blankets, blue and scarlet cloth,
Rum, powder, flour, guns, gauderies and lead.
And all about, goodbyes are being said.
Gauche girls with rainy April in their gaze
Cling to their beardless heroes, count the days
Between this parting and the wedding morn,
Unwitting how unhuman Fate may scorn

The youngling dream. For O how many a lad
Would see the face of Danger, and go mad
With her weird vixen beauty; aye, forget
This girl's face, yearning upward now and wet,
Half woman's with the first vague guess at woe!

And now commands are bellowed, boat horns blow
Haughtily in the dawn; the tumult swells.
The tow-crews, shouldering the long cordelles
Slack from the mastheads, lean upon the sag.
The keelboats answer lazily and drag
Their blunt prows slowly in the gilded tide.
A steersman sings, and up the riverside
The gay contagious ditty spreads and runs
Above the shouts, the uproar of the guns,
The nickering of horses.

                                        So, they say,
Went forth a hundred singing men that day;
And girlish April went ahead of them.
The music of her trailing garment's hem
Seemed scarce a league ahead. A little speed
Might yet almost surprise her in the deed
Of sorcery; for, ever as they strove,
A gray-green smudge in every poplar grove
Proclaimed the recent kindling. Aye, it seemed
That bird and bush and tree had only dreamed
Of song and leaf and blossom, till they heard
The young men's feet; when tree and bush and bird
Unleashed the whole conspiracy of awe!
Pale green was every slough about the Kaw;
About the Platte, pale green was every slough;
And still the pale green lingered at the Sioux,

So close they trailed the marching of the South.
But when they reached the Niobrara's mouth
The witchery of spring had taken flight
And, like a girl grown woman over night,
Young summer glowed.

                              And now the river rose,
Gigantic from a feast of northern snows,
And mightily the snub prows felt the tide;
But with the loud, sail-filling South allied,
The tow-crews battled gaily day by day;
And seldom lulled the struggle on the way
But some light jest availed to fling along
The panting lines the laughter of the strong,
For joy sleeps lightly in the hero's mood.
And when the sky-wide prairie solitude
Was darkened 'round them, and the camp was set
Secure for well-earned sleep that came not yet,
What stories shaped for marvel or for mirth!—
Tales fit to strain the supper-tightened girth,
Looped yarns, wherein the veteran spinners vied
To color with a lie more glorified
Some thread that had veracity enough,
Spun straightway out of life's own precious stuff
That each had scutched and heckled in the raw.
Then thinner grew each subsequent guffaw
While drowsily the story went the rounds
And o'er the velvet dark the summer sounds
Prevailed in weird crescendo more and more,
Until the story-teller with a snore
Gave over to a dream a tale half told.
And now the horse-guards, while the night grows old,

With intermittent singing buffet sleep
That surges subtly down the starry deep
On waves of odor from the manless miles
Of summer-haunted prairie. Now, at whiles,
The kiote's mordant clamor cleaves the drowse.
The horses stamp and blow; about the prows
Dark waters chug and gurgle; as with looms
Bugs weave a drone; a beaver's diving booms,
Whereat bluffs grumble in their sable cowls.
The devil laughter of the prairie owls
Mocks mirth anon, like unrepentant sin.
Perceptibly at last slow hours wear thin
The east, until the prairie stares with morn,
And horses nicker to the boatman's horn
That blares the music of a day begun.

So through the days of thunder and of sun
They pressed to northward. Now the river shrank,
The grass turned yellow and the men were lank
And gnarled with labor. Smooth-lipped lads matured
'Twixt moon and moon with all that they endured,
Their faces leathered by the wind and glare,
Their eyes grown ageless with the calm far stare
Of men who know the prairies or the seas.
And when they reached the village of the Rees,
One scarce might say, This man is young, this old,
Save for the beard.

                Here loitered days of gold
And days of leisure, welcome to the crews;
For recently had come the wondrous news
Of beaver-haunts beyond the Great Divide—
So rich a tale 'twould seem the tellers lied,

Had they not much fine peltry to attest.
So now the far off River of the West
Became the goal of venture for the band;
And since the farther trail lay overland
From where the Great Falls thundered to no ear,
They paused awhile to buy more ponies here
With powder, liquor, gauds and wily words.
A horse-fond people, opulent in herds,
The Rees were; and the trade was very good.

Now camped along the river-fringing wood,
Three sullen, thunder-brewing, rainless days,
Those weathered men made merry in their ways
With tipple, euchre, story, jest and song.
The marksmen matched their cleverness; the strong
Wrestled the strong; and brawling pugilists
Displayed the boasted power of their fists
In stubborn yet half amicable fights.
And whisky went hell-roaring through the nights
Among the lodges of the fuddled Rees.
Thus merrily the trappers took their ease,
Rejoicing in the thread that Clotho spun;
For it was good to feel the bright thread run,
However eager for the snipping shears.

O joy long stifled in the ruck of years!
How many came to strange and bitter ends!
And who was merrier than those three friends
Whom here a song remembers for their woe?

Will Carpenter, Mike Fink and Frank Talbeau
Were they—each gotten of a doughty breed;
For in the blood of them the ancient seed

Of Saxon, Celt and Norman grew again.
The Mississippi reared no finer men,
And rarely the Ohio knew their peers
For pluck and prowess—even in those years
When stern life yielded suck but to the strong.
Nor in the hundred Henry took along
Was found their match—and each man knew it well.
For instance, when it suited Mike to tell
A tale that called for laughter, as he thought,
The hearer laughed right heartily, or fought
And took a drubbing. Then, if more complained,
Those three lacked not for logic that explained
The situation in no doubtful way.
"Me jokes are always funny," Mike would say;
And most men freely granted that they were.

A lanky, rangy man was Carpenter,
Quite six feet two from naked heel to crown;
And, though crow-lean, he brought the steelyard down
With twice a hundred notched upon the bar.
Nor was he stooped, as tall men often are;
A cedar of a man, he towered straight.
One might have judged him lumbering of gait,
When he was still; but when he walked or ran,
He stepped it lightly like a little man—
And such a one is very good to see.
Not his the tongue for quip or repartee;
His wit seemed slow; and something of the child
Came o'er his rough-hewn features, when he smiled,
To mock the porching brow and eagle nose.
'Twas when he fought the true import of those
Grew clear, though even then his mien deceived;
For less in wrath, he seemed, than mildly grieved—

Which made his blows no whit less true or hard.
His hair was flax fresh gleaming from the card;
His eyes, the flax in bloom.

                               A match in might,
Fink lacked five inches of his comrade's height,
And of his weight scarce twenty pounds, they say.
His hair was black, his small eyes greenish gray
And restless as though feeling out of place
In such a jocund plenilunar face
That seemed made just for laughter.   Then one saw
The pert pugnacious nose, the forward jaw,
The breadth of stubborn cheekbones, and one knew
That jest and fight to him were scarcely two,
But rather shifting phases of the joy
He felt in living.   Careless as a boy,
Free handed with a gift or with a blow,
And giving either unto friend or foe
With frank good will, no man disliked him long.
They say his voice could glorify a song,
However loutish might the burden be;
And all the way from Pittsburg to the sea
The Rabelaisian stories of the rogue
Ran wedded to the richness of his brogue.
And wheresoever boatmen came to drink,
There someone broached some escapade of Fink
That well might fill the goat-hoofed with delight;
For Mike, the pantagruelizing wight,
Was happy in the health of bone and brawn
And had the code and conscience of the faun
To guide him blithely down the easy way.
A questionable hero, one might say;

And so indeed, by any civil law.
Moreover, at first glimpse of him one saw
A bull-necked fellow, seeming over stout;
Tremendous at a heavy lift, no doubt,
But wanting action. By the very span
Of chest and shoulders, one misjudged the man
When he was clothed. But when he stripped to swim,
Men flocked about to have a look at him,
Moved vaguely by that body's wonder-scheme
Wherein the shape of God's Adamic dream
Was victor over stubborn dust again!

O very lovely is a maiden, when
The old creative thrill is set astir
Along her blood, and all the flesh of her
Is shapen as to music! Fair indeed
A tall horse, lean of flank, clean-limbed for speed,
Deep-chested for endurance! Very fair
A soaring tree, aloof in violet air
Upon a hill! And 'tis a glorious thing
To see a bankfull river in the spring
Fight homeward! Children wonderful to see—
The Girl, the Horse, the River and the Tree—
As any suckled at the breast of sod;
Dissolving symbols leading back to God
Through vista after vista of the Plan!
But surely none is fairer than a man
In whom the lines of might and grace are one.

Bronzed with exposure to the wind and sun,
Behold the splendid creature that was Fink!
You see him strolling to the river's brink,

All ease, and yet tremendously alive.
He pauses, poised on tiptoe for the dive,
And momently it seems the mother mud,
Quick with a mystic seed whose sap is blood,
Mysteriously rears a human flower.
Clean as a windless flame the lines of power
Run rhythmic up the stout limbs, muscle-laced,
Athwart the ropy gauntness of the waist,
The huge round girth of chest, whereover spread
Enormous shoulders. Now above his head
He lifts his arms where big thews merge and flow
As in some dream of Michelangelo;
And up along the dimpling back there run,
Like lazy serpents stirring in the sun,
Slow waves that break and pile upon the slope
Of that great neck in swelling rolls, a-grope
Beneath the velvet softness of the skin.
Now suddenly the lean waist grows more thin,
The deep chest on a sudden grows more deep;
And with the swiftness of a tiger's leap,
The easy grace of hawks in swooping flight,
That terrible economy of might
And beauty plunges outward from the brink.

Thus God had made experiment with Fink,
As proving how 'twere best that men might grow.

One turned from Mike to look upon Talbeau—
A little man, scarce five feet six and slim—
And wondered what his comrades saw in him
To justify their being thus allied.
Was it a sort of planetary pride

In lunar adoration? Hark to Mike:
"Shure I declare I niver saw his like—
A skinny whiffet of a man! And yit—
Well, do ye moind the plisint way we mit
And how he interjooced hisself that day?
'Twas up at Pittsburg, liquor flowin' fray
And ivrybody happy as a fool.
I cracked me joke and thin, as is me rule,
Looked round to view the havoc of me wit;
And ivrywan was doubled up wid it,
Save only wan, and him a scrubby mite.
Says I, and shure me language was polite,
'And did ye hear me little joke?' says I.
'I did' says he. 'And can't ye laugh me b'y?'
'I can't' says he, the sassy little chap.
Nor did I git me hand back from the slap
I give him till he landed on me glim,
And I was countin' siventeen of him
And ivry dancin' wan of him was air!
Faith, whin I hit him he was niver there;
And shure it seemed that ivry wind that blew
Was peltin' knuckles in me face. Hurroo!
That toime, fer wance, I got me fill of fun!
God bless the little whiffet! It begun
Along about the shank of afthernoon;
And whin I washed me face, I saw the moon
A-shakin' wid its laughter in the shtrame.
And whin, betoimes, he wakened from his drame,
I says to him, 'Ye needn't laugh, me b'y:
A cliver little man ye are,' says I.
And Och, the face of me! I'm tellin' fac's—
Ye'd wonder did he do it wid an ax!
'Twas foine! 'Twas art!"

[259]

                    Thus, eloquent with pride,
Mike Fink, an expert witness, testified
To Talbeau's fistic prowess.

                              Now they say
There lived no better boatmen in their day
Than those three comrades; and the larger twain
In that wide land three mighty rivers drain
Found not their peers for skill in marksmanship.
Writes one, who made the long Ohio trip
With those boon cronies in their palmy days,
How once Mike Fink beheld a sow at graze
Upon the bank amid her squealing brood;
And how Mike, being in a merry mood,
Shot off each wiggling piglet's corkscrew tail
At twenty yards, while under easy sail
The boat moved on. And Carpenter could bore
A squirrel's eye clean at thirty steps and more—
So many say. But 'twas their dual test
Of mutual love and skill they liked the best
Of all their shooting tricks—when one stood up
At sixty paces with a whisky cup
Set'brimming for a target on his head,
And felt the gusty passing of the lead,
Hot from the other's rifle, lift his hair.
And ever was the tin cup smitten fair
By each, to prove the faith of each anew:
For 'twas a rite of love between the two,
And not a mere capricious feat of skill.
"Och, shure, and can ye shoot the whisky, Bill?"
So Mike would end a wrangle. "Damn it, Fink!
Let's bore a pair of cups and have a drink!"

So Carpenter would stop a row grown stale.
And neither feared that either love might fail
Or either skill might falter.

                                        Thus appear
The doughty three who held each other dear
For qualities they best could comprehend.

Now came the days of leisure to an end—
The days so gaily squandered, that would seem
To men at length made laughterless, a dream
Unthinkably remote; for Ilion held
Beneath her sixfold winding sheet of Eld
Seems not so hoar as bygone joy we prize
In evil days.   Now vaguely pale the skies,
The glimmer neither starlight's nor the morn's.
A rude ironic merriment of horns
Startles the men yet heavy with carouse,
And sets a Ree dog mourning in the drowse,
Snout skyward from a lodge top.   Sleepy birds
Chirp in the brush.   A drone of sullen words
Awakes and runs increasing through the camp.
Thin smoke plumes, rising in the valley damp,
Flatten among the leathern tents and make
The whole encampment like a ghostly lake
Where bobbing heads of swimmers come and go,
As with the whimsy of an undertow
That sucks and spews them.   Raising dust and din,
The horse-guards drive their shaggy rabble in
From nightlong grazing. *Voyageurs,* with packs
Of folded tents and camp gear on their backs,
Slouch boatward through the reek.   But when prevails
The smell of frying pans and coffee pails,

They cease to sulk and, greatly heartened, sing
Till ponies swell the chorus, nickering,
And race-old comrades jubilate as one.

Out of a roseless dawn the heat-pale sun
Beheld them toiling northward once again—
A hundred horses and a hundred men
Hushed in a windless swelter.   Day on day
The same white dawn o'ertook them on their way;
And daylong in the white glare sang no bird,
But only shrill grasshoppers clicked and whirred,
As though the heat were vocal.   All the while
The dwindling current lengthened, mile on mile,
Meandrous in a labyrinth of sand.

Now e'er they left the Ree town by the Grand
The revellers had seen the spent moon roam
The morning, like a tipsy hag bound home.
A bubble-laden boat, they saw it sail
The sunset river of a fairy tale
When they were camped beside the Cannonball.
A spectral sun, it held the dusk in thrall
Nightlong about the Heart.   The stars alone
Upon the cluttered Mandan lodges shone
The night they slept below the Knife.   And when
Their course, long westward, shifted once again
To lead them north, the August moon was new.

The rainless Southwest wakened now and blew
A wilting, worrying, breath-sucking gale
That roared one moment in the bellied sail,
Next moment slackened to a lazy croon.
Now came the first misfortune.   All forenoon

With line and pole the sweating boatmen strove
Along the east bank, while the horseguards drove
The drooping herd a little to the fore.
And then the current took the other shore.
Straight on, a maze of bar and shallow lay,
The main stream running half a mile away
To westward of a long low willow isle.
An hour they fought that stubborn half a mile
Of tumbled water. Down the running planks
The polesmen toiled in endless slanting ranks.
Now swimming, now a-flounder in the ooze
Of some blind bar, the naked cordelle crews
Sought any kind of footing for a pull;
While gust-bedevilled sails, now booming full,
Now flapping slack, gave questionable aid.

The west bank gained, along a ragged shade
Of straggling cottonwoods the boatmen sprawled
And panted. Out across the heat-enthralled,
Wind-fretted waste of shoal and bar they saw
The string of ponies ravelled up a draw
That mounted steeply eastward from the vale
Where, like a rampart flung across the trail,
A bluff rose sheer. Heads low, yet loath to graze,
They waxed and withered in the oily haze,
Now ponies, now a crawling flock of sheep.
Behind them three slack horseguards, half asleep,
Swayed limply, leaning on their saddle-bows.

The boat crews, lolling in a semi-doze,
Still watch the herd; nor do the gazers dream
What drama nears a climax over stream,

What others yonder may be watching too.
Now looming large upon the lucent blue,
The foremost ponies top the rim, and stare
High-headed down the vacancies of air
 Beneath them; while the herders dawdle still
And gather wool scarce halfway up the hill—
A slumbrous sight beheld by heavy eyes.

But hark! What murmuring of far-flung cries
From yonder pocket in the folded rise
That flanks the draw? The herders also hear
And with a start glance upward to the rear.
Their spurred mounts plunge! What do they see but dust
Whipped skyward yonder in a freakish gust?
What panic overtakes them? Look again!
The rolling dust cloud vomits mounted men,
A ruck of tossing heads and gaudy gears
Beneath a bristling thicket of lean spears
Slant in a gust of onset!

                                        Over stream
The boatmen stare dumfounded. Like a dream
In some vague region out of space and time
Evolves the swiftly moving pantomime
Before those loungers with ungirded loins;
Till one among them shouts *"Assiniboines!"*
And swelling to a roar, the wild word runs
Above a pellmell scramble for the guns,
Perceived as futile soon. Yet here and there
A few young hotheads fusillade the air,
And rage the more to know the deed absurd.
Some only grind their teeth without a word;
Some stand aghast, some grinningly inane,
While some, like watch-dogs rabid at the chain,

Growl curses, pacing at the river's rim.
So might unhappy spirits haunt the dim
Far shore of Styx, beholding outrage done
To loved ones in the region of the sun—
Rage goaded by its own futility!

For one vast moment strayed from time, they see
The war band flung obliquely down the slope,
The flying herdsmen, seemingly a-grope
In sudden darkness for their saddle guns.
A murmuring shock! And now the whole scene runs
Into a dusty blur of horse and man;
And now the herd's rear surges on the van
That takes the cue of panic fear and flies
Stampeding to the margin of the skies,
Till all have vanished in the deeps of air.
Now outlined sharply on the sky-rim there
The victors pause and taunt their helpless foes
With buttocks patted and with thumbs at nose
And jeers scarce hearkened for the wind's guffaw.
They also vanish. In the sunwashed draw
Remains no sign of what has come to pass,
Save three dark splotches on the yellow grass,
Where now the drowsy horseguards have their will.

At sundown on the summit of the hill
The huddled boatmen saw the burial squad
Tuck close their comrades' coverlet of sod—
Weird silhouettes on melancholy gray.
And very few found anything to say
That night; though some spoke gently of the dead,
Remembering what that one did or said

At such and such a time. And some, more stirred
With lust of vengeance for the stolen herd,
Swore vaguely now and then beneath their breath.
Some, brooding on the imminence of death,
Grew wistful of their unreturning years;
And some who found their praying in arrears
Made shift to liquidate the debt that night.

But when once more the cheerful morning light
Came on them toiling, also came the mood
Of young adventure, and the solitude
Sang with them. For 'tis glorious to spend
One's golden days large-handed to the end—
The good broadpieces that can buy so much!
And what may hoarders purchase but a crutch
Wherewith to hobble graveward?

On they pressed
To where once more the river led them west;
And every day the hot wind, puff on puff,
Assailed them; every night they heard it sough
In thickets prematurely turning sere.

Then came the sudden breaking of the year.

Abruptly in a waning afternoon
The hot wind ceased, as fallen in a swoon
With its own heat. For hours the swinking crews
Had bandied scarcely credible good news
Of clouds across the dim northwestward plain;
And they who offered wagers on the rain
Found ready takers, though the gloomy rack,
With intermittent rumbling at its back,

Had mounted slowly. Now it towered high,
A blue-black wall of night across the sky
Shot through with glacial green.

                        A mystic change!
The sun was hooded and the world went strange—
A picture world! The hollow hush that fell
Made loud the creaking of the taut cordelle,
The bent spar's groan, the plunk of steering poles.
A bodeful calm lay glassy on the shoals;
The current had the look of flowing oil.
They saw the cloud's lip billow now and boil—
Black breakers gnawing at a coast of light;
They saw the stealthy wraith-arms of the night
Grope for the day to strangle it; they saw
The up-stream reaches vanish in a flaw
Of driving sand: and scarcely were the craft
Made fast to clumps of willow fore and aft,
When with a roar the blinding fury rolled
Upon them; and the breath of it was cold.
There fell no rain.

                That night was calm and clear:
Just such a night as when the waning year
Has set aflare the old Missouri wood;
When Greenings are beginning to be good;
And when, so hollow is the frosty hush,
One hears the ripe persimmons falling—*plush!*—
Upon the littered leaves. The kindly time!
With cider in the vigor of its prime,
Just strong enough to edge the dullest wit
Should neighbor folk drop in awhile to sit
And gossip. O the dear flame-painted gloam,
The backlog's sputter on the hearth at home—

How far away that night! Thus many a lad,
Grown strangely old, remembered and was sad.
Wolves mourned among the bluffs. Like hanks of wool
Fog flecked the river. And the moon was full.

A week sufficed to end the trail. They came
To where the lesser river gives its name
And meed of waters to the greater stream.
Here, lacking horses, they must nurse the dream
Of beaver haunts beyond the Great Divide,
Build quarters for the winter trade, and bide
The coming up of Ashley and his band.

So up and down the wooded tongue of land
That thins to where the rivers wed, awoke
The sound of many axes, stroke on stroke;
And lustily the hewers sang at whiles—
The better to forget the homeward miles
In this, the homing time. And when the geese
With cacophonic councils broke the peace
Of frosty nights before they took to wing;
When cranes went over daily, southering,
And blackbirds chattered in the painted wood,
A mile above the river junction stood
The fort, adjoining the Missouri's tide.
Foursquare and thirty paces on a side,
A wall of sharpened pickets bristled 'round
A group of sod-roofed cabins. Bastions frowned
From two opposing corners, set to brave
A foe on either flank; and stout gates gave
Upon the stream, where now already came
The Indian craft, lured thither by the fame
Of traders building by the mating floods.

[268]

III

TO THE MUSSELSHELL

Now came at dawn a party of the Bloods,
Who told of having paddled seven nights
To parley for their people with the Whites,
The long way lying 'twixt a foe and foe;
For ever on their right hand lurked the Crow,
And on their left hand, the Assiniboine.
The crane-winged news, that where the waters join
The Long Knives built a village, made them sad;
Because the pastures thereabouts were bad,
Sustaining few and very scrawny herds.
So they had hastened hither, bringing words
Of kindness from their mighty men, to tell
What welcome waited on the Musselshell
Where stood the winter lodges of their band.

They rhapsodized the fatness of that land:
Lush valleys where all summer bison ran
To grass grown higher than a mounted man!
Aye, winter long on many a favored slope
The bison grazed with goat and antelope,
Nor were they ever leaner in the spring!
One heard the diving beaver's thundering
In all the streams at night; and one might hear
Uncounted bull elks whistle, when the year
Was painted for its death.   Their squaws were good,
Strong bearers of the water and the wood,

With quiet tongues and never weary hands;
Tall as the fighting men of other lands,
And good to look upon.   These things were so!
Why else then should Assiniboine and Crow
Assail the Bloods?

                              Now flaring up, they spoke
Of battles and their haters blown as smoke
Before the blizzard of their people's ire,
Devoured as grass before a prairie fire
That licks the heavens when the Northwind runs!
But, none the less, their warriors needed guns
And powder.   Wherefor, let the Great White Chief
Return with them, ere yet the painted leaf
Had fallen.   If so be he might not leave
This land of peoples skillful to deceive,
Who, needing much, had scarce a hide to sell—
Then send a party to the Musselshell
To trade and trap until the grass was young
And calves were yellow.   With no forkéd tongue
The Bloods had spoken.   Had the White Chief ears?

So Major Henry called for volunteers;
And Fink was ready on the word to go
"And chance the bloody naygurs"; then Talbeau,
Then Carpenter; and after these were nine,
In whom young blood was like a beading wine,
Who lusted for the venture.

                              Late that night
The Bloods set out for home.   With day's first light
The dozen trappers followed, paddling west
In six canoes.   And whatso suited best

The whimsies of the savage or his needs,
The slim craft carried—scarlet cloth and beads,
Some antiquated muskets, powder, ball,
Traps, knives, and little casks of alcohol
To lubricate the rusty wheels of trade!
So, singing as they went, the blithe brigade
Departed, with their galloping canoes
Heeding the tune.   They had no time to lose;
For long and stubborn was the upstream way,
And when they launched their boats at break of day
They heard a thin ice tinkle at the prows.

A bodeful silence and a golden drowse
Possessed the land.   The Four Winds held their breath
Before a vast serenity of death,
Wherein it seemed the reminiscent Year—
A yearning ghost now—wrought about its bier
Some pale hallucination of its May.
Bleak stretched the prairie to the walls of day,
So dry, that where a loping kiote broke
Its loneliness, it smouldered into smoke:
And when a herd of bison rumbled past,
'Twas like a great fire booming in a blast,
The rolling smudge whereof concealed the flame.

Proceeding in the truce of winds, they came
In five days to the vale the Poplar drains.
A trailing flight of southbound whooping cranes,
Across the fading west, was like a scrawl
Of cabalistic warning on a wall,
And counselled haste.   In seven days they reached
The point where Wolf Creek empties in, and beached

[271]

Their keels along its dusty bed. In nine,
Elk Prairie and the Little Porcupine,
Now waterless, had fallen to the rear.
The tenth sun failed them on the lone frontier
Where flows the turbid Milk by countless bends
And where Assiniboian country ends
And Blackfoot Land begins. The hollow gloom
All night resounded with the beaver's boom;
A wolf pack yammered from a distant hill;
Anon a rutting elk cried, like a shrill
Arpeggio blown upon a flageolet.
A half day more their lifting prows were set
To westward; then the flowing trail led south
Two days by many a bend to Hell Creek's mouth
Amid the Badlands. Gazing from a height,
The lookout saw the marching of the Night
Across a vast black waste of peaks and deeps
That could have been infernal cinder-heaps,
The relics of an ancient hell gone cold.

That night they saw a wild aurora rolled
Above the lifeless wilderness. It formed
Northeastwardly in upright waves that stormed
To westward, sequent combers of the bow
That gulfed Polaris in their undertow
And hurtled high upon the Ursine Isles
A surf of ghostly fire. Again, at whiles,
A shimmering silken veil, it puffed and swirled
As 'twere the painted curtain of the world
That fluttered in a rising gale of doom.
And when it vanished in the starry gloom
One said " 'Twill blow to-morrow."

                                              So it did.
Ere noon they raised the Half Way Pyramid
Southwestward; saw its wraith-like summit lift
And seem to float northwest against a drift
Of wind-whipped dust.   The lunar hills about—
Where late a bird's note startled like a shout
The hush that seemed the body of old time—
Now bellowed where the hoofs of Yotunheim
Foreran the grizzled legions of the Snow.
'Twas peep of day when it began to blow,
A zephyr growing stronger with the light,
And now by fits it churned the river white
And whipped the *voyageurs* with freezing spray.
The windward reaches took their breath away.
Ghost-white and numb with cold, from bend to bend,
Where transiently the wind became a friend
To drive them south, they battled; till at last
Around a jutting bluff they met a blast
That choked as with a hand upon their throats
The song they sang for courage; hurled their boats
Against the farther shore and held them pinned.

A sting of spitting snow was in the wind.
Southwest by west across the waste, where fell
A murky twilight, lay the Musselshell—
Two days of travel with the crow for guide.
Here must they find them shelter, and abide
The passing of the blizzard as they could.
The banks bore neither plum nor cottonwood
And all the hills were naked as a hand.
But where, debouching from the broken land,
A river in the spring was wont to flow,
A northward moving herd of buffalo

Had crossed the river, evidently bound
From failing pastures to the grazing ground
Along the Milk: and where the herd had passed
Was scattered *bois de vache* enough to last
Until the storm abated. So they packed
Great blanketfuls of sun-dried chips, and stacked
The precious fuel where the wind was stilled—
A pocket hemmed by lofty bluffs and filled
With mingled dusk and thunder; bore therein
Canoes and cargo, pitched their tents of skin
About a central heap of glowing chips,
And dined on brittle bull-meat dried in strips,
With rum to wash it down.

                                    It snowed all night.
The earth and heavens, in the morning light,
Were one white fury; and the stream ran slush.
Two days and nights the gale boomed; then a hush
Fell with the sun; and when the next dawn came—
A pale flare flanked by mockeries of flame—
The river lay as solid as the land.

Now caching half their goods, the little band
Resumed the journey, toiling under packs;
And twice they felt the morning at their backs,
A laggard traveller; and twice they saw
The sunset dwindle to a starry awe
Beyond the frozen vast, while still they pressed
The journey—bearded faces yearning west,
White as the waste they trod. Then one day more,
Southwestward, brought them to the jutting shore
That faced the goal.

                              A strip of poplars stretched
Along a winding stream, their bare boughs etched
Black line by line upon a flat of snow
Blue tinted in the failing afterglow.
Humped ponies 'mid the drifts and clumps of sage
Went nosing after grudging pasturage
Where'er it chanced the blizzard's whimsic flaws
Had swept the slough grass bare. A flock of squaws
Chopped wood and chattered in the underbrush,
Their ax strokes thudding dully in the hush,
Their nasal voices rising shrill and clear:
And, circled 'neath a bluff that towered sheer
Beside the stream, snug lodges wrought of hide,
Smoke-plumed and glowing with the fires inside,
Made glad the gazers. Even as they stood,
Content to stare a moment, from the wood
The clamor deepened, and a running shout
Among the lodges brought the dwellers out,
Braves, squaws, papooses; and the wolf dogs bayed;
And up the flat the startled ponies neighed,
Pricking their ears to question what befell.

So came Fink's party to the Musselshell,
Gaunt, bearded, yet—how gloriously young!
And then, what feasts of bison fleece and tongue,
Of browned *boudin* and steaming humprib stew!
What roaring nights of wassailing they knew—
Gargantuan regales—when through the town
The fiery liquor ravined, melting down
The tribal hoard of beaver! How they made
Their merest gewgaws mighty in the trade!
Aye, merry men they were! Nor could they know
How even then there came that wraith of woe

Amongst them; some swift-fingered Fate that span
The stuff of sorrow, wove 'twixt man and man
The tangling mesh, that friend might ruin friend
And each go stumbling to a bitter end—
A threefold doom that now the Song recalls.

IV

THE NET IS CAST

There was a woman.
      What enchantment falls
Upon that far off revel! How the din
Of jangling voices, chaffering to win
The lesser values, hushes at the words,
As dies the dissonance of brawling birds
Upon a calm before the storm is hurled!
Lo, down the age-long reaches of the world
What rose-breatht wind of ghostly music creeps!

And was she fair—this woman? Legend keeps
No answer; yet we know that she was young,
If truly comes the tale by many a tongue
That one of Red Hair's party fathered her.
What need to know her features as they were?
Was she not lovely as her lover's thought,
And beautiful as that wild love she wrought
Was fatal? Vessel of the world's desire,
Did she not glow with that mysterious fire
That lights the hearth or burns the rooftree down?
What face was hers who made the timeless town
A baleful torch forever? Hers who wailed
Upon the altar when the four winds failed
At Aulis? What the image that looked up
On Iseult from the contemplated cup

[277]

Of everlasting thirst? What wondrous face
Above the countless cradles of the race
Makes sudden heaven for the blinking eyes?
One face in truth! And once in Paradise
Each man shall stray unwittingly, and see—
In some unearthly valley where the Tree
With golden fruitage periously fraught
Still stands—that image of God's afterthought.
Then shall the world turn wonderful and strange!

Who knows how came the miracle of change
To Fink at last? For he was not of such
As tend to prize one woman overmuch;
And legend has it that, from Pittsburg down
To Baton Rouge, in many a river town
Some blowsy Ariadne pined for Mike.
"It is me rule to love 'em all alike,"
He often said, with slow, omniscient wink,
When just the proper quantity of drink
Had made him philosophic; "Glass or gourd,
Shure, now, they're all wan liquor whin they're poured!
Aye, rum is rum, me b'y!"

                              Alas, the tongue!
How glibly are its easy guesses flung
Against the knowing reticence of years,
To echo laughter in the time of tears,
Raw gusts of mocking merriment that stings!
Some logic in the seeming ruck of things
Inscrutably confutes us!

                              Now had come
The time when rum no longer should be rum,

But witchwine sweet with peril. It befell
In this wise, insofar as tongue may tell
And tongues repeat the little eyes may guess
Of what may happen in that wilderness,
The human heart. There dwelt a mighty man
Among the Bloods, a leader of his clan,
Around whose life were centered many lives,
For many sons had he of many wives;
And also he was rich in pony herds.
Wherefore, they say, men searched his lightest words
For hidden things, since anyone might see
That none had stronger medicine than he
To shape aright the stubborn stuff of life.
Among the women that he had to wife
Was she who knew the white man when the band
Of Red Hair made such marvel in the land,
She being younger then and little wise.
But in that she was pleasing to the eyes
And kept her fingers busy for her child
And bore a silent tongue, the great man smiled
Upon the woman, called her to his fire
And gave the Long Knife's girl a foster sire,
So that her maidenhood was never lean,
But like a pasture that is ever green
Because it feels a mountain's sunny flank.

Now in the season when the pale sun shrank
Far southward, like another kind of moon,
And dawns were laggard and the dark came soon,
It pleased the great man's whim to give a feast.
'Twas five days after Carpenter went east
With eight stout ponies and a band of three
To lift the cache; a fact that well might be

Sly father to the great man's festive mood—
A wistfully prospective gratitude,
Anticipating charity!

                              It chanced
That while the women sang and young men danced
About the drummers, and the pipe went round,
And ever 'twixt the songs arose the sound
Of fat dog stewing, Fink, with mournful eyes
And pious mien, lamented the demise
Of "pore owld Fido," till his comrades choked
With stifled laughter; soberly invoked
The plopping stew ("Down, Rover! Down, me lad!");
Discussed the many wives the old man had
In language more expressive than polite.
So, last of all his merry nights, that night
Fink clowned it, little dreaming he was doomed
To wear that mask of sorrow he assumed
In comic mood, thenceforward to the last.
For even as he joked, the net was cast
About him, and the mystic change had come,
And he had looked on rum that was not rum—
The Long Knife's daughter!

                           Stooped beneath a pack
Of bundled twigs, she pushed the lodge-flap back
And entered lightly; placed her load of wood
Beside the fire; then straightened up and stood
One moment there, a shapely girl and tall.
There wasn't any drama: that was all.
But when she left, the wit had died in Fink.
He seemed a man who takes the one more drink

That spoils the fun, relaxes jaw and jowl
And makes the jester, like a sunstruck owl,
Stare solemnly at nothing.

                         All next day
He moped about with scarce a word to say,
And no one dared investigate his whim.
But when the twilight came, there fell on him
A sentimental, reminiscent mood,
As though upon some frozen solitude
Within him, breathed a softening chinook,
Far strayed across the alplike years that look
On what one used to be and what one is.
And when he raised that mellow voice of his
In songs of lovers wedded to regret,
'Tis said that, unashamed, men's eyes grew wet,
So poignantly old memories were stirred.
And much his comrades marvelled as they heard
That ribald jester singing thus of love.
Nor could they solve the mystery thereof,
Until at dawn they saw him rise and take
A rifle of the latest Hawkin make,
Ball, powder, and a bolt of scarlet goods,
And hasten to the fringe of cottonwoods
Where rose the great man's lodge smoke. Then they
        knew;
For thus with gifts the Bloods were wont to woo
The daughter through the sire.

                        The white sun burned
Midmost the morning steep when he returned
Without his load and humming as he went.
And hour by hour he squatted in his tent

And stared upon the fire; save now and then
He stirred himself to lift the flap again
And cast an anxious gaze across the snows
Where stood the chieftain's lodge. And well did those
Who saw him know what sight he hoped to see;
For 'twas the custom that the bride-to-be
Should carry food to him she chose to wed.
Meanwhile, with seemly caution, be it said,
Fink's men enjoyed a comedy, and laid
Sly wagers on the coming of the maid—
She would! She wouldn't! So the brief day waned.

Now when the sun, a frosty specter maned
With corruscating vapors, lingered low
And shadows lay like steel upon the snow,
An old squaw, picking faggots in the brush,
Saw that which set her shrieking in the hush.
"They come! They come!" Then someone shouted
        "Crows!"
The town spewed tumult, men with guns and bows,
Half clad and roaring; shrill hysteric wives
With sticks of smoking firewood, axes, knives;
Dogs, bristle-necked and snarling. So they pressed
To meet a foe, as from a stricken nest
The hornet swarm boils over.
                                                    Blinking, dazed
With sudden light and panic fear, they gazed
About the frozen waste; and then they saw
Eight laden ponies filing up the draw,
Their nostrils steaming, slack of neck and slow.
Behind them, stumbling in the broken snow,
Three weary trappers trudged, while in the lead
Strode Carpenter. A goodly sight, indeed!

Upstanding, eagle-faced and eagle-eyed,
The ease of latent power in his stride,
He dwarfed the panting pony that he led;
And when the level sunlight 'round his head
Made glories in the frosted beard and hair,
Some Gothic fighting god seemed walking there,
Strayed from the dim Hercynian woods of old.

How little of a story can be told!
Let him who knows what happens in the seed
Before the sprout breaks sunward, make the deed
A plummet for the dreaming deeps that surged
Beneath the surface ere the deed emerged
For neat appraisal by the rule of thumb!
The best of Clio is forever dumb,
To human ears at least.   Nor shall the Song
Presume to guess and tell how all night long,
While roared the drunken orgy and the trade,
Doom quickened in the fancy of a maid,
The daughter of the Long knife; how she saw,
Serenely moving through a spacious awe
Behind shut lids where never came the brawl,
That shining one, magnificently tall,
A day-crowned mortal brother of the sun.
Suffice it here that, when the night was done
And morning, like an uproar in the east,
Aroused the town still heavy with the feast,
All men might see what whimsic, fatal bloom
A soil, dream-plowed and seeded in the gloom,
Had nourished unto blowing in the day.
'Twas then the girl appeared and took her way
Across the snow with hesitating feet.
She bore a little pot of steaming meat;

And when midmost the open space, she turned
And held it up to where the morning burned,
As one who begs a blessing of the skies.
Unconscious of the many peeping eyes,
Erect, with wrapt uplifted face she stood—
A miracle of shapely maidenhood—
Before the flaming god.   And many heard,
Or seemed to hear by piecing word to word,
The prayer she muttered to the wintry sky:
"O Sun, behold a maiden!   Pure am I!
Look kindly on the little gift I give;
For, save you smile upon it, what can live?
Bright Father, hear a maiden!"   Then, as one
Who finds new courage for a task begun,
She turned and hastened to the deed.

                                                    They say
There was no dearth of gossiping that day
Among the lodges.   Shrewish tongues there were
That clacked no happy prophecies of her.
And many wondered at the chieftain's whim.
The Long Knife's girl had wrought a spell on him;
Why else then was he silent?   See her shrink
A moment there before the tent of Fink,
As one who feels a sudden sleety blast!
But look again!   She starts, and hurries past!
All round the circled village, lodges yawn
To see how brazen in the stare of dawn
A petted girl may be.   For now, behold!
Was ever maiden of the Bloods so bold?
She stops before another tent and stoops,
Her fingers feeling for the buckskin loops

[284]

That bind the rawhide flap.   'Tis opened wide.
The slant white light of morning falls inside,
And half the town may witness at whose feet
She sets the little pot of steaming meat—
'Tis Carpenter!

V

THE QUARREL

                         Perceptibly, at length,
The days grew longer, and the winter's strength
Increased to fury. Down across the flat
The blizzards bellowed; and the people sat
Fur-robed about the smoky fires that stung
Their eyes to streaming, when a freak gust flung
The sharp reek back with flaws of powdered snow.
And much the old men talked of long ago,
Invoking ghostly Winters from the Past,
Till cold snap after cold snap followed fast,
And none might pile his verbal snow so deep
But some athletic memory could heap
The drifts a trifle higher; give the cold
A greater rigor in the story told;
Put bellows to a wind already high.
And ever greater reverence thereby
The old men won from gaping youths, who heard,
Like marginalia to the living word,
The howling of the poplars tempest-bent,
The smoke-flap cracking sharply at the vent,
The lodge poles creaking eerily. And O!
The happy chance of living long ago,
Of having wrinkles now and being sires
With many tales to tell around the fires
Of days when things were bigger! All night long
White hands came plucking at the buckskin thong

That bound the door-flap, and the writhing dark
Was shrill with spirits. By the snuffling bark
Of dogs men knew that homesick ghosts were there.
And often in a whirl of chilling air
The weird ones entered, though the flap still held,
Built up in smoke the shapes they knew of eld,
Grew thin and long to vanish as they came.

Now had the scandal, like a sudden flame
Fed fat with grasses, perished in the storm.
The fundamental need of keeping warm
Sufficed the keenest gossip for a theme;
And whimsies faded like a warrior's dream
When early in the dawn the foemen cry.

The time when calves are black had blustered by—
A weary season—since the village saw
The chief's wife pitching for her son-in-law
The nuptial lodge she fashioned. Like a bow
That feels the arrow's head, the moon hung low
That evening when they gave the wedding gifts;
And men had seen it glaring through the rifts
Of wintry war as up the east it reeled,
A giant warrior's battle-bitten shield—
But now it braved no more the charging air.
Meanwhile the lodge of Carpenter stood there
Beside the chieftain's, huddled in the snows,
And, like a story everybody knows,
Was little heeded now.

                              But there was one
Who seldom noted what was said or done
Among his comrades; he would sit and look
Upon the fire, as one who reads a book

Of woeful doings, ever on the brink
Of ultimate disaster. It was Fink:
And seeing this, Talbeau was sick at heart
With dreading that his friends might drift apart
And he be lost, because he loved them both.
But, knowing well Mike's temper, he was loath
To broach the matter. Also, knowing well
That silence broods upon the hottest hell,
He prayed that Fink might curse.

                        So worried past
The days of that estrangement. Then at last
One night when 'round their tent the blizzard roared
And, nestled in their robes, the others snored,
Talbeau could bear the strain no more and spoke.
He opened with a random little joke,
Like some starved hunter trying out the range
Of precious game where all the land is strange;
And, as the hunter, missing, hears the grim
And spiteful echo-rifles mocking him,
His own unmirthful laughter mocked Talbeau.
He could have touched across the ember-glow
Mike's brooding face—yet Mike was far away.
And O that nothing more than distance lay
Between them—any distance with an end!
How tireless then in running to his friend
A man might be! For suddenly he knew
That Mike would have him choose between the two.
How could he choose 'twixt Carpenter and Fink?
How idle were a choice 'twixt food and drink
When, choosing neither, one were sooner dead!
Thus torn within, and hoarse with tears unshed,

He strove again to find his comrade's heart:
"O damn it, Mike, don't make us drift apart!
Don't do it, Mike!   This ain't a killin' fuss,
And hadn't ought to faze the three of us
That's weathered many a rough-and-tumble fight!
W'y don't you mind that hell-a-poppin' night
At Baton Rouge three years ago last fall—
The time we fit the whole damned dancin' hall
And waded out nigh belly-deep in men?
O who'd have said a girl could part us, then?
And, Mike, that fracas in the Vide Poche dive!
Can you forget it long as you're alive?—
A merry time!   Us strollin' arm-in-arm
From drink to drink, not calculatin' harm,
But curious, because St. Louis town
Fair boiled with greasy mountain men, come down
All brag and beaver, howlin' for a spree!
And then—you mind?—a feller jostled me—
'Twas at the bar—a chap all bones and big.
Says he in French: 'You eater of a pig,
Make room for mountain men!'   And then says you
In Irish, aimin' where the whiskers grew,
And landin' fair: 'You eater of a dog,
Make room for boatmen!'   Like a punky log
That's water-soaked, he dropped.   What happened then?
A cyclone in a woods of mountain men—
That's what!   O Mike you can't forget it now!
And what in hell's a woman, anyhow,
To memories like that?''

So spoke Talbeau,
And, pausing, heard the hissing of the snow,

[289]

The snoring of the sleepers and the cries
Of blizzard-beaten poplars.   Still Fink's eyes
Upon the crumbling embers pored intent.
Then momently, or so it seemed, there went
Across that alien gaze a softer light,
As when bleak windows in a moony night
Flush briefly with a candle borne along.
And suddenly the weary hope grew strong
In him who saw the glimmer, and he said:
"O Mike, I see the good old times ain't dead!
Why don't you fellers shoot the whisky cup
The way you used to do?"

                                    Then Fink looked up.
'Twas bad the way the muscles twitched and worked
About his mouth, and in his eyes there lurked
Some crouchant thing.   "To hell wid you!" he cried.
So love and hate that night slept side by side;
And hate slept well, but love lay broad awake
And, like a woman, for the other's sake
Eked out the lonely hours with worrying.

Now came a heartsick yearning for the spring
Upon Talbeau; for surely this bad dream
Would vanish with the ice upon the stream,
Old times be resurrected with the grass!
But would the winter ever, ever pass,
The howling of the blizzard ever cease?
So often now he dreamed of hearing geese
Remotely honking in the rain-washed blue;
And ever when the blur of dawn broke through

[290]

The scudding rack, he raised the flap to see,
By sighting through a certain forked tree,
How much the sun made northward.

                                    Then, one day,
The curtain of the storm began to fray;
The poplars' howling softened to a croon;
The sun set clear, and dusk revealed the moon—
A thin-blown bubble in a crystal bowl.
All night, as 'twere the frozen prairie's soul
That voiced a hopeless longing for the spring,
The wolves assailed with mournful questioning
The starry deeps of that tremendous hush.
Dawn wore the mask of May—a rosy flush.
It seemed the magic of a single bird
Might prove the seeing of the eye absurd
And make the heaped-up winter billow green.
On second thought, one knew the air was keen—
A whetted edge in gauze.   The village fires
Serenely builded tenuous gray spires
That vanished in the still blue deeps of awe.
All prophets were agreed upon a thaw.
And when the morning stood a spearlength high,
There grew along the western rim of sky
A bank of cloud that had a rainy look.
It mounted slowly.   Then the warm chinook
Began to breathe a melancholy drowse
And sob among the naked poplar boughs,
As though the prairie dreamed a dream of June
And knew it for a dream.   All afternoon
The gale increased.   The sun went down blood-red;
The young moon, perilously fragile, fled
To early setting.   And the long night roared.

Tempestuously broke the day and poured
An intermittent glory through the rifts
Amid the driven fog. The sodden drifts
Already grooved and withered in the blast;
And when the flying noon stared down aghast,
The bluffs behind the village boomed with flood.
What magic in that sound to stir the blood
Of winter-weary men! For now the spring
No longer seemed a visionary thing,
But that which any morning might bestow.
And most of all that magic moved Talbeau;
For, scrutinizing Fink, he thought he saw
Some reflex of that February thaw—
A whit less curling of the upper lip.
O could it be returning comradeship,
That April not beholden to the moon
Nor chatteled to the sun?

                                        That afternoon
They played at euchre. Even Fink sat in;
And though he showed no eagerness to win,
Forgot the trumps and played his bowers wild,
There were not lacking moments when he smiled,
A hesitating smile 'twixt wan and grim.
It seemed his stubborn mood embarrassed him
Because regret now troubled it with shame.

The great wind died at midnight. Morning came,
Serene and almost indolently warm—
As when an early April thunder storm
Has cleansed the night and vanished with the gloom;
When one can feel the imminence of bloom

As 'twere a spirit in the orchard trees;
When, credulous of blossom, come the bees
To grumble 'round the seepages of sap.
So mused Talbeau while, pushing back the flap,
Instinctively he listened for a bird
To fill the hush. Then presently he heard—
And 'twas the only sound in all the world—
The trickle of the melting snow that purled
And tinkled in the bluffs above the town.
The sight of ragged Winter patched with brown,
The golden peace and, palpitant therein,
That water note, spun silverly and thin,
Begot a wild conviction in the man:
The wounded Winter weakened! Now began
The reconciliation! Hate would go
And, even as the water from the snow,
Old comradeship come laughing back again!

All morning long he pondered, while the men
Played seven-up. And scarce a trick was played
But someone sang a snatch of song or made
A merry jest. And when the game was balked
By one who quite forgot his hand, and talked
Of things in old St. Louis, none demurred.
And thus, by noon, it seemed the lightest word
Of careless salutation would avail
To give a happy ending to the tale
Of clouded friendship. So he 'rose and went,
By studied indirection, to the tent
Of Carpenter, as one who takes the air.
And, as he raised the flap and entered there,
A sudden gale of laughter from the men
Blew after him. What music in it then!

[293]

What mockery, when memory should raise
So often in the coming nights and days
The ruthless echo of it!

                   Click on click
Amid the whirlwind finish of a trick
The cards fell fast, while King and Queen and Ace,
With meaner trumps for hounds, pursued the chase
Of wily Knave and lurking Deuce and Ten;
When suddenly the game-enchanted men
Were conscious of a shadow in the place,
And glancing up they saw the smiling face
Of Carpenter, thrust in above Talbeau's.
"How goes it, Boys?" said he; and gaily those
Returned the greeting. "Howdy, Mike!" he said;
And with a sullen hanging of the head
Fink mumbled "Howdy!" Gruff—but what of that?
One can not doff displeasure like a hat—
'Twould dwindle snow-like.

                   Nothing else would do
But Carpenter should play. Now Fink played too;
And, having brought his cherished ones together,
Talbeau surrendered to the languid weather
And, dreamily contented, watched the sport.
All afternoon the pictured royal court
Pursued its quarry in the mimic hunt;
And Carpenter, now gayer than his wont,
Lost much; while Fink, with scarce a word to say,
His whole attention fixed upon the play,
Won often. So it happened, when the sun
Was near to setting, that the day seemed won
For friendliness, however stood the game.
But even then that Unseen Player came

Who stacks the shuffled deck of circumstance
And, playing wild the Joker men call Chance,
Defeats the Aces of our certainty.

The cards were dealt and Carpenter bid three.
The next man passed the bid, and so the next.
Then Fink, a trifle hesitant and vexed,
Bid four on spades. And there was one who said
In laughing banter: "Mike, I'll bet my head
As how them spades of your'n 'll dig a hole!"
And in some subtle meaning of the soul
The wag was more a prophet than he knew.

Fink held the Ace and Deuce, and that made two:
His black King scored another point with Knave.
But Carpenter, to whom that Weird One gave
A band of lesser trumps to guard his Ten,
Lay low until the Queen had passed, and then
Swept in a last fat trick for Game, and scored.
And now the players slapped their knees and roared:
"You're set! You're in the hole! He set you, Mike!"

Then suddenly they saw Fink crouch to strike;
And ere they comprehended what they saw,
There came a thud of knuckles on a jaw
And Carpenter rolled over on the ground.
One moment in a breathless lapse of sound
The stricken man strove groggily to 'rise,
The emptiness of wonder in his eyes
Turned dreamily with seeming unconcern
Upon Mike's face, where now began to burn
The livid murder-lust. 'Twixt breath and breath
The hush and immobility of death

Made there a timeless picture.   Then a yell,
As of a wild beast charging, broke the spell.
Fink sprang to crush, but midway met Talbeau
Who threw him as a collie dog may throw
A raging bull.   But Mike was up again,
And wielding thrice the might of common men,
He gripped the little man by nape and thigh
And lightly lifted him and swung him high
And flung him; and the smitten tent went down.
Then 'rose a roar that roused the teeming town,
And presently a shouting rabble surged
About the wreck, whence tumblingly emerged
A knot of men who grappled Fink and clung.
Prodigiously he rose beneath them, flung
His smashing arms, man-laden, forth and back;
But stubbornly they gripped him, like a pack
That takes uncowed the maulings of a bear.
"Let Carpenter get up!" they cried.   "Fight fair!
Fight fair!   Fight fair!"

                                    Quite leisurely the while
The stricken man arose, a sleepy smile
About his quiet eyes.   Indeed, he seemed
As one but lately wakened, who has dreamed
A pleasing dream.   But when he stroked his beard
And gazed upon his fingers, warmly smeared
With crimson from the trickle at his jaw,
His eyes went eagle-keen with what they saw.
The stupor passed.   He hastily untied
His buckskin shirt and, casting it aside,
Stood naked to the hips.   The tumult ceased
As, panting hard, the *voyageurs* released

Their struggling charge and, ducking to a swing
Of those freed arms, sought safely, scampering.

Fink also stripped his shirt; and as the man
Stood thus revealed, a buzz of wonder ran
Amid the jostling rabble. Few there were
Who in that moment envied Carpenter,
Serenely poised and waiting placid browed:
For shall a lonely cedar brave a cloud
Bulged big and shapen to the cyclone's whirl?
Lo, even as the body of a girl,
The body of the blond was smooth and white;
But vaguely, as one guesses at the might
Of silent waters running swift and deep,
One guessed what stores of power lay asleep
Beneath the long fleet lines of trunk and limb.
Thus God had made experiment with him;
And, groping for the old Adamic dream,
Had found his patterns in the tree and stream,
As Fink's in whirling air and hungry flame.

Now momently the picture there became
A blur of speed. Mike rushed. The tiptoe town
Craned eagerly to see a man go down
Before that human thunder gust. But lo!
As bends a sapling when the great winds blow,
The other squatted, deftly swayed aside,
And over him the slashing blows went wide.
Fink sprawled. But hardly had a spreading roar
O'errun the town, when silence as before
Possessed the scene; for Mike flashed back again
With flame-like speed, and suddenly the men
Clenched, leaning neck to neck.

                              Without a word,
Like horn-locked bulls that strive before the herd,
They balanced might with might; till Mike's hands
        whipped
Beneath the other's arm-pits, met and gripped
Across the broad white shoulders. Then began
The whole prodigious engine of the man
To bulge and roll and darken with the strain.
Like rivulets fed suddenly with rain,
The tall one's thews rose ropily and flowed
Converging might against the growing load
Of those tremendous arms that strove to crush.
Their labored breathing whistled in the hush.
One saw the blond man's face go bluish red,
As deeper, deeper sank Fink's shaggy head
Amid his heaped-up shoulder brawn. One knew
That very soon the taller of the two
Must yield and take that terrible embrace.
A tense hypnotic quiet filled the place.
The men were like two wrestlers in a dream
That holds an endless moment; till a scream
Fell stab-like on the hush. One saw Talbeau,
Jaws set, hands clenched, eyes wild, and bending low,
As though he too were struggling, slowly bowed
Beneath Fink's might. And then—

                              What ailed the crowd?
Swept over by a flurry of surprise,
They swayed and jostled, shouting battle-cries
And quips and jeers of savage merriment.
One moment they had seen the tall man bent,

About to break: then, falling back a-haunch,
His feet had plunged against the other's paunch
And sent Fink somersaulting.

                                    Once again
A silence fell as, leaping up, the men
Were mingled briefly in a storm of blows.
Now, tripping like a dancer on his toes,
The blond man sparred; while, like a baited bear,
Half blinded with the lust to crush and tear,
Fink strove to clutch that something lithe and sleek
That stung and fled and stung. Upon his cheek
A flying shadow laid a vivid bruise;
Another—and his brow began to ooze
Slow drops that spattered on his bearded jaw.
Again that shadow passed—his mouth went raw,
And like a gunshot wound it gaped and bled.
Fink roared with rage and plunged with lowered head
Upon this thing that tortured, hurled it back
Amid the crowd. One heard a thud and smack
Of rapid blows on bone and flesh—and then
One saw the tall man stagger clear again
With gushing nostrils and a bloody grin,
And down his front the' whiteness of the skin
Was striped with flowing crimson to the waist.
Unsteadily he wheeled about and faced
The headlong hate of his antagonist.
Now toe to toe and fist to flying fist,
They played at give and take; and all the while
The blond man smiled that riddle of a smile,
As one who meditates upon a jest.

Yet surely he was losing! Backward pressed,
He strove in vain to check his raging foe.

Fink lunged and straightened to a shoulder blow
With force enough to knock a bison down.
The other dodged it, squatting.   Then the town
Discovered what a smile might signify.
For, even as the futile blow went by,
One saw the lithe white form shoot up close in,
A hooked white arm jab upward to the chin—
Once—twice—and yet again.   With eyes a-stare,
His hands aloft and clutching at the air,
Fink tottered backward, limply lurched and fell.

Then came to pass what stilled the rabble's yell,
So strange it was.   And 'round the fires that night
The wisest warriors, talking of the fight,
Could not explain what happened at the end.
No friend, they said, makes war upon a friend;
Nor does a foe have pity on a foe:
And yet the tall white chief had bathed with snow
The bloody mouth and battered cheek and brow
Of him who fell!

                    Queer people, anyhow,
The Long Knives were—and hard to understand!

VI

THE SHOOTING OF THE CUP

BULL-ROARING March had swept across the land,
And now the evangelic goose and crane,
Forerunners of the messianic Rain,
Went crying through the wilderness aloft.
Fog hid the sun, and yet the snow grew soft.
The monochrome of sky and poplar bough,
Drab tracery on drab, was stippled now
With swelling buds; and slushy water ran
Upon the ice-bound river that began
To stir and groan as one about to wake.

Now, while they waited for the ice to break,
The trappers fashioned bull-boats—willow **wrought**
To bowl-like frames, and over these drawn taut
Green bison hides with bison sinew sewn.
And much they talked about the Yellowstone:
How fared their comrades yonder since the fall?
And would they marvel at the goodly haul
Of beaver pelts these crazy craft would bring?
And what of Ashley starting north that spring
With yet another hundred?   Did his prows
Already nose the flood?—Ah, cherry boughs
About St. Louis now were loud with bees
And white with bloom, and wading to the knees,
The cattle browsed along the fresh green sloughs!
Yes, even now the leaning cordelle crews

With word from home (so far away, alas!)
Led north the marching armies of the grass,
As 'twere the heart of Summertime they towed!

So while they shaped the willow frames and sewed
The bison hides, the trappers' hearts were light.
They talked no longer now about the fight.
That story, shaped and fitted part by part,
Unwittingly was rounded into art,
And, being art, already it was old.
When this bleak time should seem the age of gold,
These men, grown gray and garrulous, might tell
Of wondrous doings on the Musselshell—
How Carpenter, the mighty, fought, and how
Great Fink went down.   But spring was coming now,
And who's for backward looking in the spring?

Yet one might see that Mike still felt the sting
Of that defeat; for often he would brood,
Himself the center of a solitude
Wherein the friendly chatter of the band
Was like a wind that makes a lonely land
Seem lonelier.   And much it grieved Talbeau
To see a haughty comrade humbled so;
And, even more, he feared what wounded pride
Might bring to pass, before their boats could ride
The dawnward reaches of the April floods
And leave behind the village of the Bloods;
For now it seemed a curse was on the place.
Talbeau was like a man who views a race
With all to lose: so slowly crept the spring,
So surely crawled some formless fatal thing,

[302]

He knew not what it was.   But should it win,
Life could not be again as it had been
And spring would scarcely matter any more.
The daybreak often found him at the shore,
A ghostly figure in the muggy light,
Intent to see what progress over night
The shackled river made against the chain.

And then at last, one night, a dream of rain
Came vividly upon him.   How it poured!
A witch's garden was the murk that roared
With bursting purple bloom.   'Twas April weather,
And he and Mike and Bill were boys together
Beneath the sounding shingle roof at home.
He smelled the odor of the drinking loam
Still rolling mellow from the recent share;
And he could feel the meadow greening there
Beyond the apple orchard.   Then he 'woke
And raised the flap.   A wraith of thunder-smoke
Was trailing off along the prairie's rim.
Half dreaming yet, the landscape puzzled him.
What made the orchard seem so tall and lean?
And surely yonder meadow had been green
A moment since!   What made it tawny now?
And yonder where the billows of the plow
Should glisten fat and sleek——?

                                    The drowsy spell
Dropped off and left him on the Musselshell
Beneath the old familiar load of care.
He looked aloft.   The stars had faded there.
The sky was cloudless.   No, one lonely fleece
Serenely floated in the spacious peace

And from the distance caught prophetic light.
In truth he had heard thunder in the night
And dashing rain; for all the land was soaked,
And where the withered drifts had lingered, smoked
The naked soil.   But since the storm was gone,
How strange that still low thunder mumbled on—
An unresolving cadence marred at whiles
By dull explosions!   Now for miles and miles
Along the vale he saw a trail of steam
That marked the many windings of the stream,
As though the river simmered.   Then he knew.
It was the sound of April breaking through!
The resurrection thunder had begun!
The ice was going out, and spring had won
The creeping race with dread!

                                      His ringing cheers
Brought out the blinking village by the ears
To share the news; and though they could not know
What ecstasy of triumph moved Talbeau,
Yet lodge on lodge took up the joyous cry
That set the dogs intoning to the sky,
The drenched cayuses shrilly nickering.
So man and beast proclaimed the risen Spring
Upon the Musselshell.

                              And all day long
The warring River sang its ocean song.
And all that night the spirits of the rain
Made battle music with a shattered chain
And raged upon the foe.   And did one gaze
Upon that struggle through the starry haze,
One saw enormous bodies heaved and tossed,
Where stubbornly the Yotuns of the Frost

With shoulder set to shoulder strove to stem
The wild invasion rolling over them.
Nor in the morning was the struggle done.
Serenely all that day the doughty Sun,
A banished king returning to his right,
Beheld his legions pouring to the fight,
Exhaustless; and his cavalries that rode—
With hoofs that rumbled and with manes that flowed
White in the war gust—crashing on the foe.
And all that night the din of overthrow
Arose to heaven from the stricken field;
A sound as of the shock of spear and shield,
Of wheels that trundled and the feet of hordes,
Of shrieking horses mad among the swords,
Hurrahing of attackers and attacked,
And sounds as of a city that is sacked
When lust for loot runs roaring through the night.
Dawn looked upon no battle, but a flight.
And when the next day broke, the spring flood flowed
Like some great host that takes the homeward road
With many spoils—a glad triumphal march,
Of which the turquoise heaven was the arch.

Now comes a morning when the tents are down
And packed for travel; and the whole Blood town
Is out along the waterfront to see
The trappers going.   Dancing as with glee,
Six laden bull-boats feel the April tide
And sweep away.   Along the riverside
The straggling, shouting rabble keeps abreast
A little while; but, longer than the rest,
A weeping runner races with the swirl
And loses slowly.   'Tis the Long Knife's girl,

Whom love perhaps already makes aware
How flows unseen a greater river there—
The never-to-be-overtaken days.
And now she pauses at the bend to gaze
Upon the black boats dwindling down the long
Dawn-gilded reach.   A merry trapper's song
Comes liltingly to mock her, and a hand
Waves back farewell.   Now 'round a point of land
The bull-boats disappear; and that is all—
Save only that long waiting for the fall
When he would come again.

                                   All day they swirled
Northeastwardly.   The undulating world
Flowed by them—wooded headland, greening vale
And naked hill—as in a fairy tale
Remembered in a dream.   And when the flare
Of sunset died behind them, and the air
Went weird and deepened to a purple gloom,
They saw the white Enchanted Castles loom
Above them, slowly pass and drift a-rear,
Dissolving in the starry crystal sphere
'Mid which they seemed suspended.

                                   Late to camp,
They launched while yet the crawling valley damp,
Made islands of the distant hills and hid
The moaning flood.   The Half Way Pyramid
That noon stared in upon them from the south.
'Twas starlight when they camped at Hell Creek's mouth,
Among those hills where evermore in vain
The Spring comes wooing, and the April rain

Is tears upon a tomb.   And once again
The dead land echoed to the songs of men
Bound dayward when the dawn was but a streak.
Halfway to noon they sighted Big Dry Creek,
Not choked with grave dust now, but carolling
The universal music of the spring.
Then when the day was midway down the sky,
They reached the Milk.   And howsoe'er the eye
Might sweep that valley with a far-flung gaze,
It found no spot uncovered with a maze
Of bison moving lazily at browse—
Scarce wilder than a herd of dairy cows
That know their herdsmen.

                     Now the whole band willed
To tarry.   So they beached their boats and killed
Three fatling heifers; sliced the juicy rumps
For broiling over embers; set the humps
And loins to roast on willow spits, and threw
The hearts and livers in a pot to stew
Against the time of dulling appetites.
And when the stream ran opalescent lights
And in a scarlet glow the new moon set,
The feast began.   And some were eating yet,
And some again in intervals of sleep,
When upside down above the polar steep
The Dipper hung.   And many tales were told
And there was hearty laughter as of old,
With Fink's guffaw to swell it now and then.
It seemed old times were coming back again;
That truly they had launched upon a trip
Whereof the shining goal was comradeship:

And tears were in the laughter of Talbeau,
So glad was he.   For how may mortals know
Their gladness, save they sense it by the fear
That whispers how the very thing held dear
May pass away?

                         The smoky dawn was lit,
And, suddenly become aware of it,
A flock of blue cranes, dozing on the sand,
With startled cries awoke the sprawling band
And took the misty air with moaning wings.
Disgruntled with the chill drab scheme of things,
Still half asleep and heavy with the feast,
The trappers launched their boats.   But when the east
Burned rosily, therefrom a raw wind blew,
And ever with the growing day it grew
Until the stream rose choppily and drove
The fleet ashore.   Camped snugly in a grove
Of cottonwoods, they slept.   And when the gale,
Together with the light, began to fail,
They 'rose and ate and set-a-drift again.

It seemed the solid world that mothers men
With twilight and the falling moon had passed,
And there was nothing but a hollow vast,
By time-outlasting stars remotely lit,
And they who at the central point of it
Hung motionless; while, rather sensed than seen,
The phantoms of a world that had been green
Stole by in silence—shapes that once were trees,
Black wraiths of bushes, airy traceries
Remembering the hills.   Then sleep made swift
The swinging of the Dipper and the lift

Of stars that dwell upon the day's frontier;
Until at length the wheeling hollow sphere
Began to fill. And just at morningshine
They landed at the Little Porcupine.
Again they slept and, putting off at night,
They passed the Elk Horn Prairie on the right
Halfway to dawn and Wolf Creek. One night more
Had vanished when they slept upon the shore
Beside the Poplar's mouth. And three had fled
When, black against the early morning red,
The Fort that Henry builded heard their calls,
And sentries' rifles spurting from the walls
Spilled drawling echoes. Then the gates swung wide
And shouting trappers thronged the riverside
To welcome back the homing *voyageurs*.

That day was spent in sorting out the furs,
With eager talk of how the winter went;
And with the growing night grew merriment.
The hump and haunches of a bison cow
Hung roasting at the heaped-up embers now
On Henry's hearth. The backlog whined and popped
And, sitting squat or lounging elbow-propped,
Shrewd traders in the merchandise of tales
Held traffic, grandly careless how the scales
Tiptilted with a slight excessive weight.
And when the roast was finished, how they ate!
And there was that which set them singing too
Against the deep bass music of the flue,
While catgut screamed ecstatic in the lead,
Encouraging the voices used and keyed
To vast and windy spaces.

Later came
A gentler mood when, staring at the flame,
Men ventured reminiscences and spoke
About Kentucky people or the folk
Back yonder in Virginia or the ways
They knew in old St. Louis; till the blaze
Fell blue upon the hearth, and in the gloom
And melancholy stillness of the room
They heard the wind of midnight wail outside.

Then there was one who poked the logs and cried:
"Is this a weeping drunk? I swear I'm like
To tear my hair! Sing something lively, Mike!"
And Fink said nought; but after poring long
Upon the logs, began an Irish song—
A gently grieving thing like April rain,
That while it wakes old memories of pain,
Wakes also odors of the violet.
A broken heart, it seemed, could ne'er forget
The eyes of Nora, dead upon the hill.
And when he ceased the men sat very still,
As hearing yet the low caressing note
Of some lost angel mourning in his throat.
And afterwhile Mike spoke: "Shure, now," said he,
" 'Tis in a woman's eyes shtrong liquors be;
And if ye drink av thim—and if ye drink—"
For just a moment in the face of Fink
Talbeau beheld that angel yearning through;
And wondering if Carpenter saw too,
He looked, and lo! the guileless fellow—grinned!

[310]

As dreaming water, stricken by a wind,
Gives up the imaged heaven that it knows,
So Fink's face lost the angel.   He arose
And left the place without a word to say.

The morrow was a perfect April day;
Nor might one guess—so friendly was the sun,
So kind the air—what thread at length was spun,
What shears were opened now to sever it.
No sullen mood was Mike's.   His biting wit
Made gay the trappers busy with the fur;
Though more and ever more on Carpenter
His sallies fell, with ever keener whet.
And Carpenter, unskilled in banter, met
The sharper sally with the broader grin.
But, by and by, Mike made a jest, wherein
Some wanton innuendo lurked and leered,
About the Long Knife's girl.   The place went weird
With sudden silence as the tall man strode
Across the room, nor lacked an open road
Among the men.   A glitter in his stare
Belied the smile he bore; and, pausing there
With stiffened index finger raised and held
Before the jester's eyes, as though he spelled
The slow words out, he said: "We'll have no jokes
In just that way about our women folks!"
And Fink guffawed.
                        They would have fought again,
Had not the Major stepped between the men
And talked the crisis by.   And when 'twas past,
Talbeau, intent to end the strife at last,
Somehow persuaded Fink to make amends,
And, as a proof that henceforth they were friends,

[311]

Proposed the shooting of the whisky cup.
"Shure, b'y," said Mike, "we'll toss a copper up
And if 'tis heads I'll thry me cunning first.
As fer me joke, the tongue of me is cursed
Wid double j'ints——so let it be forgot!"
And so it was agreed.

                                  They cleared a spot
And flipped a coin that tinkled as it fell.
A tiny sound——yet, like a midnight bell
That sets wild faces pressing at the pane,
Talbeau would often hear that coin again,
In vivid dreams, to waken terrified.
'Twas heads.

                       And now the tall man stepped aside
And, beckoning Talbeau, he whispered: "Son,
If anything should happen, keep my gun
For old time's sake.   And when the Major pays
In old St. Louis, drink to better days
When friends were friends, with what he's owing me."
Whereat the little man laughed merrily
And said: "Old Horse, you're off your feed to-day;
But if you've sworn an oath to blow your pay,
I guess the three of us can make it good!
Mike couldn't miss a target if he would."
"Well, maybe so," said Carpenter, and smiled.

A windless noon was brooding on the wild
And in the clearing, eager for the show,
The waiting trappers chatted.   Now Talbeau
Stepped off the range.   The tall man took his place,
The grin of some droll humor on his face;

And when his friend was reaching for his head
To set the brimming cup thereon, he said:
"You won't forget I gave my gun to you
And all my blankets and my fixin's too?"
The small man laughed and, turning round, he cried:
"We're ready, Mike!"

                              A murmur ran and died
Along the double line of eager men.
Fink raised his gun, but set it down again
And blew a breath and said: "I'm gittin' dhry!
So howld yer noddle shtiddy, Bill, me b'y,
And don't ye shpill me whisky!" Cedar-straight
The tall man stood, the calm of brooding Fate
About him.   Aye, and often to the end
Talbeau would see that vision of his friend—
A man-flower springing from the fresh green sod,
While, round about, the bushes burned with God
And mating peewees fluted in the brush.

They heard a gun lock clicking in the hush.
They saw Fink sighting—heard the rifle crack,
And saw beneath the spreading powder rack
The tall man pitching forward.

                              Echoes fled
Like voices in a panic.   Then Mike said:
"Bejasus, and ye've shpilled me whisky, Bill!"

A catbird screamed.   The crowd stood very still
As though bewitched.

          "And can't ye hear?" bawled Fink;
"I say, I'm dhry—and now ye've shpilled me drink!"
He stooped to blow the gases from his gun.

[313]

And now men saw Talbeau. They saw him run
And stoop to peer upon the prostrate man
Where now the mingling blood and whisky ran
From oozing forehead and the tilted cup.
And in the hush a sobbing cry grew up:
"My God! You've killed him, Mike!"

                                    Then growing loud,
A wind of horror blew among the crowd
And set it swirling round about the dead.
And over all there roared a voice that said:
"I niver mint to do it, b'ys, I swear!
The divil's in me gun!" Men turned to stare
Wild-eyed upon the center of that sound,
And saw Fink dash his rifle to the ground,
As 'twere the hated body of his wrong.

Once more arose that wailing, like a song,
Of one who called and called upon his friend.

VII

THE THIRD RIDER

It seemed the end, and yet 'twas not the end.
A day that wind of horror and surprise
Blew high; and then, as when the tempest dies
And only aspens prattle, as they will,
Though pines win silence and the oaks are still,
By furtive twos and threes the talk survived.
To some it seemed that men were longer lived
Who quarreled not over women.   Others guessed
That love was bad for marksmanship at best—
The nerves, you know!   Still others pointed out
Why Mike should have the benefit of doubt;
For every man, who knew a rifle, knew
That there were days you'd split a reed in two,
Off-hand at fifty paces; then, one day,
Why, somehow, damn your eyes, you'd blaze away
And miss a bull!   No doubt regarding that!
"But," one replied, " 'tis what you're aiming at,
Not what you hit, determines skill, you know!"—
An abstract observation, apropos
Of nothing in particular, but made
As just a contribution to the trade
Of gunnery!   And others would recall
The center of that silence in the hall
The night one lay there waiting, splendid, still,
And nothing left to wait for.   Poor old Bill!

There went a man, by God! Who knew his like—
So meek in might? And some remembered Mike—
The hearth-lit room—the way he came to look
Upon that face—and how his shoulders shook
With sobbing as he moaned: "My friend! My friend!"

It seemed the end, and yet 'twas not the end,
Though men cared less to know what cunning gnome
Or eyeless thing of doom had ridden home
The deadly slug. And then there came a day
When Major Henry had a word to say
That seemed, at last, to lay the ghost to rest.
He meant to seek the River of the West
Beyond the range, immensely rich in furs,
And for the wiving prows of *voyageurs*
A virgin yearning. Yonder one might glide
A thousand miles to sunset, where the tide
Is tempered with an endless dream of May!
So much and more the Major had to say—
Words big with magic for the young men's ears.
And finally he called for volunteers—
Two men to hasten to the Moreau's mouth,
Meet Ashley's party coming from the south
And bid them buy more horses at the Grand
Among the Rees. Then, pushing through the band,
Mike Fink stood forth, and after him, Talbeau.

Now Henry thought 'twere wiser they should go
By land, although the river trail, he knew,
Were better. But a wind of rumor blew
Up stream. About the region of the Knife,
It seemed, the Grovans tarried, nursing strife

Because the Whites were favoring their foes
With trade for guns; and, looking on their bows,
The Grovans hated.   So the rumor said.
And thus it came to pass the new trail led
About six days by pony to the south;
Thence eastward, five should find the Moreau's mouth
And Ashley toiling up among the bars.

The still white wind was blowing out the stars
When yawning trappers saw the two men row
Across the river with their mounts in tow—
A red roan stallion and a buckskin mare.
And now the ponies gain the far bank there
And flounder up and shake themselves like dogs.
And now the riders mount and breast the fogs
Flung down as wool upon the flat.   They dip
And rise and float, submerging to the hip,
Turn slowly into shadow men, and fade.
And some have said that when the ponies neighed,
'Twas like a strangled shriek; and far ahead
Some ghostly pony, ridden by the dead,
Called onward like a bugle singing doom.
And when the valley floor, as with a broom,
Was swept by dawn, men saw the empty land.

Not now the Song shall tell of Henry's band
Ascending to the Falls, nor how they crossed
The Blackfoot trail, nor how they fought and lost,
Thrown back upon the Yellowstone to wait
In vain for Ashley's hundred.   Yonder, Fate
Led southward through the fog, and thither goes
The prescient Song.

                              The April sun arose
And fell; and all day long the riders faced
A rolling, treeless, melancholy waste
Of yellow grass; for 'twas a rainless time,
Nor had the baby green begun to climb
The steep-kneed hills, but kept the nursing draws.
And knee to knee they rode with scarce a pause,
Save when the ponies drank; and scarce a word,
As though the haunting silence of a third,
Who rode between them, shackled either tongue.
And when along the sloughs the twilight flung
Blue haze, and made the hills seem doubly bleak,
They camped beside a songless little creek
That crawled among the clumps of stunted plum
Just coming into bud. And both sat dumb
Beside a mewing fire, until the west
Was darkenèd and the shadows leaped and pressed
About their little ring of feeble light.
Then, moved by some vague menace in the night,
Fink forced a laugh that wasn't glad at all,
And joked about a certain saddle gall
That troubled him——a Rabelaisian quip
That in the good old days had served to strip
The drooping humor from the dourest jowl.
He heard the laughter of the prairie owl,
A goblin jeering. Gazing at the flame,
Talbeau seemed not to hear. But when there came
A cry of kiotes, peering all about
He said: "You don't suppose they'll dig him out?
I carried heavy stones till break of day.
You don't suppose they'll come and paw away
The heavy stones I packed, and pester Bill?"
"Huh uh," Fink grunted; but the evening chill

Seemed doubled on a sudden; so he sought
His blanket, wrapped it closely, thought and thought
Till drowsy nonsense tumbled through his skull.

Now at that time of night when comes a lull
On stormy life; when even sorrow sleeps,
And sentinels upon the stellar steeps
Sight morning, though the world is blind and dumb,
Fink wakened at a whisper: "Mike! He's come!
Look! Look!" And Mike sat up and blinked and saw.
It didn't walk—it burned along the draw—
Tall, radiantly white! It wasn't dead—
It smiled—it had a tin cup on its head—
Eh?—Gone!

        Fink stirred the embers to a flare.
What dream was this? The world seemed unaware
That anything at all had come to pass.
Contentedly the ponies nipped the grass
There in the darkness; and the night was still.
They slept no more, but nursed the fire until
The morning broke; then ate and rode away.

They weren't any merrier that day.
And each spoke little, save when Fink would swear
And smirch the virtue of the buckskin mare
For picking quarrels with the roan he rode.
(Did not the Northwind nag her like a goad,
And was there any other horse to blame?)

The worried day dragged on and twilight came—
A dusty gray. They climbed a hill to seek
Some purple fringe of brush that marked a creek.

[319]

The prairie seemed an endless yellow blur:
Nor might they choose but tarry where they were
And pass the cheerless night as best they could,
For they had seen no water-hole or wood
Since when the sun was halfway down the sky;
And there would be no stars to travel by,
So thick a veil of dust the great wind wove.
They staked their ponies in a leeward cove,
And, rolling in their blankets, swooned away.

Talbeau awoke and stared.   'Twas breaking day!
So soon?   It seemed he scarce had slept a wink!
He'd have another snooze, for surely Fink
Seemed far from waking, sprawled upon the ground,
His loose mouth gaping skyward with a sound
As of a bucksaw grumbling through a knot.
Talbeau dropped back and dreamed the sun was hot
Upon his face.   He tried but failed to stir;
Whereat he knew that he was Carpenter
And hot-breatht wolves were sniffing round his head!
He wasn't dead!   He really wasn't dead!
Would no one come, would no one drive them off?
His cry for help was nothing but a cough,
For something choked him.   Then a shrill long scream
Cut knife-like through the shackles of his dream,
And once again he saw the lurid flare
Of morning on the hills.

                                    What ailed the mare?
She strained her tether, neighing.   And the roan?
He squatted, trembling, with his head upthrown,
And lashed his tail and snorted at the blast.
Perhaps some prowling grizzly wandered past.

Talbeau sat up. What stifling air! How warm!
What sound was that? Perhaps a thunder storm
Was working up. He coughed; and then it broke
Upon him how the air was sharp with smoke;
And, leaping up, he turned and looked and knew
What birdless dawn, unhallowed by the dew,
Came raging from the northwest! Half the earth
And half the heavens were a burning hearth
Fed fat with grass inflammable as tow!

He shook Fink, yelling: "Mike, we've got to go!
All hell's broke loose!"

                                    They cinched the saddles on
With hands that fumbled; mounted and were gone,
Like rabbits fleeing from a kiote pack.
They crossed the valley, topped a rise, looked back,
Nor dared to gaze. The firm, familiar world,
It seemed, was melting down, and Chaos swirled
Once more across the transient realms of form
To scatter in the primal atom-storm
The earth's rich dust and potency of dreams.
Infernal geysers gushed, and sudden streams
Of rainbow flux went roaring up the skies
Through ghastly travesties of Paradise,
Where, drowsy in a tropic summertide,
Strange gaudy flowers bloomed and aged and died—
Whole seasons in a moment. Bloody rain,
Blown slant like April silver, spewed the plain
To mock the fallow sod; and where it fell
Anemones and violets of hell
Foreran the fatal summer.

Spurs bit deep.
Now down the hill where shadow-haunted sleep
Fell from the broken wind's narcotic breath,
The ponies plunged.   A sheltered draw, where death
Seemed brooding in the silence, heard them pass.
A hollow, deep with tangled jointed grass,
Snatched at the frantic hoofs.   Now up a slope
They clambered, blowing, at a stumbling lope
And, reined upon the summit, wheeled to stare.
The stallion snorted, and the rearing mare
Screamed at the sight and bolted down the wind.
The writhing Terror, scarce a mile behind,
Appeared to gain; while far to left and right
Its flanks seemed bending in upon the night—
A ten-league python closing on its prey.

No guiding hand was needed for the way;
Blind speed was all.   So little Nature heeds
The fate of men, these blew as tumbleweeds
Before that dwarfing, elemental rage.
A gray wolf bounded from a clump of sage;
A rabbit left its bunchgrass nest and ran
Beside its foe; and neither dreaded Man,
The deadliest of all earth's preying things.
A passing knoll exploded into wings,
And prairie owls, befuddled by the light,
Went tumbling up like patches of the night
The burning tempest tattered.

Leaning low,
The gasping riders let the ponies go,
The little buckskin leading, while the roan
Strove hard a-flank, afraid to be alone

[322]

And nickering at whiles.   And he who led,
By brief hypnotic lapses comforted,
Recalled the broad Ohio, heard the horns
The way they used to sing those summer morns
When he and Mike and——.   There the dream went wrong
And through his head went running, like a song
That sings itself: 'He tried so hard to come
And warn us; but the grave had made him dumb,
And 'twas to show he loved us that he smiled.'
And of the other terror made a child
Whom often, for a panic moment's span,
Projections from the conscience of the man
Pursued with glaring eyes and claws of flame.
For this the dead arose, for this he came——
That grin upon his face!

                                A blinding gloom
Crushed down; then, followed by a rolling boom,
There broke a scarlet hurricane of light
That swept the farthest reaches of the night
Where unsuspected hills leaped up aghast.
Already through the hollow they had passed
So recently, the hounding Terror sped!
And now the wind grew hotter.   Overhead
Inverted seas of color rolled and broke,
And from the combers of the litten smoke
A stinging spindrift showered.

                                On they went,
Unconscious of duration or extent,
Of everything but that from which they fled.
Now, sloping to an ancient river bed,
The prairie flattened.   Plunging downward there,
The riders suddenly became aware

How surged, beneath, a mighty shadow-stream—
As though the dying Prairie dreamed a dream
Of yesterage when all her valleys flowed
With Amazons, and monster life abode
Upon her breast and quickened in her womb.
And from that rushing in the flame-smeared gloom
Unnumbered outcries blended in a roar.
The headlong ponies struck the sounding shore
And reared upon their haunches. Far and near,
The valley was a-flood with elk and deer
And buffalo and wolves and antelope
And whatsoever creature slough and slope
Along the path of terror had to give.
Torrential with the common will to live,
The river of unnumbered egos swept
The ponies with it. But the buckskin kept
The margin where the rabble frayed and thinned
And, breathing with the wheeze of broken wind,
The stallion clung to her.

                                   It came to pass
The valley yawned upon a sea of grass
That seemed to heave, as waves of gloom and glare
Ran over it; and, rising here and there,
Tall buttes made islands in the living tide
That roared about them. Still with swinging stride
And rhythmic breath the little buckskin ran
Among the herd, that opened like a fan
And scattered. But the roan was losing ground.
His breathing gave a gurgling, hollow sound,
As though his life were gushing from his throat.
His whole frame quivered like a scuttled boat

That slowly sinks; nor did he seem to feel
Upon his flank the biting of the steel
That made him bleed. Fink cut the rifle-boot
And saddle-bags away, to give the brute
Less burden.

             Now it happened, as they neared
A lofty butte whose summit glimmered weird
Beneath the lurid boiling of the sky,
Talbeau was startled by a frantic cry
Behind him; noted that he rode alone,
And, turning in the saddle, saw the roan
Go stumbling down and wither to a heap.
And momently, between a leap and leap,
The love of self was mighty in the man;
For now the Terror left the hills and ran
With giant strides along the grassy plains.
Dear Yesterdays fought wildly for the reins,
To-morrows for the spur.   And then the mare
Heeled to the sawing bit and pawed the air
And halted, prancing.

                 Once again Talbeau
Looked back to where the sparks were blown as snow
Before that blizzard blast of scorching light,
And saw Fink running down the painted night
Like some lost spirit fleeing from the Wrath.

One horse—and who should ride it.   All he hath
A man will give for life!   But shall he give
For living that which makes it good to live—
The consciousness of fellowship and trust?
Let fools so prize a pinch of throbbing dust!

[325]

Now Fink should ride, and let the rest be hid.
He bounded from the mare; but, as he did,
The panic-stricken pony wheeled about,
Won freedom with a lunge, and joined the rout
Of fleeing shadows.

                          Well, 'twas over now—
Perhaps it didn't matter anyhow—
They'd go together now and hunt for Bill!
And momently the world seemed very still
About Talbeau. Then Fink was at his side,
Blank horror in his face. "Come on!" he cried;
"The butte! We'll climb the butte!" And once again
Talbeau knew fear.

                       Now, gripping hands, the men
Scuttled and dodged athwart the scattered flight
Of shapes that drifted in the flood of light,
A living flotsam; reached the bare butte's base,
Went scrambling up its leaning leeward face
To where the slope grew sheer, and huddled there.
And hotter, hotter, hotter grew the air,
Until their temples sang a fever tune.
The April night became an August noon.
Then, near to swooning in a blast of heat,
They heard the burning breakers boom and beat
About their lofty island, as they lay,
Their gaping mouths pressed hard against the clay,
And fought for every breath. Nor could they tell
How long upon a blistered scarp in hell
They gasped and clung. But suddenly at last—
An age in passing, and a moment, passed—

The torture ended, and the cool air came;
And, looking out, they saw the long slant flame
Devour the night to leeward.

                                    By and by
Drab light came seeping through the sullen sky.
They waited there until the morning broke,
And, like a misty moon amid the smoke,
The sun came stealing up.

                              They found a place
Where rain had scarred the butte wall's western face
With many runnels; clambered upward there—
And viewed a panorama of despair.
The wind had died, and not a sound arose
Above those blackened leagues; for even crows
(The solitude embodied in a bird)
Had fled that desolation.   Nothing stirred,
Save here and there a thin gray column grew
From where some draw still smouldered.   And they knew
How universal quiet may appal
As violence, and, even as a wall,
Sheer vacancy confine.

                              No horse, no gun!
Nay, worse; no hint of water hole or run
In all the flat or back among the hills!
Mere hunger is a goad that, ere it kills,
May drive the lean far down the hardest road:
But thirst is both a snaffle and a load;
It gripped them now.   When Mike made bold to speak,
His tongue was like a stranger to his cheek.
"Shure, b'y," he croaked; " 'tis Sunday morn in hell!"
The sound seemed profanation; on it fell
The vast, rebuking silence.

Long they gazed
About them, standing silent and amazed
Upon the summit.   West and north and east
They saw too far.   But mystery, at least,
Was in the south, where still the smoke concealed
The landscape.   Vistas of the unrevealed
Invited Hope to stray there as it please.
And presently there came a little breeze
Out of the dawn.   As of a crowd that waits
Some imminent revealment of the Fates
That toil behind the scenes, a murmur 'woke
Amid the hollow hush.   And now the smoke
Mysteriously stirs, begins to flow,
And giant shadow bulks that loom below
Seem crowding dawnward.   One by one they lift
Above the reek, and trail the ragged drift
About their flanks.   A melancholy scene!
Gray buttes and giddy gulfs that yawn between—
A Titan's labyrinth!   But see afar
Where yonder canyon like a purple scar
Cuts zigzag through the waste!   Is that a gleam
Of water in its deeps?

                              A stream!   A stream!
Now scrambling down the runnels of the rain,
They struck across the devastated plain
Where losers of the night's mad race were strewn
To wait the wolves and crows.

                              Mid-afternoon
Beheld them stripping at the river's bank.
They wallowed in the turbid stream and drank

Delicious beakers in the liquid mud;
Nor drank alone, for here the burning flood
Had flung its panting driftage in the dark.
The valley teemed with life, as though some Ark
That rode the deluge, spewed its cargo here:
Elk, antelope, wolves, bison, rabbits, deer,
Owls, crows—the greatest mingled with the least.
And when the men had drunk, they had a feast
Of liver, bolted dripping from a cow
Dead at the water's lip.

                                    Blue shadow now
Was mounting slowly up the canyon steep;
So, seeking for a better place to sleep,
They wandered down the margin of the stream.
'Twas scarce more real than walking in a dream
Of lonely craters in a lunar land
That never thrilled with roots.   On either hand
The dwarfing summits soared, grotesque, austere,
And jaggéd fissures, sentinelled with fear,
Led back to mysteries of purple gloom.

They came to where a coulee, like a flume,
Rose steeply to the prairie.   Thither hurled,
A roaring freshet of the herd had swirled,
Cascading to the river bed; and there,
Among the trampled carcasses, the mare
Lay bloated near the water.   She had run
With saddle, panniers, powder-horn and gun
Against the wind-thewed fillies of the fire,
And won the heat, to perish at the wire—
A plucky little brute!

VIII

VENGEANCE

                              They made a camp
Well up above the crawling valley damp,
And where no prowling beast might chance to come.
There was no fuel; but a flask of rum,
Thanks to the buckskin, dulled the evening chill.
And both grew mellow. Memories of Bill
And other nights possessed the little man;
And on and on his reminiscence ran,
As 'twere the babble of a brook of tears
Gone groping for the ocean of dead years
Too far away to reach. And by and by
The low voice sharpened to an anguished cry:
"O Mike! I said you couldn't miss the cup!"

Then something snapped in Fink and, leaping up,
He seized Talbeau and shook him as a rat
Is shaken by a dog. "Enough of that!"
He yelled; "And, 'faith, I'll sind ye afther Bill
Fer wan more wurrd! Ye fool! I mint to kill!
And, moind me now, ye'd better howld yer lip!"

Talbeau felt murder shudder in the grip
That choked and shook and flung him. Faint and dazed,
He sprawled upon the ground. And anger blazed
Within him, like the leaping Northern Light
That gives no heat. He wished to rise and fight,

But could not for the horror of it all.
Wild voices thronged the further canyon wall
As Fink raved on; and every word he said
Was like a mutilation of the dead
By some demonic mob.

                    And when at length
He heard Mike snoring yonder, still the strength
To rise and kill came not upon Talbeau.
So many moments of the Long Ago
Came pleading; and the gentle might thereof
United with the habit of old love
To weave a spell about the sleeping man.
Then drowsily the pondered facts began
To merge and group, as running colors will,
In new and vaguer patterns. Mike and Bill
Were bickering again. And someone said:
"Let's flip a copper; if it's tails, he's dead;
If heads, he's living. That's the way to tell!"
A spinning copper jangled like a bell.
But even as he stooped to pick it up,
Behold! the coin became a whisky cup
Bored smoothly through the center! "Look at this!"
He seemed to shout: "I knew Mike couldn't miss!
Bill only played at dying for a joke!"

Then laughter filled his dream, and he awoke.
The dawn was like a stranger's cold regard
Across the lifeless land, grotesquely scarred
As by old sorrow; and the man's dull sense
Of woe, become objective and immense,
Seemed waiting there to crush him.

                              Still Fink slept;
And even now, it seemed, his loose mouth kept
A shape for shameless words, as though a breath,
Deep drawn, might set it gloating o'er the death
Of one who loved its jesting and its song.
And while Talbeau sat pondering the wrong
So foully done, and all that had been killed,
And how the laughter of the world was stilled
And all its wine poured out, he seemed to hear
As though a spirit whispered in his ear:
You won't forget I gave my gun to you!
And instantly the deep conviction grew
That 'twas a plea for justice from the slain.
Ah, not without a hand upon the rein,
Nor with an empty saddle, had the mare
Outrun the flame that she might carry there
The means of vengeance!

                         Yet—if Mike were dead!
He shuddered, gazing where the gray sky bled
With morning, like a wound. He couldn't kill;
Nor did it seem to be the way of Bill
To bid him do it. Yet the gun was sent.
For what?—To make Mike suffer and repent?
But how?

                         Awhile his apathetic gaze
Explored yon thirst- and hunger-haunted maze,
As though he might surprise the answer there.
The answer came. That region of despair
Should be Mike's Purgatory! More than Chance
Had fitted circumstance to circumstance

That this should be! He knew it! And the plan,
Thus suddenly conceived, possessed the man.
It seemed the might of Bill had been reborn
In him.

He took the gun and powder horn,
The water flasks and sun-dried bison meat
The panniers gave; then climbing to a seat
Above the sleeper, shouted down to him:
"Get up!" Along the further canyon rim
A multitude of voices swelled the shout.
Fink started up and yawned and looked about,
Bewildered. Once again the clamor ran
Along the canyon wall. The little man,
Now squinting down the pointed rifle, saw
The lifted face go pale, the stubborn jaw
Droop nervelessly. A twinge of pity stirred
Within him, and he marvelled as he heard
His own voice saying what he wished unsaid:
"It's Bill's own rifle pointing at your head;
Go east, and think of all the wrong you've done!"

Fink glanced across his shoulder where the sun
Shone level on the melancholy land;
And, feigning that he didn't understand,
Essayed a careless grin that went awry.
"Bejasus, and we'll not go there, me b'y,"
He said; "for shure 'tis hell widout the lights!"
That one-eyed stare along the rifle sights
Was narrowed to a slit. A sickening shock
Ran through him at the clucking of the lock.
He clutched his forehead, stammering: "Talbe
I've been yer frind——."

[333]

"I'll give you three to go,"
The other said, "or else you'll follow Bill!
One—two—."

Fink turned and scuttled down the hill;
And at the sight the watcher's eyes grew dim,
For something old and dear had gone from him—
His pride in one who made a clown of Death.
Alas, how much the man would give for breath!
How easily Death made of him the clown!

Now scrambling for a grip, now rolling down,
Mike landed at the bottom of the steep,
And, plunging in the river belly deep,
Struck out in terror for the other shore.
At any moment might the rifle's roar
Crash through that rearward silence, and the lead
Come snarling like a hornet at his head—
He felt the spot!   Then presently the flood
Began to cool the fever in his blood,
And furtive self-derision stung his pride.
He clambered dripping up the further side
And felt himself a fool!   He wouldn't go!
That little whiffet yonder was Talbeau!
And who was this that he, Mike Fink, had feared?
He'd go and see.

A spurt of smoke appeared
Across the river, and a bullet struck—
Spat ping—beside him, spewing yellow muck
Upon his face.   Then every cliff and draw
Rehearsed the sullen thunders of the law

He dared to question.   Stricken strangely weak,
He clutched the clay and watched the powder reek
Trail off with glories of the level sun.
He saw Talbeau pour powder in his gun
And ram the wad.   A second shot might kill!
That brooding like a woman over Bill
Had set the fellow daft.   *A crazy man!*
The notion spurred him.   Springing up, he ran
To where a gully cleft the canyon rim
And, with that one-eyed fury after him,
Fled east.

           The very buttes, grotesque and weird,
Seemed startled at the sight of what he feared
And powerless to shield him in his need.
'Twas more than man he fled from; 'twas a deed,
Become alive and subtle as the air,
That turned upon the doer.   Everywhere
It gibbered in the echoes as he fled.
A stream of pictures flitted through his head:
The quiet body in the hearth-lit hall,
The grinning ghost, the flight, the stallion's fall,
The flame-girt isle, the spectral morning sun,
And then the finding of the dead man's gun
Beside the glooming river.   Flowing by,
These fused and focused in the deadly eye
He felt behind him.

           Suddenly the ground
Heaved up and smote him with a crashing sound;
And in the vivid moment of his fall
He thought he heard the snarling rifle ball
And felt the one-eyed fury crunch its mark.
Expectant of the swooping of the dark,

He raised his eyes.——The sun was shining still;
It peeped about the shoulder of a hill
And viewed him with a quizzifying stare.
He looked behind him.   Nothing followed there;
But Silence, big with dread-begotten sound,
Dismayed him; and the steeps that hemmed him round
Seemed plotting with a more than human guile.
He rose and fled; but every little while
A sense of eyes behind him made him pause;
And always down the maze of empty draws
It seemed a sound of feet abruptly ceased.

Now trotting, walking now, he labored east;
And when at length the burning zenith beat
Upon him, and the summits swam with heat,
And on the winding gullies fell no shade,
He came to where converging gulches made
A steep-walled basin for the blinding glare.
Here, fanged and famished, crawled the prickly pear;
Malevolent with thirst, the soap weed thrust
Its barbed stilettos from the arid dust,
Defiant of the rain-withholding blue:
And in the midst a lonely scrub oak grew,
A crookéd dwarf that, in the pictured bog
Of its own shadow, squatted like a frog.
Fink, panting, flung himself beneath its boughs.

A mighty magic in the noonday drowse
Allayed the driving fear.   A waking dream
Fulfilled a growing wish.   He saw the stream
Far off as from a space-commanding height.
And now a phantasy of rapid flight

Transported him above the sagging land,
And with a sudden swoop he seemed to stand
Once more upon the shimmering river's brink.
His eyes drank deep; but when his mouth would drink,
A giant hornet from the other shore—
The generating center of a roar
That shook the world—snarled by.

He started up,
And saw the basin filling as a cup
With purple twilight!   Gazing all around
Where still the flitting ghost of some great sound
Troubled the crags a moment, then was mute,
He saw along the shoulder of a butte,
A good three hundred paces from the oak,
A slowly spreading streak of rifle smoke
And knew the deadly eye was lurking there.
He fled again.

About him everywhere
Amid the tangled draws now growing dim,
Weird witnesses took cognizance of him
And told abroad the winding way he ran.
He halted only when his breath began
To stab his throat.   And lo, the staring eye
Was quenched with night!   No further need he fly
Till dawn.   And yet—.   He held his breath to hear
If footsteps followed.   Silence smote his ear,
The gruesome silence of the hearth-lit hall,
More dread than sound.   Against the gully wall
He shrank and huddled with his eyes shut tight,
For fear a presence, latent in the night,
Should walk before him.

[337]

                              Then it seemed he ran
Through regions alien to the feet of Man,
A weary way despite the speed of sleep,
And came upon a river flowing deep
Between black crags that made the sky a well.
And eerily the feeble starlight fell
Upon the flood with water lilies strown.
But when he stooped, the stream began to moan,
And suddenly from every lily pad
A white face bloomed, unutterably sad
And bloody browed.

                              A swift, erasing flame
Across the dusky picture, morning came.
Mike lay a moment, blinking at the blue;
And then the fear of yesterday broke through
The clinging drowse. For lo, on every side
The paling summits watched him, Argus-eyed,
In hushed anticipation of a roar.
He fled.

                              All day, intent to see once more
The open plain before the night should fall,
He labored on. But many a soaring wall
Annulled some costly distance he had won;
And misdirected gullies, white with sun,
Seemed spitefully to baffle his desire.

The deeps went blue; on mimic dome and spire
The daylight faded to a starry awe.
Mike slept; and lo, they marched along the draw—
Or rather burned—tall, radiantly white!
A hushed procession, tunnelling the night,

They came, with lips that smiled and brows that bled,
And each one bore a tin cup on its head,
A brimming cup. But ever as they came
Before him, like a draught-struck candle flame
They shuddered and were snuffed.

                              'Twas deep night yet
When Mike awoke and felt the terror sweat
Upon his face, the prickling of his hair.
Afraid to sleep, he paced the gully there
Until the taller buttes were growing gray.

He brooded much on flowing streams that day.
As with a weight, he stooped; his feet were slow;
He shuffled. Less and less he feared Talbeau
Behind him. More and more he feared the night
Before him. Any hazard in the light,
Or aught that might befall 'twixt living men,
Were better than to be alone again
And meet that dream!

                          The deeps began to fill
With purple haze. Bewildered, boding ill,
A moaning wind awoke. 'Twould soon be dark.
Mike pondered. Twice Talbeau had missed the mark.
Perhaps he hadn't really meant to hit.
And surely now that flaring anger fit
Had burned away. It wasn't like the man
To hold a grudge. Mike halted, and began
To grope for words regretful of the dead,
Persuasive words about a heart that bled
For Bill. 'Twas all a terrible mistake.
"Plase now, a little dhrop fer owld toime's sake!"

[339]

With troublesome insistence, that refrain
Kept running through the muddle of his brain
And disarranged the words he meant to speak.
The trickle of a tear along his cheek
Consoled him. Soon his suffering would end.
Talbeau would see him weeping for his friend—
Talbeau had water!

        Now the heights burned red
To westward. With a choking clutch of dread
He noted how the dusk was gathering
Along the draws—a trap about to spring.
He cupped his hands about his mouth and cried:
"Talbeau! Talbeau!" Despairing voices died
Among the summits, and the lost wind pined.
It made Talbeau seem infinitely kind—
The one thing human in a ghostly land.
Where was he? Just a touch of that warm hand
Would thwart the dark! Mike sat against a wall
And brooded.

        By and by a skittering fall
Of pebbles at his back aroused the man.
He scrambled to his feet and turned to scan
The butte that sloped above him. Where the glow
Still washed the middle height, he saw Talbeau
Serenely perched upon a ledge of clay!
And Mike forgot the words he meant to say,
The fitted words, regretful of his deed.
A forthright, stark sincerity of need
Rough hewed the husky, incoherent prayer
He shouted to that Lord of water there
Above the gloom. A little drop to drink
For old time's sake!

                              Talbeau regarded Fink
Awhile in silence; then his thin lips curled.
"You spilled the only drink in all the world!
Go on," he said, "and think of what you've done!"
Beyond the pointed muzzle of his gun
He saw the big man wither to a squat
And tremble, like a bison when the shot
Just nips the vital circle.   Then he saw
A stooping figure hurry down the draw,
Grow dim, and vanish in the failing light.

'Twas long before Talbeau could sleep that night.
Some questioner, insistently perverse,
Assailed him and compelled him to rehearse
The justifying story of the friend
Betrayed and slain.   But when he reached the end,
Still unconvinced the questioner was there
To taunt him with that pleading of despair—
For old time's sake!   Sleep brought him little rest;
For what the will denied, the heart confessed
In mournful dreams.   And when the first faint gray
Aroused him, and he started on his way,
He knew the stubborn questioner had won.
No brooding on the wrong that Mike had done
Could still that cry: "Plase now, fer owld toime's sake,
A little dhrop!"   It made his eyeballs ache
With tears of pity that he couldn't shed.
No other dawn, save that when Bill lay dead
And things began to stare about the hall,
Had found the world so empty.   After all,
What man could know the way another trod?
And who was he, Talbeau, to play at God?

Let one who curbs the wind and brews the rain
Essay the subtler portioning of pain
To souls that err! Talbeau would make amends!
Once more they'd drink together and be friends.
How often they had shared!

                     He struck a trot,
Eyes fixed upon the trail. The sun rose hot;
Noon poured a blinding glare along the draws;
And still the trail led on, without a pause
To show where Mike had rested. Thirst began
To be a burden on the little man;
His progress dwindled to a dragging pace.
But when he tipped the flask, that pleading face
Arose before him, and a prayer denied
Came mourning back to thrust his need aside—
A little drop! How Mike must suffer now!
"I'm not so very thirsty, anyhow,"
He told himself. And almost any bend
Might bring him on a sudden to his friend.
He'd wait and share the water.

                     Every turn
Betrayed a hope. The west began to burn;
Flared red; went ashen; and the stars came out.
Dreams, colored by an unacknowledged doubt,
Perplexed the trail he followed in his sleep;
And dreary hours before the tallest steep
Saw dawn, Talbeau was waiting for the day.

Till noon he read a writing in the clay
That bade him haste; for now from wall to wall
The footmarks wandered, like the crabbéd scrawl

An old man writes.   They told a gloomy tale.
And then the last dim inkling of a trail
Was lost upon a patch of hardened ground!

The red west saw him, like a nervous hound
That noses vainly for the vanished track,
Still plunging into gullies, doubling back,
And pausing now and then to hurl a yell
Among the ululating steeps.   Night fell.
The starlit buttes still heard him panting by,
And summits weird with midnight caught his cry
To answer, mocking.

                          Morning brought despair;
Nor did he get much comfort of his prayer:
"God, let me find him!   Show me where to go!"
Some greater, unregenerate Talbeau
Was God that morning; for the lesser heard
His own bleak answer echoed word for word:
Go on, and think of all the wrong you've done!

His futile wish to hasten sped the sun.
That day, as he recalled it in the dark,
Was like the spinning of a burning arc.
He nodded, and the night was but a swoon;
And morning neighbored strangely with the noon;
And evening was the noon's penumbral haze.

No further ran the reckoning of days.
'Twas evening when at last he stooped to stare
Upon a puzzling trail.   A wounded bear,
It seemed, had dragged its rump across the sands
That floored the gullies now.   But sprawling hands

Had marked the margin! Why was that? No doubt
Mike too had tarried here to puzzle out
What sort of beast had passed. And yet—how queer—
'Twas plain no human feet had trodden here!
A trail of hands! That throbbing in his brain
Confused his feeble efforts to explain;
And hazily he wondered if he slept
And dreamed again. Tenaciously he kept
His eyes upon the trail and labored on,
Lest, swooping like a hawk, another dawn
Should snatch that hope away.

                    A sentry crow,
Upon a sunlit summit, saw Talbeau
And croaked alarm. The noise of many wings,
In startled flight, and raucous chatterings
Arose. What feast was interrupted there
A little way ahead? 'Twould be the bear!
He plodded on. The intervening space
Sagged under him; and, halting at the place
Where late the flock had been, he strove to break
A grip of horror. Surely now he'd wake
And see the morning quicken in the skies!

The thing remained!—It hadn't any eyes—
The pilfered sockets bore a pleading stare!

A long, hoarse wail of anguish and despair
Aroused the echoes. Answering, arose
Once more the jeering chorus of the crows.

THE SONG OF HUGH GLASS
(1915)

TO SIGURD, SCARCELY THREE

When you are old enough to know
The joys of kite and boat and bow
And other suchlike splendid things
That boyhood's rounded decade brings,
I shall not give you trope and rhymes;
But, rising to those rousing times,
I shall ply well the craft I know
Of shaping kite and boat and bow,
For you shall teach me once again
The goodly art of being ten.

Meanwhile, as on a rainy day
When 'tis not possible to play,
The while you do your best to grow
I ply the other craft I know
And strive to build for you the mood
Of daring and of fortitude
With fitted word and shapen phrase,
Against those later wonder-days
When first you glimpse the world of men
Beyond the bleaker side of ten.

SONG OF HUGH GLASS

I

GRAYBEARD AND GOLDHAIR

The year was eighteen hundred twenty three.

'TWAS when the guns that blustered at the Ree
Had ceased to brag, and ten score martial clowns
Retreated from the unwhipped river towns,
Amid the scornful laughter of the Sioux.
A withering blast the arid South still blew,
And creeks ran thin beneath the glaring sky;
For 'twas a month ere honking geese would fly
Southward before the Great White Hunter's face:
And many generations of their race,
As bow-flung arrows, now have fallen spent.

It happened then that Major Henry went
With eighty trappers up the dwindling Grand,
Bound through the weird, unfriending barren-land
For where the Big Horn meets the Yellowstone;
And old Hugh Glass went with them.

                      Large of bone,
Deep-chested, that his great heart might have play,
Gray-bearded, gray of eye and crowned with gray
Was Glass. It seemed he never had been young;
And, for the grudging habit of his tongue,

None knew the place or season of his birth.
Slowly he 'woke to anger or to mirth;
Yet none laughed louder when the rare mood fell,
And hate in him was like a still, white hell,
A thing of doom not lightly reconciled.
What memory he kept of wife or child
Was never told; for when his comrades sat
About the evening fire with pipe and chat,
Exchanging talk of home and gentler days,
Old Hugh stared long upon the pictured blaze,
And what he saw went upward in the smoke.

But once, as with an inner lightning stroke,
The veil was rent, and briefly men discerned
What pent-up fires of selfless passion burned
Beneath the still gray smoldering of him.
There was a rakehell lad, called Little Jim,
Jamie or Petit Jacques; for scarce began
The downy beard to mark him for a man.
Blue-eyed was he and femininely fair.
A maiden might have coveted his hair
That trapped the sunlight in its tangled skein:
So, tardily, outflowered the wild blond strain
That gutted Rome grown overfat in sloth.
A Ganymedes haunted by a Goth
Was Jamie. When the restive ghost was laid,
He seemed some fancy-ridden child who played
At manliness among those bearded men.
The sternest heart was drawn to Jamie then.
But his one mood ne'er linked two hours together.
To schedule Jamie's way, as prairie weather,
Was to get fact by wedding doubt and whim;
For very lightly slept that ghost in him.

No cloudy brooding went before his wrath
That, like a thunder-squall, recked not its path,
But raged upon what happened in its way.
Some called him brave who saw him on that day
When Ashley stormed a bluff town of the Ree,
And all save beardless Jamie turned to flee
For shelter from that steep, lead-harrowed slope.
Yet, hardly courage, but blind rage agrope
Inspired the foolish deed.

                  'Twas then old Hugh
Tore off the gray mask, and the heart shone through
For, halting in a dry, flood-guttered draw,
The trappers rallied, looked aloft and saw
That travesty of war against the sky.
Out of a breathless hush, the old man's cry
Leaped shivering, an anguished cry and wild
As of some mother fearing for her child,
And up the steep he went with mighty bounds.
Long afterward the story went the rounds,
How old Glass fought that day.   With gun for club,
Grim as a grizzly fighting for a cub,
He laid about him, cleared the way, and so,
Supported by the firing from below,
Brought Jamie back.   And when the deed was done,
Taking the lad upon his knee: "My Son,
Brave men are not ashamed to fear," said Hugh,
"And I've a mind to make a man of you;
So here's your first acquaintance with the law!"
Whereat he spanked the lad with vigorous paw
And, having done so, limped away to bed;
For, wounded in the hip, the old man bled.

[351]

It was a month before he hobbled out,
And Jamie, like a fond son, hung about
The old man's tent and waited upon him.
And often would the deep gray eyes grow dim
With gazing on the boy; and there would go—
As though Spring-fire should waken out of snow—
A wistful light across that mask of gray.
And once Hugh smiled his enigmatic way,
While poring long on Jamie's face, and said:
"So with their sons are women brought to bed,
Sore wounded!"

                Thus united were the two:
And some would dub the old man 'Mother Hugh';
While those in whom all living waters sank
To some dull inner pool that teemed and stank
With formless evil, into that morass
Gazed, and saw darkly there, as in a glass,
The foul shape of some weakly envied sin.
For each man builds a world and dwells therein;
Nor could these know what mocking ghost of Spring
Stirred Hugh's gray world with dreams of blossoming
That wooed no seed to swell or bird to sing.
So might a dawn-struck digit of the moon
Dream back the rain of some old lunar June
And ache through all its craters to be green.
Little they know what life's one love can mean,
Who shrine it in a bower of peace and bliss:
Pang dwelling in a puckered cicatrice
More truly figures this belated love.
Yet very precious was the hurt thereof,
Grievous to bear, too dear to cast away.
Now Jamie went with Hugh; but who shall say

[352]

If 'twas a warm heart or a wind of whim,
Love, or the rover's teasing itch in him,
Moved Jamie? Howsoe'er, 'twas good to see
Graybeard and Goldhair riding knee to knee,
One age in young adventure. One who saw
Has likened to a February thaw
Hugh's mellow mood those days; and truly so,
For when the tempering Southwest wakes to blow
A phantom April over melting snow,
Deep in the North some new white wrath is brewed.
Out of a dim-trailed inner solitude
The old man summoned many a stirring story,
Lived grimly once, but now shot through with glory
Caught from the wondering eyes of him who heard—
Tales jaggéd with the bleak unstudied word,
Stark saga-stuff. "A fellow that I knew,"
So nameless went the hero that was Hugh—
A mere pelt merchant, as it seemed to him;
Yet trailing epic thunders through the dim,
Whist world of Jamie's awe.

                            And so they went,
One heart, it seemed, and that heart well content
With tale and snatch of song and careless laughter.
Never before, and surely never after,
The gray old man seemed nearer to his youth—
That myth that somehow had to be the truth,
Yet could not be convincing any more.

Now when the days of travel numbered four
And nearer drew the barrens with their need,
On Glass, the hunter, fell the task to feed

Those four score hungers when the game should fail.
For no young eye could trace so dim a trail,
Or line the rifle sights with speed so true.
Nor might the wistful Jamie go with Hugh;
"For," so Hugh chaffed, "my trick of getting game
Might teach young eyes to put old eyes to shame.
An old dog never risks his only bone."
'Wolves prey in packs, the lion hunts alone'
Is somewhat nearer what he should have meant.

And so with merry jest the old man went;
And so they parted at an unseen gate
That even then some gust of moody fate
Clanged to betwixt them; each a tale to spell—
One in the nightmare scrawl of dreams from hell,
One in the blistering trail of days a-crawl,
Venomous footed.   Nor might it ere befall
These two should meet in after days and be
Graybeard and Goldhair riding knee to knee,
Recounting with a bluff, heroic scorn
The haps of either tale.

                                    'Twas early morn
When Hugh went forth, and all day Jamie rode
With Henry's men, while more and more the goad
Of eager youth sore fretted him, and made
The dusty progress of the cavalcade
The journey of a snail flock to the moon;
Until the shadow-weaving afternoon
Turned many fingers nightward—then he fled,
Pricking his horse, nor deigned to turn his head
At any dwindling voice of reprimand;
For somewhere in the breaks along the Grand

Surely Hugh waited with a goodly kill.
Hoofbeats of ghostly steeds on every hill,
Mysterious, muffled hoofs on every bluff!
Spurred echo horses clattering up the rough
Confluent draws! These flying Jamie heard.
The lagging air droned like the drowsy word
Of one who tells weird stories late at night.
Half headlong joy and half delicious fright,
His day-dream's pace outstripped the plunging steed's.

Lean galloper in a wind of splendid deeds,
Like Hugh's, he seemed unto himself, until,
Snorting, a-haunch above a breakneck hill,
The horse stopped short—then Jamie was aware
Of lonesome flatlands fading skyward there
Beneath him, and, zigzag on either hand,
A purple haze denoted how the Grand
Forked wide 'twixt sunset and the polar star.

A-tiptoe in the stirrups, gazing far,
He saw no Hugh nor any moving thing,
Save for a welter of cawing crows, a-wing
About some banquet in the further hush.
One faint star, set above the fading blush
Of sunset, saw the coming night, and grew.
With hand for trumpet, Jamie gave halloo;
And once again. For answer, the horse neighed.
Some vague mistrust now made him half afraid—
Some formless dread that stirred beneath the will
As far as sleep from waking.

                                    Down the hill,
Close-footed in the skitter of the shale,
The spurred horse floundered to the solid vale

[355]

And galloped to the northwest, whinnying.
The outstripped air moaned like a wounded thing;
But Jamie gave the lie unto his dread.
"The old man's camping out to-night," he said,
"Somewhere about the forks, as like as not;
And there'll be hunks of fresh meat steaming hot,
And fighting stories by a dying fire!"

The sunset reared a luminous phantom spire
That, crumbling, sifted ashes down the sky.

Now, pausing, Jamie sent a searching cry
Into the twilit river-skirting brush,
And in the vast denial of the hush
The champing of the snaffled horse seemed loud.

Then, startling as a voice beneath a shroud,
A muffled boom woke somewhere up the stream
And, like vague thunder hearkened in a dream,
Drawled back to silence. Now, with heart a-bound,
Keen for the quarter of the perished sound,
The lad spurred gaily; for he doubted not
His cry had brought Hugh's answering rifle shot.
The laggard air was like a voice that sang,
And Jamie half believed he sniffed the tang
Of woodsmoke and the smell of flesh a-roast;
When presently before him, like a ghost,
Upstanding, huge in twilight, arms flung wide,
A gray form loomed. The wise horse reared and shied,
Snorting his inborn terror of the bear!
And in the whirlwind of a moment there,
Betwixt the brute's hoarse challenge and the charge,
The lad beheld, upon the grassy marge

[356]

Of a small spring that bullberries stooped to scan,
A ragged heap that should have been a man,
A huddled, broken thing—and it was Hugh!

There was no need for any closer view.
As, on the instant of a lightning flash
Ere yet the split gloom closes with a crash,
A landscape stares with every circumstance
Of rock and shrub—just so the fatal chance
Of Hugh's one shot, made futile with surprise,
Was clear to Jamie.   Then before his eyes
The light whirled in a giddy dance of red;
And, doubting not the crumpled thing was dead
That was a friend, with but a skinning knife
He would have striven for the hated life
That triumphed there: but with a shriek of fright
The mad horse bolted through the falling night,
And Jamie, fumbling at his rifle boot,
Heard the brush crash behind him where the brute
Came headlong, close upon the straining flanks.
But when at length low-lying river banks—
White rubble in the gloaming—glimmered near,
A swift thought swept the mind of Jamie clear
Of anger and of anguish for the dead.
Scarce seemed the raging beast a thing to dread,
But some foul-playing braggart to outwit.
Now hurling all his strength upon the bit,
He sank the spurs, and with a groan of pain
The plunging horse, obedient to the rein,
Swerved sharply streamward.   Sliddering in the sand,
The bear shot past.   And suddenly the Grand

Loomed up beneath and rose to meet the pair
That rode a moment upon empty air,
Then smote the water in a shower of spray.
And when again the slowly ebbing day
Came back to them, a-drip from nose to flank,
The steed was scrambling up the further bank,
And Jamie saw across the narrow stream,
Like some vague shape of fury in a dream,
The checked beast ramping at the water's rim.
Doubt struggled with a victor's thrill in him,
As, hand to buckle of the rifle-sheath,
He thought of dampened powder; but beneath
The rawhide flap the gun lay snug and dry.
Then as the horse wheeled and the mark went by—
A patch of shadow dancing upon gray—
He fired. A sluggish thunder trailed away;
The spreading smoke-rack lifted slow, and there,
Floundering in a seethe of foam, the bear
Hugged yielding water for the foe that slew!

Triumphant, Jamie wondered what old Hugh
Would think of such a "trick of getting game"!
"Young eyes" indeed!—And then that memory came,
Like a dull blade thrust back into a wound.
One moment 'twas as though the lad had swooned
Into a dream-adventure, waking there
To sicken at the ghastly land, a-stare
Like some familiar face gone strange at last.
But as the hot tears came, the moment passed.
Song snatches, broken tales—a troop forlorn,
Like merry friends of eld come back to mourn—

O'erwhelmed him there.   And when the black bulk
        churned
The star-flecked stream no longer, Jamie turned,
Recrossed the river and rode back to Hugh.

A burning twist of valley grasses threw
Blear light about the region of the spring.
Then Jamie, torch aloft and shuddering,
Knelt there beside his friend, and moaned: "O Hugh,
If I had been with you—just been with you!
We might be laughing now—and you are dead."

With gentle hand he turned the hoary head
That he might see the good gray face again.
The torch burned out, the dark swooped back, and then
His grief was frozen with an icy plunge
In horror.   'Twas as though a bloody sponge
Had wiped the pictured features from a slate!
So, pillaged by an army drunk with hate,
Home stares upon the homing refugee.
A red gout clung where either brow should be;
The haughty nose lay crushed amid the beard,
Thick with slow ooze, whence like a devil leered
The battered mouth convulsed into a grin.

Nor did the darkness cover, for therein
Some torch, unsnuffed, with blear funereal flare,
Still painted upon black that alien stare
To make the lad more terribly alone.

Then in the gloom there rose a broken moan,
Quick stifled; and it seemed that something stirred
About the body.   Doubting that he heard,

The lad felt, with a panic catch of breath,
Pale vagrants from the legendry of death
Potential in the shadows there. But when
The motion and the moaning came again,
Hope, like a shower at daybreak, cleansed the dark,
And in the lad's heart something like a lark
Sang morning. Bending low, he crooned: "Hugh,
        Hugh,
It's Jamie—don't you know?—I'm here with you."

As one who in a nightmare strives to tell—
Shouting across the gap of some dim hell—
What things assail him; so it seemed Hugh heard,
And flung some unintelligible word
Athwart the muffling distance of his swoon.

Now kindled by the yet unrisen moon,
The East went pale; and like a naked thing
A little wind ran vexed and shivering
Along the dusk, till Jamie shivered too
And worried lest 'twere bitter cold where Hugh
Hung clutching at the bleak, raw edge of life.
So Jamie rose, and with his hunting-knife
Split wood and built a fire. Nor did he fear
The staring face now, for he found it dear
With the warm presence of a friend returned.
The fire made cozy chatter as it burned,
And reared a tent of light in that lone place.
Then Jamie set about to bathe the face
With water from the spring, oft crooning low,
"It's Jamie here beside you—don't you know?"

Yet came no answer save the labored breath
Of one who wrestled mightily with Death
Where watched no referee to call the foul.

The moon now cleared the world's end, and the owl
Gave voice unto the wizardry of light;
While in some dim-lit chancel of the night,
Snouts to the goddess, wolfish corybants
Intoned their wild antiphonary chants—
The oldest, saddest worship in the world.

And Jamie watched until the firelight swirled
Softly about him.   Sound and glimmer merged
To make an eerie void, through which he urged
With frantic spur some whirlwind of a steed
That made the way as glass beneath his speed,
Yet scarce kept pace with something dear that fled
On, ever on—just half a dream ahead:
Until it seemed, by some vague shape dismayed,
He cried aloud for Hugh, and the steed neighed—
A neigh that was a burst of light, not sound.
And Jamie, sprawling on the dewy ground,
Knew that his horse was sniffing at his hair,
While, mumbling through the early morning air,
There came a roll of many hoofs—and then
He saw the swinging troop of Henry's men
A-canter up the valley with the sun.

Of all Hugh's comrades crowding round, not one
But would have given heavy odds on Death;
For, though the graybeard fought with sobbing breath,
No man, it seemed, might break upon the hip
So stern a wrestler with the strangling grip

That made the neck veins like a purple thong
Tangled with knots. Nor might Hugh tarry long
There where the trail forked outward far and dim;
Or so it seemed. And when they lifted him,
His moan went treble like a song of pain,
He was so tortured. Surely it were vain
To hope he might endure the toilsome ride
Across the barrens. Better let him bide
There on the grassy couch beside the spring.
And, furthermore, it seemed a foolish thing
That eighty men should wait the issue there;
For dying is a game of solitaire
And all men play the losing hand alone.

But when at noon he had not ceased to moan,
And fought still like the strong man he had been,
There grew a vague mistrust that he might win,
And all this be a tale for wondering ears.
So Major Henry called for volunteers,
Two men among the eighty who would stay
To wait on Glass and keep the wolves away
Until he did whatever he might do.
All quite agreed 'twas bitter bread for Hugh,
Yet none, save Jamie, felt in duty bound
To run the risk—until the hat went round,
And pity wakened, at the silver's clink,
In Jules Le Bon.

                              'He would not have them think
That mercenary motives prompted him.
But somehow just the grief of Little Jim
Was quite sufficient—not to mention Hugh.
He weighed the risk. As everybody knew,

The Rickarees were scattered to the West:
The late campaign had stirred a hornet's nest
To fill the land with stingers (which was so),
And yet—'
           Three days a southwest wind may blow
False April with no drop of dew at heart.
So Jules ran on, while, ready for the start,
The pawing horses nickered and the men,
Impatient in their saddles, yawned. And then,
With brief advice, a round of bluff good-byes
And some few reassuring backward cries,
The troop rode up the valley with the day.

Intent upon his friend, with naught to say,
Sat Jamie; while Le Bon discussed at length
The reasonable limits of man's strength—
A self-conducted dialectic strife
That made absurd all argument for life
And granted but a fresh-dug hole for Hugh.
'Twas half like murder. Yet it seemed Jules knew
Unnumbered tales accordant with the case,
Each circumstantial as to time and place
And furnished with a death's head colophon.

Vivaciously despondent, Jules ran on.
'Did he not share his judgment with the rest?
You see, 'twas some contusion of the chest
That did the trick—heart, lungs and all that, mixed
In such a way they never could be fixed.
A bear's hug—ugh!'

                And often Jamie winced
At some knife-thrust of reason that convinced

Yet left him sick with unrelinquished hope.
As one who in a darkened room might grope
For some belovéd face, with shuddering
Anticipation of a clammy thing;
So in the lad's heart sorrow fumbled round
For some old joy to lean upon, and found
The stark, cold something Jamie knew was there.
Yet, womanlike, he stroked the hoary hair
Or bathed the face; while Jules found tales to tell—
Lugubriously garrulous.

                                        Night fell.
At sundown, day-long winds are like to veer;
So, summoning a mood of relished fear,
Le Bon remembered dire alarms by night—
The swoop of savage hordes, the desperate fight
Of men outnumbered: and, like him of old,
In all that made Jules shudder as he told,
His the great part—a man by field and flood
Fate-tossed.   Upon the gloom he limned in blood
Their situation's possibilities:
Two men against the fury of the Rees—
A game in which two hundred men had failed!
He pointed out how little it availed
To run the risk for one as good as dead;
Yet, Jules Le Bon meant every word he said,
And had a scalp to lose, if need should be.

That night through Jamie's dreaming swarmed the Ree.
Gray-souled, he wakened to a dawn of gray,
And felt that something strong had gone away,
Nor knew what thing.   Some whisper of the will
Bade him rejoice that Hugh was living still;

But Hugh, the real, seemed somehow otherwhere.
Jules, snug and snoring in his blanket there,
Was half a life the nearer.   Just so, pain
Is nearer than the peace we seek in vain,
And by its very sting compels belief.
Jules woke, and with a fine restraint of grief
Saw early dissolution.   'One more night,
And then the poor old man would lose the fight—
Ah, such a man!'

A day and night crept by,
And yet the stubborn fighter would not die,
But grappled with the angel.   All the while,
With some conviction, but with more of guile,
Jules colonized the vacancy with Rees;
Till Jamie felt that looseness of the knees
That comes of oozing courage.   Many men
May tower for a white-hot moment, when
The wild blood surges at a sudden shock;
But when, insistent as a ticking clock,
Blind peril haunts and whispers, fewer dare.
Dread hovered in the hushed and moony air
The long night through; nor might a fire be lit,
Lest some far-seeing foe take note of it.
And day-long Jamie scanned the blank sky rim
For hoof-flung dust clouds; till there woke in him
A childish anger—dumb for ruth and shame—
That Hugh so dallied.
But the fourth dawn came
And with it lulled the fight, as on a field
Where broken armies sleep but will not yield.
Or had one conquered?   Was it Hugh or Death?
The old man breathed with faintly fluttering breath,

Nor did his body shudder as before.
Jules triumphed sadly. 'It would soon be o'er;
So men grew quiet when they lost their grip
And did not care. At sundown he would slip
Into the deeper silence.'
                                        Jamie wept,
Unwitting how a furtive gladness crept
Into his heart that gained a stronger beat.
So cities, long beleaguered, take defeat—
Unto themselves half traitors.
                                        Jules began
To dig a hole that might conceal a man;
And, as his sheath knife broke the stubborn sod,
He spoke in kindly vein of Life and God
And Mutability and Rectitude.
The immemorial funerary mood
Brought tears, mute tribute to the mother-dust;
And Jamie, seeing, felt each cutting thrust
Less like a stab into the flesh of Hugh.
The sun crept up and down the arc of blue
And through the air a chill of evening ran;
But, though the grave yawned, waiting for the man,
The man seemed scarce yet ready for the grave.

Now prompted by a coward or a knave
That lurked in him, Le Bon began to hear
Faint sounds that to the lad's less cunning ear
Were silence; more like tremors of the ground
They were, Jules said, than any proper sound—
Thus one detected horsemen miles away.
For many moments big with fate, he lay,
Ear pressed to earth; then rose and shook his head
As one perplexed. "There's something wrong," he said.

And—as at daybreak whiten winter skies,
Agape and staring with a wild surmise—
The lad's face whitened at the other's word.
Jules could not quite interpret what he heard;
A hundred horse might noise their whereabouts
In just that fashion; yet he had his doubts.
It could be bison moving, quite as well.
But if 'twere Rees—there'd be a tale to tell
That two men he might name would never hear.
He reckoned scalps that Fall were selling dear,
In keeping with the limited supply.
Men, fit to live, were not afraid to die!

Then, in that caution suits not courage ill,
Jules saddled up and cantered to the hill,
A white dam set against the twilight stream;
And as a horseman riding in a dream
The lad beheld him; watched him clamber up
To where the dusk, as from a brimming cup,
Ran over; saw him pause against the gloom,
Portentous, huge—a brooder upon doom.
What did he look upon?

                        Some moments passed;
Then suddenly it seemed as though a blast
Of wind, keen-cutting with the whips of sleet,
Smote horse and rider. Haunched on huddled feet,
The steed shrank from the ridge, then, rearing, wheeled
And took the rubbly incline fury-heeled.

Those days and nights, like seasons creeping slow,
Had told on Jamie. Better blow on blow

Of evil hap, with doom seen clear ahead,
Than that monotonous, abrasive dread,
Blind gnawer at the soul-thews of the blind.
Thin-worn, the last heart-string that held him kind;
Strung taut, the final tie that kept him true
Now snapped in Jamie, as he saw the two
So goaded by some terrifying sight.
Death riding with the vanguard of the Night,
Life dwindling yonder with the rear of Day!
What choice for one whom panic swept away
From moorings in the sanity of will?

Jules came and summed the vision of the hill
In one hoarse cry that left no word to say:
"Rees!   Saddle up!   We've got to get away!"

Small wit had Jamie left to ferret guile,
But fumblingly obeyed Le Bon; the while
Jules knelt beside the man who could not flee:
For big hearts lack not time for charity
However thick the blows of fate may fall.
Yet, in that Jules Le Bon was practical,
He could not quite ignore a hunting knife,
A flint, a gun, a blanket—gear of life
Scarce suited to the customs of the dead!

And Hugh slept soundly in his ample bed,
Star-canopied and blanketed with night,
Unwitting how Venality and Fright
Made hot the westward trail of Henry's men.

II

THE AWAKENING

No one may say what time elapsed, or when
The slumbrous shadow lifted over Hugh:
But some globose immensity of blue
Enfolded him at last, within whose light
He seemed to float, as some faint swimmer might,
A deep beneath and overhead a deep.
So one late plunged into the lethal sleep,
A spirit diver fighting for his breath,
Swoops through the many-fathomed glooms of death,
Emerging in a daylight strange and new.

Rousing a languid wonder, came on Hugh
The quiet, steep-arched splendor of the day.
Agrope for some dim memory, he lay
Upon his back, and watched a lucent fleece
Fade in the blue profundity of peace
As did the memory he sought in vain.
Then with a stirring of mysterious pain,
Old habit of the body bade him rise;
But when he would obey, the hollow skies
Broke as a bubble punctured, and went out.

Again he woke, and with a drowsy doubt,
Remote unto his horizontal gaze
He saw the world's end kindle to a blaze

And up the smoky steep pale heralds run.
And when at length he knew it for the sun,
Dawn found the darkling reaches of his mind,
Where in the twilight he began to find
Strewn shards and torsos of familiar things.
As from the rubble in a place of kings
Men school the dream to build the past anew,
So out of dream and fragment builded Hugh,
And came upon the reason of his plight:
The bear's attack—the shot—and then the night
Wherein men talked as ghosts above a grave.

Some consciousness of will the memory gave:
He would get up.   The painful effort spent
Made the wide heavens billow as a tent
Wind-struck, the shaken prairie sag and roll.
Some moments with an effort at control
He swayed, half raised upon his arms, until
The dizzy cosmos righted, and was still.

Then would he stand erect and be again
The man he was: an overwhelming pain
Smote him to earth, and one unruly limb
Refused the weight and crumpled under him.

Sickened with torture he lay huddled there,
Gazing about him with a great despair
Proportioned to the might that felt the chain.
Far-flung as dawn, collusive sky and plain
Stared bleak denial back.

                              Why strive at all?—
That vacancy about him like a wall,

Yielding as light, a granite scarp to climb!
Some little waiting on the creep of time,
Abandonment to circumstance; and then—

Here flashed a sudden thought of Henry's men
Into his mind and drove the gloom away.
They would be riding westward with the day!
How strange he had forgot!   That battered leg
Or some scalp wound, had set his wits a-beg!
Was this Hugh Glass to whimper like a squaw?
Grimly amused, he raised his head and saw—
The empty distance: listened long and heard—
Naught but the twitter of a lonely bird
That emphasized the hush.

                              Was something wrong?
'Twas not the Major's way to dally long,
And surely they had camped not far behind.
Now woke a query in his troubled mind—
Where was his horse?   Again came creeping back
The circumstances of the bear's attack.
He had dismounted, thinking at the spring
To spend the night—and then the grisly thing—
Of course the horse had bolted; plain enough!
But why was all the soil about so rough
As though a herd of horses had been there?
The riddle vexed him till his vacant stare
Fell on a heap of earth beside a pit.
What did that mean?   He wormed his way to it,
The newly wakened wonder dulling pain.
No paw of beast had scooped it—that was plain.
'Twas squared; indeed, 'twas like a grave, he thought.
A grave—a grave—the mental echo wrought

Sick fancies! Who had risen from the dead?
Who, lying there, had heard above his head
The ghostly talkers deaf unto his shout?

Now searching all the region round about,
As though the answer were a lurking thing,
He saw along the margin of the spring
An ash-heap and the litter of a camp.
Suspicion, like a little smoky lamp
That daubs the murk but cannot fathom it,
Flung blear grotesques before his groping wit.
Had Rees been there? And he alive? Who then?
And were he dead, it might be Henry's men!
How many suns had risen while he slept?
The smoky glow flared wildly, and he crept,
The dragged limb throbbing, till at length he found
The trail of many horses westward bound;
And in one breath the groping light became
A gloom-devouring ecstasy of flame,
A dazing conflagration of belief!

Plunged deeper than the seats of hate and grief,
He gazed about for aught that might deny
Such baseness; saw the non-committal sky,
The prairie apathetic in a shroud,
The bland complacence of a vagrant cloud—
World-wide connivance! Smilingly the sun
Approved a land wherein such deeds were done;
And careless breezes, like a troop of youth,
Unawed before the presence of such truth,
Went scampering amid the tousled brush.
Then by and by came on him with a rush

His weakness and the consciousness of pain,
While, with the chill insistence of a rain
That pelts the sodden wreck of Summer's end,
His manifest betrayal by a friend
Beat in upon him. Jamie had been there;
And Jamie—Jamie—Jamie did not care!

What no man yet had witnessed the wide sky
Looked down and saw; a light wind idling by
Heard what no ear of mortal yet had heard:
For he—whose name was like a magic word
To conjure the remote heroic mood
Of valiant deed and splendid fortitude,
Wherever two that shared a fire might be,—
Gave way to grief and wept unmanfully.
Yet not as they for whom tears fall like dew
To green a frosted heart again, wept Hugh.
So thewed to strive, so engined to prevail
And make harsh fate the zany of a tale,
His own might shook and tore him.

                                    For a span
He lay, a gray old ruin of a man
With all his years upon him like a snow.
And then at length, as from the long ago,
Remote beyond the other side of wrong,
The old love came like some remembered song
Whereof the strain is sweet, the burden sad.
A retrospective vision of the lad
Grew up in him, as in a foggy night
The witchery of semilunar light
Mysteriously quickens all the air.
Some memory of wind-blown golden hair,

[373]

The boyish laugh, the merry eyes of blue,
Wrought marvelously in the heart of Hugh,
As under snow the dæmon of the Spring.
And momently it seemed a little thing
To suffer; nor might treachery recall
The miracle of being loved at all,
The privilege of loving to the end.
And thereupon a longing for his friend
Made life once more a struggle for a prize—
To look again upon the merry eyes,
To see again the wind-blown golden hair.
Aye, one should lavish very tender care
Upon the vessel of a hope so great,
Lest it be shattered, and the precious freight,
As water on the arid waste, poured out.
Yet, though he longed to live, a subtle doubt
Still turned on him the weapon of his pain:
Now, as before, collusive sky and plain
Outstared his purpose for a puny thing.

Praying to live, he crawled back to the spring,
With something in his heart like gratitude
That by good luck his gun might furnish food,
His blanket, shelter, and his flint, a fire.

For, after all, what thing do men desire
To be or have, but these condition it?
These with a purpose and a little wit,
And howsoever smitten, one might rise,
Push back the curtain of the curving skies,
And come upon the living dream at last.
Exhausted, by the spring he lay and cast

Dull eyes about him. What did it portend?
Naught but the footprints of a fickle friend,
A yawning grave and ashes met his eyes!
Scarce feeling yet the shock of a surprise,
He searched about him for his flint and knife;
Knew vaguely that his seeking was for life,
And that the place was empty where he sought.
No food, no fire, no shelter! Dully wrought
The bleak negation in him, slowly crept
To where, despite the pain, his love had kept
A shrine for Jamie undefiled of doubt.
Then suddenly conviction, like a shout,
Aroused him. Jamie—Jamie was a thief!
The very difficulty of belief
Was fuel for the simmering of rage,
That grew and grew, the more he strove to gage
The underlying motive of the deed.
Untempered youth might fail a friend in need;
But here had wrought some devil of the will,
Some heartless thing, too cowardly to kill,
That left to Nature what it dared not do!

So bellowsed, all the kindled soul of Hugh
Became a still white hell of brooding ire,
And through his veins regenerating fire
Ran, driving out the lethargy of pain.
Now once again he scanned the yellow plain,
Conspirant with the overbending skies;
And lo, the one was blue as Jamie's eyes,
The other of the color of his hair—
Twin hues of falseness merging to a stare,

As though such guilt, thus visibly immense,
Regarded its effect with insolence!

Alas for those who fondly place above
The act of loving, what they chance to love;
Who prize the goal more dearly than the way!
For time shall plunder them, and change betray,
And life shall find them vulnerable still.

A bitter-sweet narcotic to the will,
Hugh's love increased the peril of his plight;
But anger broke the slumber of his might,
Quickened the heart and warmed the blood that ran
Defiance for the treachery of Man,
Defiance for the meaning of his pain,
Defiance for the distance of the plain
That seemed to gloat, 'You can not master me.'
And for one burning moment he felt free
To rise and conquer in a wind of rage.
But as a tiger, conscious of the cage,
A-smoulder with a purpose, broods and waits,
So with the sullen patience that is hate's
Hugh taught his wrath to bide expedience.

Now cognizant of every quickened sense,
Thirst came upon him. Leaning to the spring,
He stared with fascination on a thing
That rose from giddy deeps to share the draught—
A face, it was, so tortured that it laughed,
A ghastly mask that Murder well might wear;
And while as one they drank together there,
It was as though the deed he meant to do
Took shape and came to kiss the lips of Hugh,

Lest that revenge might falter.   Hunger woke;
And from the bush with leafage gray as smoke,
Wherein like flame the bullberries glinted red
(Scarce sweeter than the heart of him they fed),
Hugh feasted.

                              And the hours of waiting crept,
A-gloom, a-glow; and though he waked or slept,
The pondered purpose or a dream that wrought,
By night, the murder of his waking thought,
Sustained him till he felt his strength returned.
And then at length the longed-for morning burned
And beckoned down the vast way he should crawl—
That waste to be surmounted as a wall,
Sky-rims and yet more sky-rims steep to climb—
That simulacrum of enduring Time—
The hundred empty miles 'twixt him and where
The big Missouri ran!

                              Yet why not dare?
Despite the useless leg, he could not die
One hairsbreadth farther from the earth and sky,
Or more remote from kindness.

III

THE CRAWL

STRAIGHT away
Beneath the flare of dawn, the Ree land lay,
And through it ran the short trail to the goal.
Thereon a grim turnpikeman waited toll:
But 'twas so doomed that southering geese should flee
Nine times, ere yet the vengeance of the Ree
Should make their foe the haunter of a tale.

Midway to safety on the northern trail
The scoriac region of a hell burned black
Forbade the crawler. And for all his lack,
Hugh had no heart to journey with the suns:
No suppliant unto those faithless ones
Should bid for pity at the Big Horn's mouth.

The greater odds for safety in the South
Allured him; so he felt the midday sun
Blaze down the coulee of a little run
That dwindled upward to the watershed
Whereon the feeders of the river head—
Scarce more than deep-carved runes of vernal rain.
The trailing leg was like a galling chain,
And bound him to a doubt that would not pass.
Defiant clumps of thirst-embittered grass

[378]

That bit parched earth with bared and fang-like roots;
Dwarf thickets, jealous for their stunted fruits,
Harsh-tempered by their disinheritance—
These symbolized the enmity of Chance
For him who, with his fate unreconciled,
Equipped for travel as a weanling child,
Essayed the journey of a mighty man.

Like agitated oil the heat-waves ran
And made the scabrous gulch appear to shake
As some reflected landscape in a lake
Where laggard breezes move. A taunting reek
Rose from the grudging seepage of the creek,
Whereof Hugh drank and drank, and still would drink.
And where the mottled shadow dripped as ink
From scanty thickets on the yellow glare,
The crawler faltered with no heart to dare
Again the torture of that toil, until
The master-thought of vengeance 'woke the will
To goad him forth. And when the sun quiesced
Amid ironic heavens in the West—
The region of false friends—Hugh gained a rise
Whence to the fading cincture of the skies
A purpling panorama swept away.
Scarce farther than a shout might carry, lay
The place of his betrayal. He could see
The yellow blotch of earth where treachery
Had digged his grave. O futile wrath and toil!
Tucked in beneath yon coverlet of soil,
Turned back for him, how soundly had he slept!
Fool, fool! to struggle when he might have crept

So short a space, yet farther than the flight
Of swiftest dreaming through the longest night,
Into the quiet house of no false friend.

Alas for those who seek a journey's end—
They have it ever with them like a ghost:
Nor shall they find, who deem they seek it most,
But crave the end of human ends—as Hugh.

Now swoopingly the world of dream broke through
The figured wall of sense. It seemed he ran
As wind above the creeping ways of man,
And came upon the place of his desire,
Where burned, far-luring as a beacon-fire,
The face of Jamie. But the vengeful stroke
Bit air. The darkness lifted like a smoke—
And it was early morning.

                              Gazing far,
From where the West yet kept a pallid star
To thinner sky where dawn was wearing through,
Hugh shrank with dread, reluctant to renew
The war with that serene antagonist.
More fearsome than a smashing iron fist
Seemed that vast negativity of might;
Until the frustrate vision of the night
Came moonwise on the gloom of his despair.
And lo, the foe was naught but yielding air,
A vacancy to fill with his intent!
So from his spacious bed he 'rose and went
Three-footed; and the vision goaded him.
All morning southward to the bare sky rim

The rugged coulee zigzagged, mounting slow;
And ever as it 'rose, the lean creek's flow
Dwindled and dwindled steadily, until
At last a scooped-out basin would not fill;
And henceforth 'twas a way of mocking dust.
But, in that Hugh still kept the driving lust
For vengeance, this new circumstance of fate
Served but to brew more venom for his hate,
And nerved him to avail the most with least.

Ere noon the crawler chanced upon a feast
Of bread-root sunning in a favored draw.
A sentry gopher from his stronghold saw
Some three-legged beast, bear-like, yet not a bear,
With quite misguided fury digging where
No hapless brother gopher might be found.
And while, with stripéd nose above his mound,
The sentinel chirped shrilly to his clan
Scare-tales of that anomaly, the man
Devoured the chance-flung manna of the plains
That some vague reminiscence of old rains
Kept succulent, despite the burning drouth.

So with new vigor Hugh assailed the South,
His pockets laden with the precious roots
Against that coming traverse, where no fruits
Of herb or vine or shrub might brave the land
Spread rooflike 'twixt the Moreau and the Grand.

The coulee deepened; yellow walls flung high,
Sheer to the ragged strip of blinding sky,
Dazzled and sweltered in the glare of day.

Capricious draughts that woke and died away
Into the heavy drowse, were breatht as flame.
And midway down the afternoon, Hugh came
Upon a little patch of spongy ground.
His thirst became a rage.   He gazed around,
Seeking a spring; but all about was dry
As strewn bones bleaching to a desert sky;
Nor did a clawed hole, bought with needed strength,
Return a grateful ooze.   And when at length
Hugh sucked the mud, he spat it in disgust.
It had the acrid tang of broken trust,
The sweetish, tepid taste of feigning love!

Still hopeful of a spring somewhere above,
He crawled the faster for his taunted thirst.
More damp spots, no less grudging than the first,
Occurred with growing frequence on the way,
Until amid the purple wane of day
The crawler came upon a little pool!
Clear as a friend's heart, 'twas, and seeming cool—
A crystal bowl whence skyey deeps looked up.
So might a god set down his drinking cup
Charged with a distillation of haut skies.
As famished horses, thrusting to the eyes
Parched muzzles, take a long-sought water-hole,
Hugh plunged his head into the brimming bowl
As though to share the joy with every sense.
And lo, the tang of that wide insolence
Of sky and plain was acrid in the draught!
How ripplingly the lying water laughed!
How like fine sentiment the mirrored sky
Won credence for a sink of alkali!

So with false friends.   And yet, as may accrue
From specious love some profit of the true,
One gift of kindness had the tainted sink.
Stripped of his clothes, Hugh let his body drink
At every thirsting pore.   Through trunk and limb
The elemental blessing solaced him;
Nor did he rise till, vague with stellar light,
The lone gulch, buttressing an arch of night,
Was like a temple to the Holy Ghost.
As priests in slow procession with the Host,
A gusty breeze intoned—now low, now loud,
And now, as to the murmur of a crowd,
Yielding the dim-torched wonder of the nave.
Aloft along the dusky architrave
The wander-tale of drifting stars evolved;
And Hugh lay gazing till the whole resolved
Into a haze.

It seemed that Little Jim
Had come to share a merry fire with him,
And there had been no trouble 'twixt the two.
And Jamie listened eagerly while Hugh
Essayed a tangled tale of bears and men,
Bread-root and stars.   But ever now and then
The shifting smoke-cloud dimmed the golden hair,
The leal blue eyes; until with sudden flare
The flame effaced them utterly—and lo,
The gulch bank-full with morning!

Loath to go,
Hugh lay beside the pool and pondered fate.
He saw his age-long pilgrimage of hate

Stretch out—a fool's trail; and it made him cringe;
For still amid the nightly vision's fringe
His dull wit strayed, companioned with regret.
But when the sun, a tilted cauldron set
Upon the gulch rim, poured a blaze of day,
He rose and bathed again, and went his way,
Sustaining wrath returning with the toil.

At noon the gulch walls, hewn in lighter soil,
Fell back; and coulees dense with shrub and vine
Climbed zigzag to the sharp horizon line,
Whence one might choose the pilotage of crows.
He labored upward through the noonday doze
Of breathless shade, where plums were turning red
In tangled bowers, and grapevines overhead
Purpled with fruit to taunt the crawler's thirst.
With little effort Hugh attained the first;
The latter bargained sharply ere they sold
Their luscious clusters for the hoarded gold
Of strength that had so very much to buy.
Now, having feasted, it was sweet to lie
Beneath a sun-proof canopy; and sleep
Came swiftly.

              Hugh awakened to some deep
Star-snuffing well of night.   Awhile he lay
And wondered what had happened to the day
And where he was and what were best to do.
But when, fog-like, the drowse dispersed, he knew
How from the rim above the plain stretched far
To where the evening and the morning are,
And that 'twere better he should crawl by night,
Sleep out the glare.   With groping hands for sight,

Skyward along the broken steep he crawled,
And saw at length, immense and purple-walled—
Or sensed—the dusky mystery of plain.
Gazing aloft, he found the capsized Wain
In mid-plunge down the polar steep. Thereto
He set his back; and far ahead there grew,
As some pale blossom from a darkling root,
The star-blanched summit of a lonely butte,
And thitherward he dragged his heavy limb.

It seemed naught moved. Time hovered over him,
An instant of incipient endeavor.
'Twas ever thus, and should be thus forever—
This groping for the same armful of space,
An insubstantial essence of one place,
Extentless on a weird frontier of sleep.
Sheer deep upon unfathomable deep
The flood of dusk bore down without a sound,
As ocean on the spirits of the drowned
Awakened headlong leagues beneath the light.

So lapsed the drowsy æon of the night—
A strangely tensile moment in a trance.
And then, as quickened to somnambulance,
The heavens, imperceptibly in motion,
Were altered as the upward deeps of ocean
Diluted with a seepage of the moon.
The butte-top, late a gossamer balloon
In mid-air tethered hovering, grew down
And rooted in a blear expanse of brown,
That, lifting slowly with the ebb of night,
Took on the harsh solidity of light—

And day was on the prairie like a flame.
Scarce had he munched the hoarded roots, when came
A vertigo of slumber. Snatchy dreams
Of sick pools, inaccessible cool streams,
Lured on through giddy vacancies of heat
In swooping flights; now hills of roasting meat
Made savory the oven of the world,
Yet kept remote peripheries and whirled
About a burning center that was Hugh.
Then all were gone, save one, and it turned blue
And was a heap of cool and luscious fruit,
Until at length he knew it for the butte
Now mantled with a weaving of the gloam.

It was the hour when cattle straggle home.
Across the clearing in a hush of sleep
They saunter, lowing; loiter belly-deep
Amid the lush grass by the meadow stream.
How like the sound of water in a dream
The intermittent tinkle of yon bell.
A windlass creaks contentment from a well,
And cool deeps gurgle as the bucket sinks.
Now blowing at the trough the plow-team drinks;
The shaken harness rattles. Sleepy quails
Call far. The warm milk hisses in the pails
There in the dusky barn-lot. Crickets cry.
The meadow twinkles with the glowing fly.
One hears the horses munching at their oats.
The green grows black. A veil of slumber floats
Across the haunts of home-enamored men.

Some freak of memory brought back again
The boyhood world of sight and scent and sound:
It perished, and the prairie ringed him round,

Blank as the face of fate.   In listless mood
Hugh set his face against the solitude
And met the night.   The new moon, low and far,
A frail cup tilted, nor the high-swung star,
It seemed, might glint on any stream or spring
Or touch with silver any toothsome thing.
The kiote voiced the universal lack.
As from a nether fire, the plain gave back
The swelter of the noon-glare to the gloom.
In the hot hush Hugh heard his temples boom.
Thirst tortured.   Motion was a languid pain.
Why seek some further nowhere on the plain?
Here might the kiotes feast as well as there.
So spoke some loose-lipped spirit of despair;
And still Hugh moved, volitionless—a weight
Submissive to that now unconscious hate,
As darkling water to the hidden moon.

Now when the night wore on in middle swoon,
The crawler, roused from stupor, was aware
Of some strange alteration in the air.
To breathe became an act of conscious will.
The starry waste was ominously still.
The far-off kiote's yelp came sharp and clear
As through a tunnel in the atmosphere—
A ponderable, resonating mass.
The limp leg dragging on the sun-dried grass
Produced a sound unnaturally loud.

Crouched, panting, Hugh looked up but saw no cloud.
An oily film seemed spread upon the sky
Now dully staring as the open eye

[387]

Of one in fever.   Gasping, choked with thirst,
A childish rage assailed Hugh, and he cursed:
'Twas like a broken spirit's outcry, tossed
Upon hell's burlesque sabbath for the lost,
And briefly space seemed crowded with the voice.

To wait and die, to move and die—what choice?
Hugh chose not, yet he crawled; though more and more
He felt the futile strife was nearly o'er.
And as he went, a muffled rumbling grew,
More felt than heard; for long it puzzled Hugh.
Somehow 'twas coextensive with his thirst,
Yet boundless; swollen blood-veins ere they burst
Might give such warning, so he thought.   And still
The drone seemed heaping up a phonic hill
That towered in a listening profound.
Then suddenly a mountain peak of sound
Came toppling to a heaven-jolting fall!
The prairie shuddered, and a raucous drawl
Ran far and perished in the outer deep.

As one too roughly shaken out of sleep,
Hugh stared bewildered.   Still the face of night
Remained the same, save where upon his right
The moon had vanished 'neath the prairie rim.
Then suddenly the meaning came to him.
He turned and saw athwart the northwest sky,
Like some black eyelid shutting on an eye,
A coming night to which the night was day!
Star-hungry, ranged in regular array,
The lifting mass assailed the Dragon's lair,
Submerged the region of the hounded Bear,

Out-topped the tall Ox-Driver and the Pole.
And all the while there came a low-toned roll,
Less sound in air than tremor in the earth,
From where, like flame upon a windy hearth,
Deep in the further murk sheet-lightning flared.
And still the southern arc of heaven stared,
A half-shut eye, near blind with fever rheum;
And still the plain lay tranquil as a tomb
Wherein the dead reck not a menaced world.

What turmoil now? Lo, ragged columns hurled
Pell-mell up stellar slopes! Swift blue fires leap
Above the wild assailants of the steep!
Along the solid rear a dull boom runs!
So light horse squadrons charge beneath the guns.
Now once again the night is deathly still.
What ghastly peace upon the zenith hill,
No longer starry? Not a sound is heard.
So poised the hush, it seems a whispered word
Might loose all noises in an avalanche.
Only the black mass moves, and far glooms blanch
With fitful flashes. The capricious flare
Reveals the butte-top tall and lonely there
Like some gray prophet contemplating doom.

But hark! What spirits whisper in the gloom?
What sibilation of conspiracies
Ruffles the hush—or murmuring of trees,
Ghosts of the ancient forest—or old rain,
In some hallucination of the plain,
A frustrate phantom mourning? All around,
That e'er evolving, ne'er resolving sound

[389]

Gropes in the stifling hollow of the night.
Then—once—twice—thrice—a blade of blinding light
Ripped up the heavens, and the deluge came—
A burst of wind and water, noise and flame
That hurled the watcher flat upon the ground.
A moment past Hugh famished; now, half drowned,
He gasped for breath amid the hurtling drench.

So might a testy god, long sought to quench
A puny thirst, pour wassail, hurling after
The crashing bowl with wild sardonic laughter
To see man wrestle with his answered prayer!

Prone to the roaring flaw and ceaseless flare,
The man drank deeply with the drinking grass;
Until it seemed the storm would never pass
But ravin down the painted murk for aye.
When had what dreamer seen a glaring day
And leagues of prairie pantingly aquiver?
Flame, flood, wind, noise and darkness were a river
Tearing a cosmic channel to no sea.

The tortured night wore on; then suddenly
Peace fell. Remotely the retreating Wrath
Trailed dull, reluctant thunders in its path,
And up along a broken stair of cloud
The dawn came creeping whitely. Like a shroud
Gray vapors clung along the sodden plain.
Up rose the sun to wipe the final stain
Of fury from the sky and drink the mist.
Against a flawless arch of amethyst
The butte soared, like a soul serene and white
Because of the katharsis of the night.

All day Hugh fought with sleep and struggled on
Southeastward; for the heavy heat was gone
Despite the naked sun. The blank Northwest
Breathed coolly; and the crawler thought it best
To move while yet each little break and hollow
And shallow basin of the bison-wallow
Begrudged the earth and air its dwindling store.
But now that thirst was conquered, more and more
He felt the gnaw of hunger like a rage.
And once, from dozing in a clump of sage,
A lone jackrabbit bounded. As a flame
Hope flared in Hugh, until the memory came
Of him who robbed a sleeping friend and fled.
Then hate and hunger merged; the man saw red,
And momently the hare and Little Jim
Were one blurred mark for murder unto him—
Elusive, taunting, sweet to clutch and tear.
The rabbit paused to scan the crippled bear
That ground its teeth as though it chewed a root.
But when, in witless rage, Hugh drew his boot
And hurled it with a curse, the hare loped off,
Its critic ears turned back, as though to scoff
At silly brutes that threw their legs away.

Night like a shadow on enduring day
Swooped by. The dream of crawling and the act
Were phases of one everlasting fact:
Hugh woke, and he was doing what he dreamed.
The butte, outstripped at eventide, now seemed
Intent to follow. Ever now and then
The crawler paused to calculate again

What dear-bought yawn of distance dwarfed the hill.
Close in the rear it soared, a Titan still,
Whose hand-in-pocket saunter kept the pace.

Distinct along the southern rim of space
A sharp ridge lay, the crest of the divide.
What rest and plenty on the other side!
Through what lush valleys ran what crystal brooks!
And there in virgin meadows wayside nooks
With leaf and purple cluster dulled the light!

All day it seemed that distant Pisgah Height
Retreated, and the tall butte dogged the rear.
At eve a stripéd gopher chirping near
Gave Hugh an inspiration.   Now, at least,
No thieving friend should rob him of a feast.
His great idea stirred him as a shout.
Off came a boot, a sock was ravelled out.
The coarse yarn, fashioned to a running snare,
He placed about the gopher's hole with care,
And then withdrew to hold the yarn and wait.
The night-bound moments, ponderous with fate,
Crept slowly by.   The battered gray face leered
In expectation.   Down the grizzled beard
Ran slaver from anticipating jaws.
Evolving twilight hovered to a pause.
The light wind fell.   Again and yet again
The man devoured his fancied prey: and then
Within the noose a timid snout was thrust.
His hand unsteadied with the hunger lust,
Hugh jerked the yarn.   It broke.

                    Down swooped the night,
A shadow of despair. Bleak height on height,
It seemed, a sheer abyss enclosed him round.
Clutching a strand of yarn, he heard the sound
Of some infernal turmoil under him.
Grimly he strove to reach the ragged rim
That snared a star, until the skyey space
Was darkened with a roof of Jamie's face,
And then the yarn was broken, and he fell.
A-tumble like a stricken bat, his yell
Woke hordes of laughers down the giddy yawn
Of that black pit—and suddenly 'twas dawn.

Dream-dawn, dream-noon, dream-twilight! Yet, possest
By one stern dream more clamorous than the rest,
Hugh headed for a gap that notched the hills,
Wherethrough a luring murmur of cool rills,
A haunting smell of verdure seemed to creep.
By fits the wild adventure of his sleep
Became the cause of all his waking care,
And he complained unto the empty air
How Jamie broke the yarn.

                    The sun and breeze
Had drunk all shallow basins to the lees,
But now and then some gully, choked with mud,
Retained a turbid relict of the flood.
Dream-dawn, dream-noon, dream-night! And still ob-
        sessed
By that one dream more clamorous than the rest,
Hugh struggled for the crest of the divide.
And when at length he saw the other side,

'Twas but a rumpled waste of yellow hills!
The deep-sunk, wiser self had known the rills
And nooks to be the facture of a whim;
Yet had the pleasant lie befriended him,
And now the brutal fact had come to stare.

Succumbing to a langorous despair,
He mourned his fate with childish uncontrol
And nursed that deadly adder of the soul,
Self-pity. Let the crows swoop down and feed,
Aye, batten on a thing that died of need,
A poor old wretch betrayed of God and Man!
So peevishly his broken musing ran,
Till, glutted with the luxury of woe,
He turned to see the butte, that he might know
How little all his striving could avail
Against ill-luck. And lo, a finger-nail,
At arm-length held, could blot it out of space!
A goading purpose and a creeping pace
Had dwarfed the Titan in a haze of blue!
And suddenly new power came to Hugh
With gazing on his masterpiece of will.
So fare the wise on Pisgah.

                                        Down the hill,
Unto the higher vision consecrate,
Now sallied forth the new triumvirate—
A Weariness, a Hunger and a Glory—
Against tyrannic Chance. As in a story
Some higher Hugh observed the baser part.
So sits the artist throned above his art,
Nor recks the travail so the end be fair.
It seemed the wrinkled hills pressed in to stare,

The arch of heaven was an eye a-gaze.
And as Hugh went, he fashioned many a phrase
For use when, by some friendly ember-light,
His tale of things endured should speed the night
And all this gloom grow golden in the sharing.
So wrought the old evangel of high daring,
The duty and the beauty of endeavor,
The privilege of going on forever,
A victor in the moment.
                  Ah, but when
The night slipped by and morning came again,
The sky and hill were only sky and hill
And crawling but an agony of will.
So once again the old triumvirate,
A buzzard Hunger and a viper Hate
Together with the baser part of Hugh,
Went visionless.
              That day the wild geese flew,
Vague in a gray profundity of sky;
And on into the night their muffled cry
Haunted the moonlight like a far farewell.
It made Hugh homesick, though he could not tell
For what he yearned; and in his fitful sleeping
The cry became the sound of Jamie weeping,
Immeasurably distant.

                        Morning broke,
Blear, chilly, through a fog that drove as smoke
Before the booming Northwest.   Sweet and sad
Came creeping back old visions of the lad—
Some trick of speech, some merry little lilt,
The brooding blue of eyes too clear for guilt,

The wind-blown golden hair. Hate slept that day,
And half of Hugh was half a life away,
A wandering spirit wistful of the past;
And half went drifting with the autumn blast
That mourned among the melancholy hills;
For something of the lethargy that kills
Came creeping close upon the ebb of hate.
Only the raw wind, like the lash of Fate,
Could have availed to move him any more.
At last the buzzard beak no longer tore
His vitals, and he ceased to think of food.
The fighter slumbered, and a maudlin mood
Foretold the dissolution of the man.
He sobbed, and down his beard the big tears ran.
And now the scene is changed; the bleak wind's cry
Becomes a flight of bullets snarling by
From where on yonder summit skulk the Rees.
Against the sky, in silhouette, he sees
The headstrong Jamie in the leaden rain.
And now serenely beautiful and slain
The dear lad lies within a gusty tent.

Thus vexed with doleful whims the crawler went
Adrift before the wind, nor saw the trail;
Till close on night he knew a rugged vale
Had closed about him; and a hush was there,
Though still a moaning in the upper air
Told how the gray-winged gale blew out the day.
Beneath a clump of brush he swooned away
Into an icy void; and waking numb,
It seemed the still white dawn of death had come
On this, some cradle-valley of the soul.
He saw a dim, enchanted hollow roll

Beneath him, and the brush thereof was fleece;
And, like the body of the perfect peace
That thralled the whole, abode the break of day.
It seemed no wind had ever come that way,
Nor sound dwelt there, nor echo found the place.
And Hugh lay lapped in wonderment a space,
Vexed with a snarl whereof the ends were lost,
Till, shivering, he wondered if a frost
Had fallen with the dying of the blast.
So, vaguely troubled, listlessly he cast
A gaze about him.   Lo, above his head
The gray-green curtain of his chilly bed
Was broidered thick with plums!   Or so it seemed,
For he was half persuaded that he dreamed;
And with a steady stare he strove to keep
That treasure for the other side of sleep.

Returning hunger bade him rise.   In vain
He struggled with a fine-spun mesh of pain
That trammelled him, until a yellow stream
Of day flowed down the white vale of a dream
And left it disenchanted in the glare.
Then, warmed and soothed, Hugh rose and feasted there,
And thought once more of reaching the Moreau.

To southward with a painful pace and slow
He went stiff-jointed; and a gnawing ache
In that hip-wound he had for Jamie's sake
Oft made him groan—nor wrought a tender mood.
The rankling weapon of ingratitude
Was turned again with every puckering twinge.
Far down the vale a narrow winding fringe

Of wilted green betokened how a spring
There sent a little rill meandering;
And Hugh was greatly heartened, for he knew
What fruits and herbs might flourish in the slough,
And thirst, henceforth, should torture not again.

So day on day, despite the crawler's pain,
All in the windless, golden autumn weather,
These two, as comrades, struggled south together—
The homeless graybeard and the homing rill:
And one was sullen with the lust to kill,
And one went crooning of the moon-wooed vast.
For each the many-fathomed peace at last,
But O the boon of singing on the way!
So came these in the golden fall of day
Unto a sudden turn in the ravine,
Wherefrom Hugh saw a flat of cluttered green
Beneath the further bluffs of the Moreau.

With sinking heart he paused and gazed below
Upon the goal of so much toil and pain.
Yon green had seemed a paradise to gain
The while he thirsted where the lonely butte
Looked far and saw no toothsome herb or fruit
In all that yellow barren dim with heat.
But now the wasting body cried for meat,
And sickness was upon him. Game would pass,
Nor deign to fear the mighty hunter Glass,
But curiously sniffing, pause to stare.

Now while thus musing, Hugh became aware
Of some low murmur, phasic and profound,
Scarce risen o'er the border line of sound.

It might have been the coursing of his blood,
Or thunder heard remotely, or a flood
Flung down a wooded valley far away.
Yet that had been no weather-breeding day;
'Twould frost that night; amid the thirsty land
All streams ran thin; and when he pressed a hand
On either ear, the world seemed very still.

The deep-worn channel of the little rill
Here fell away to eastward, rising, rough
With old rain-furrows, to a lofty bluff
That faced the river with a yellow wall.
Thereto, perplexed, Hugh set about to crawl,
Nor reached the summit till the sun was low.
Far-spread, shade-dimpled in the level glow,
The still land told not whence the murmur grew;
But where the green strip melted into blue
Far down the winding valley of the stream,
Hugh saw what seemed the tempest of a dream
At mimic havoc in the timber-glooms.
As from the sweeping of gigantic brooms,
A dust cloud deepened down the dwindling river;
Upon the distant tree-tops ran a shiver
And huddled thickets writhed as in a gale.

On creeps the windless tempest up the vale,
The while the murmur deepens to a roar,
As with the wider yawning of a door.
And now the agitated green gloom gapes
To belch a flood of countless dusky shapes
That mill and wrangle in a turbid flow—
Migrating myriads of the buffalo

Bound for the winter pastures of the Platte!
Exhausted, faint with need of meat, Hugh sat
And watched the mounting of the living flood.
Down came the night, and like a blot of blood
The lopped moon weltered in the dust-bleared East.
Sleep came and gave a Barmecidal feast.
About a merry flame were simmering
Sweet haunches of the calving of the Spring,
And tender tongues that never tasted snow,
And marrow bones that yielded to a blow
Such treasure! Hugh awoke with gnashing teeth,
And heard the mooing drone of cows beneath,
The roll of hoofs, the challenge of the bull.
So sounds a freshet when the banks are full
And bursting brush-jams bellow to the croon
Of water through green leaves. The ragged moon
Now drenched the valley in an eerie rain:
Below, the semblance of a hurricane;
Above, the perfect calm of brooding frost,
Through which the wolves in doleful tenson tossed
From hill to hill the ancient hunger-song.
In broken sleep Hugh rolled the chill night long,
Half conscious of the flowing flesh below.
And now he trailed a bison in the snow
That deepened till he could not lift his feet.
Again, he battled for a chunk of meat
With some gray beast that fought with icy fang.
And when he woke, the wolves no longer sang;
White dawn athwart a white world smote the hill,
And thunder rolled along the valley still.

Morn, wiping up the frost as with a sponge,
Day on the steep and down the nightward plunge,

And Twilight saw the myriads moving on.
Dust to the westward where the van had gone,
And dust and muffled thunder in the east!
Hugh starved while gazing on a Titan feast.
The tons of beef, that eddied there and swirled,
Had stilled the crying hungers of the world,
Yet not one little morsel was for him.

The red sun, pausing on the dusty rim,
Induced a panic aspect of his plight:
The herd would pass and vanish in the night
And be another dream to cling and flout.
Now scanning all the summit round about,
Amid the rubble of the ancient drift
He saw a bowlder. 'Twas too big to lift,
Yet he might roll it. Painfully and slow
He worked it to the edge, then let it go
And breathlessly expectant watched it fall.
It hurtled down the leaning yellow wall,
And bounding from a brushy ledge's brow,
It barely grazed the buttocks of a cow
And made a moment's eddy where it struck.

In peevish wrath Hugh cursed his evil luck,
And seizing rubble, gave his fury vent
By pelting bison till his strength was spent:
So might a child assail the crowding sea!
Then, sick at heart and musing bitterly,
He shambled down the steep way to the creek,
And having stayed the tearing buzzard beak
With breadroot and the waters of the rill,
Slept till the white of morning o'er the hill

[401]

Was like a whisper groping in a hush.
The stream's low trill seemed loud. The tumbled brush
And rumpled tree-tops in the flat below,
Upon a fog that clung like spectral snow,
Lay motionless; nor any sound was there.
No frost had fallen, but the crystal air
Smacked of the autumn, and a heavy dew
Lay hoar upon the grass. There came on Hugh
A picture, vivid in the moment's thrill,
Of marshaled corn-shocks marching up a hill
And spiked fields dotted with the pumpkin's gold.
It vanished; and, a-shiver with the cold,
He brooded on the mockeries of Chance,
The shrewd malignity of Circumstance
That either gave too little or too much.

Yet, with the fragment of a hope for crutch,
His spirit rallied, and he rose to go,
Though each stiff joint resisted as a foe
And that old hip-wound battled with his will.
So down along the channel of the rill
Unto the vale below he fought his way.
The frore fog, rifting in the risen day,
Revealed the havoc of the living flood—
The river shallows beaten into mud,
The slender saplings shattered in the crush,
All lower leafage stripped, the tousled brush
Despoiled of fruitage, winter-thin, aghast.
And where the avalanche of hoofs had passed
It seemed nor herb nor grass had ever been.
And this the hard-won paradise, wherein
A food-devouring plethora of food
Had come to make a starving solitude!

Yet hope and courage mounted with the sun.
Surely, Hugh thought, some ill-begotten one
Of all that striving mass had lost the strife
And perished in the headlong stream of life—
A feast to fill the bellies of the strong,
That still the weak might perish. All day long
He struggled down the stricken vale, nor saw
What thing he sought. But when the twilight awe
Was creeping in, beyond a bend arose
A din as though the kiotes and the crows
Fought there with shrill and raucous battle cries.

Small need had Hugh to ponder and surmise
What guerdon beak and fang contended for.
Within himself the oldest cause of war
Brought forth upon the instant fang and beak.
He too would fight! Nor had he far to seek
Amid the driftwood strewn about the sand
For weapons suited to a brawny hand
With such a purpose. Armed with club and stone
He forged ahead into the battle zone,
And from a screening thicket spied his foes.

He saw a bison carcass black with crows,
And over it a welter of black wings,
And round about, a press of tawny rings
That, like a muddy current churned to foam
Upon a snag, flashed whitely in the gloam
With naked teeth; while close about the prize
Red beaks and muzzles bloody to the eyes
Betrayed how worth a struggle was the feast.
Then came on Hugh the fury of the beast—

To eat or to be eaten! Better so
To die contending with a living foe,
Than fight the yielding distance and the lack.
Masked by the brush he opened the attack,
And ever where a stone or club fell true,
About the stricken one an uproar grew
And brute tore brute, forgetful of the prey,
Until the whole pack tumbled in the fray
With bleeding flanks and lacerated throats.
Then, as the leader of a host who notes
The cannon-wrought confusion of the foe,
Hugh seized the moment for a daring blow.

The wolf's a coward, that, in good packs,
May counterfeit the courage that he lacks
And with a craven's fury crush the bold.
But when the disunited mass that rolled
In suicidal strife, became aware
How some great beast that shambled like a bear
Bore down with roaring challenge, fell a hush
Upon the pack, some slinking to the brush
With tails a-droop; while some that whined in pain
Writhed off on reddened trails. With bristled mane
Before the flying stones a bolder few
Snarled menace at the foe as they withdrew
To fill the outer dusk with clamorings.
Aloft upon a moaning wind of wings
The crows with harsh, vituperative cries
Now saw a gray wolf of prodigious size
Devouring with the frenzy of the starved.
Thus fell to Hugh a bison killed and carved;

And so Fate's whims mysteriously trend—
Woe in the silken meshes of the friend,
Weal in the might and menace of the foe.

But with the fading of the afterglow
The routed wolves found courage to return.
Amid the brush Hugh saw their eye-balls burn;
And well he knew how futile stick and stone
Would prove by night to keep them from their own.
Better is less with safety, than enough
With ruin. He retreated to a bluff,
And scarce had reached it when the pack swooped in
Upon the carcass.

                All night long, the din
Of wrangling wolves assailed the starry air,
While high above them in a brushy lair
Hugh dreamed of gnawing at the bloody feast.

Along about the blanching of the east,
When sleep is weirdest and a moment's flight,
Remembered coextensive with the night,
May teem with hapful years; as light in smoke,
Upon the jumble of Hugh's dreaming broke
A buzz of human voices. Once again
He rode the westward trail with Henry's men—
Hoof-smitten leagues consuming in a dust.
And now the nightmare of that broken trust
Was on him, and he lay beside the spring,
A corpse, yet heard the muffled parleying
Above him of the looters of the dead.
But when he might have riddled what they said,

The babble flattened to a blur of gray—
And lo, upon a bleak frontier of day,
The spent moon staring down!   A little space
Hugh scrutinized the featureless white face,
As though 'twould speak.   But when again the sound
Grew up, and seemed to come from under ground,
He cast the drowse, and peering down the slope,
Beheld what set at grapple fear and hope—
Three Indian horsemen riding at a jog!
Their ponies, wading belly-deep in fog,
That clung along the valley, seemed to swim,
And through a thinner vapor moving dim,
The men were ghost-like.

                   Could they be the Sioux?
Almost the wish became belief in Hugh.
Or were they Rees?   As readily the doubt
Withheld him from the hazard of a shout.
And while he followed them with baffled gaze,
Grown large and vague, dissolving in the haze,
They vanished westward.

                 Knowing well the wont
Of Indians moving on the bison-hunt,
Forthwith Hugh guessed the early riders were
The outflung feelers of a tribe a-stir
Like some huge cat gone mousing.   So he lay
Concealed, impatient with the sleepy day
That dawdled in the dawning.   Would it bring
Good luck or ill?   His eager questioning,
As crawling fog, took on a golden hue
From sunrise.   He was waiting for the Sioux,
Their parfleche panniers fat with sun-dried maize
And wasna!   From the mint of evil days

He would coin tales and be no begging guest
About the tribal feast-fires burning west,
But kinsman of the blood of daring men.
And when the crawler stood erect again—
O Friend-Betrayer at the Big Horn's mouth,
Beware of someone riding from the South
To do the deed that he had lived to do!

Now when the sun stood hour-high in the blue,
From where a cloud of startled blackbirds rose
Down stream, a panic tumult broke the doze
Of windless morning. What unwelcome news
Embroiled the conference of feathered shrews?
A boiling cloud against the sun they lower,
Flackering strepent; now a sooty shower,
Big-flaked, squall-driven westward, down they flutter
To set a clump of cottonwoods a-sputter
With cold black fire! And once again, some shock
Of sight or sound flings panic in the flock—
Gray boughs exploding in a ruck of birds!

What augury in orniscopic words
Did yon swart sibyls on the morning scrawl?

Now broke abruptly through the clacking brawl
A camp-dog's barking and a pony's neigh;
Whereat a running nicker fled away,
Attenuating to a rearward hush.
And lo! in hailing distance 'round the brush
That fringed a jutting bluff's base like a beard
Upon a stubborn chin out-thrust, appeared
A band of mounted warriors! In their van
Aloof and lonely rode a gnarled old man

Upon a piebald stallion.   Stooped was he
Beneath his heavy years, yet haughtily
He wore them like the purple of a king.
Keen for a goal, as from the driving string
A barbed and feathered arrow truly sped,
His face was like a flinty arrow-head,
And brooded westward in a steady stare.
There was a sift of winter in his hair,
The bleakness of brown winter in his look.

Hugh saw, and huddled closer in his nook.
Fled the bright dreams of safety, feast and rest
Before that keen, cold brooder on the West,
As gaudy leaves before the blizzard flee.
'Twas Elk Tongue, fighting chieftain of the Ree,
With all his people at his pony's tail—
Full two-score lodges emptied on the trail
Of hunger!

             On they came in ravelled rank,
And many a haggard eye and hollow flank
Made plain how close and pitilessly pressed
The enemy that drove them to the West—
Such foeman as no warrior ever slew.
A tale of cornfields plundered by the Sioux
Their sagging panniers told.   Yet rich enough
They seemed to him who watched them from the bluff;
Yea, pampered nigh the limit of desire!
No friend had filched from them the boon of fire
And hurled them shivering back upon the beast.
Erect they went, full-armed to strive, at least;
And nightly in a cozy ember-glow
Hope fed them with a dream of buffalo

Soon to be overtaken.   After that,
Home with their Pawnee cousins on the Platte,
Much meat and merry-making till the Spring.

On dragged the rabble like a fraying string
Too tautly drawn.   The rich-in-ponies rode,
For much is light and little is a load
Among all heathen with no Christ to save!
Gray seekers for the yet begrudging grave,
Bent with the hoeing of forgotten maize,
Wood-hewers, water-bearers all their days,
Toiled 'neath the life-long hoarding of their packs.
And nursing squaws, their babies at their backs
Whining because the milk they got was thinned
In dugs of famine, strove as with a wind.
Invincibly equipped with their first bows
The striplings strutted, knowing, as youth knows,
How fair life is beyond the beckoning blue.
Cold-eyed the grandsires plodded, for they knew,
As frosted heads may know, how all trails merge
In what lone land.   Raw maidens on the verge
Of some half-guessed-at mystery of life,
In wistful emulation of the wife
Stooped to the fancied burden of the race;
Nor read upon the withered grandam's face
The scrawled tale of that burden and its woe.
Slant to the sagging poles of the travaux,
Numb to the squaw's harsh railing and the goad,
The lean cayuses toiled.   And children rode
A-top the household plunder, wonder-eyed
To see a world flow by on either side,

From blue air sprung to vanish in blue air,
A river of enchantments.

                              Here and there
The camp-curs loped upon a vexing quest
Where countless hoofs had left a palimpsest,
A taunting snarl of broken scents. And now
They sniff the clean bones of the bison cow,
Howl to the skies; and now with manes a-rough
They nose the man-smell leading to the bluff;
Pause puzzled at the base and sweep the height
With questioning yelps. Aloft, crouched low in fright,
Already Hugh can hear the braves' guffaws
At their scorned foeman yielded to the squaws'
Inverted mercy and a slow-won grave.
Since Earth's first mother scolded from a cave
And that dear riddle of her love began,
No man has wrought a weapon against man
To match the deadly venom brewed above
The lean, blue, blinding heart-fires of her love.
Well might the hunted hunter shrink aghast!
But thrice three seasons yet should swell the past,
So was it writ, ere Fate's keen harriers
Should run Hugh Glass to earth.

                              The hungry curs
Took up again the tangled scent of food.
Still flowed the rabble through the solitude—
A thinning stream now of the halt, the weak
And all who had not very far to seek
For that weird pass whereto the fleet are slow,
And out of it keen winds and numbing blow,

Shrill with the fleeing voices of the dead.
Slowly the scattered stragglers, making head
Against their weariness as up a steep,
Fled westward; and the morning lay asleep
Upon the valley fallen wondrous still.

Hugh kept his nook, nor ventured forth, until
The high day toppled to the blue descent,
When thirst became a master, and he went
With painful scrambling down the broken scarp,
Lured by the stream, that like a smitten harp
Rippled a muted music to the sun.

Scarce had he crossed the open flat, and won
The half-way fringe of willows, when he saw,
Slow plodding up the trail, a tottering squaw
Whose years made big the little pack she bore.
Crouched in the brush, Hugh watched her. More and more
The little burden tempted him. Why not?
A thin cry throttled in that lonely spot
Could bring no succor. None should ever know,
Save him, the feasted kiote and the crow,
Why one poor crone found not the midnight fire.
Nor would the vanguard, quick with young desire,
Devouring distance westward like a flame,
Regret this ash dropped rearward.

                         On she came,
Slow-footed, staring blankly on the sand—
So close now that it needed but a hand
Out-thrust to overthrow her; aye, to win
That priceless spoil, a little tent of skin,

[411]

A flint and steel, a kettle and a knife!
What did the dying with the means of life,
That thus the fit-to-live should suffer lack?

Poised for the lunge, what whimsy held him back?
Why did he gaze upon the passing prize,
Nor seize it? Did some gust of ghostly cries
Awaken 'round her—whisperings of Eld,
Wraith-voices of the babies she had held,
Guarding the milkless paps, the withered womb?
Far down a moment's cleavage in the gloom
Of backward years Hugh saw her now—nor saw
The little burden and the feeble squaw,
But someone sitting haloed like a saint
Beside a hearth long cold. The dream grew faint;
And when he looked again, the crone was gone
Beyond a clump of willow.

                                              Crawling on,
He reached the river. Leaning to a pool
Calm in its cup of sand, he saw—a fool!
A wild, wry mask of mirth, a-grin, yet grim,
Rose there to claim identity with him
And ridicule his folly. Pity? Faugh!
Who pitied this, that it should spare a squaw
Spent in the spawning of a scorpion brood?

He drank and hastened down the solitude,
Fleeing that thing which fleered him, and was Hugh.
And as he went his self-accusing grew
And with it, anger; till it came to seem
That somehow some sly Jamie of a dream

[412]

Had plundered him again; and he was strong
With lust of vengeance and the sting of wrong,
So that he travelled faster than for days.

Now when the eve in many-shaded grays
Wove the day's shroud, and through the lower lands
Lean fog-arms groped with chilling spirit hands,
Hugh paused perplexed.   Elusive, haunting, dim,
As though some memory that stirred in him,
Invasive of the real, outgrew the dream,
There came upon the breeze that stole up stream
A whiff of woodsmoke.

                'Twixt a beat and beat
Of Hugh's deluded heart, it seemed the sweet
Allure of home.—A brief way, and one came
Upon the clearing where the sumach flame
Ran round the forest-fringe; and just beyond
One saw the slough grass nodding in the pond
Unto the sleepy troll the bullfrogs sung.
And then one saw the place where one was young—
The log-house sitting on a stumpy rise.
Hearth-lit within, its windows were as eyes
That love much and are faded with old tears.
It seemed regretful of a life's arrears,
Yet patient, with a self-denying poise,
Like some old mother for her bearded boys
Waiting sweet-hearted and a little sad.—
So briefly dreamed a recrudescent lad
Beneath gray hairs, and fled.

              Through chill and damp
Still groped the odor, hinting at a camp,

A two-tongued herald wooing hope and fear.
Was hospitality or danger near?
A Sioux war-party hot upon the trail,
Or laggard Rees?   Hugh crawled across the vale,
Toiled up along à zigzag gully's bed
And reached a bluff's top.   In a smudge of red
The West burned low.   Hill summits, yet alight,
And pools of gloom anticipating night
Mottled the landscape to the dull blue rim.
What freak of fancy had imposed on him?
Could one smell home-smoke fifty years away?
He saw no fire; no pluming spire of gray
Rose in the dimming air to woo or warn.

He lay upon the bare height, fagged, forlorn,
And old times came upon him with the creep
Of subtle drugs that put the will to sleep
And wreak doom to the soothing of a dream.
So listlessly he scanned the sombrous stream,
Scarce seeing what he scanned.   The dark increased;
A chill wind wakened from the frowning east
And soughed along the vale.

                     Then with a start
He saw what broke the torpor of his heart
And set the wild blood free.   From where he lay
An easy point-blank rifle-shot away,
Appeared a mystic germinating spark
That in some secret garden of the dark
Upreared a frail, blue, nodding stem, whereon
A ruddy lily flourished—and was gone!

What miracle was this?   Again it grew,
The scarlet blossom on the stem of blue,
And withered back again into the night.

With pounding heart Hugh crawled along the height
And reached a point of vantage whence, below,
He saw capricious witch-lights dim and glow
Like far-spent embers quickened in a breeze.
'Twas surely not a camp of laggard Rees,
Nor yet of Siouan warriors hot in chase.
The dusk and quiet bivouacked in that place.
A doddering vagrant with numb hands, the Wind
Fumbled the dying ashes there, and whined.
It was the day-old camp-ground of the foe!

Glad-hearted now, Hugh gained the vale below,
Keen to possess once more the ancient gift.
Nearing the glow, he saw vague shadows lift
Out of the painted gloom of smouldering logs—
Distorted bulks that bristled, and were dogs
Snarling at this invasion of their lair.
Hugh charged upon them, growling like a bear,
And sent them whining.

                                    Now again to view
The burgeoning of scarlet, gold and blue,
The immemorial miracle of fire!
From heaped-up twigs a tenuous smoky spire
Arose, and made an altar of the place.
The spark-glow, faint upon the grizzled face,
Transformed the kneeling outcast to a priest;
And, native of the light-begetting East,

The Wind became a chanting acolyte.
These two, entempled in the vaulted night,
Breathed conjuries of interwoven breath.
Then, hark!—the snapping of the chains of Death!
From dead wood, lo!—the epiphanic god!

Once more the freightage of the fennel rod
Dissolved the chilling pall of Jovian scorn.
The wonder of the resurrection morn,
The face apocalyptic and the sword,
The glory of the many-symboled Lord,
Hugh, lifting up his eyes about him, saw!
And something in him like a vernal thaw,
Voiced with the sound of many waters, ran
And quickened to the laughter of a man.

Light-heartedly he fed the singing flame
And took its blessing: till a soft sleep came
With dreaming that was like a pleasant tale.

The far white dawn was peering up the vale
When he awoke to indolent content.
A few shorn stars in pale astonishment
Were huddled westward; and the fire was low.
Three scrawny camp-curs, mustered in a row
Beyond the heap of embers, heads askew,
Ears pricked to question what the man might do,
Sat wistfully regardant.   He arose;
And they, grown canny in a school of blows,
Skulked to a safer distance, there to raise
A dolorous chanting of the evil days,
Their gray breath like the body of a prayer.
Hugh nursed the sullen embers to a flare,

Then set about to view an empty camp
As once before; but now no smoky lamp
Of blear suspicion searched a gloom of fraud
Wherein a smirking Friendship, like a bawd,
Embraced a coward Safety; now no grief,
'Twixt hideous revelation and belief,
Made womanish the man; but glad to strive,
With hope to nerve him and a will to drive,
He knew that he could finish in the race.
The staring impassivity of space
No longer mocked; the dreadful skyward climb,
Where distance seemed identical with time,
Was past now; and that mystic something, luck,
Without which worth may flounder in the ruck,
Had turned to him again.

                                        So flamelike soared
Rekindled hope in him as he explored
Among the ash-heaps; and the lean dogs ran
And barked about him, for the love of man
Wistful, yet fearing. Surely he could find
Some trifle in the hurry left behind—
Or haply hidden in the trampled sand—
That to the cunning of a needy hand
Should prove the master-key of circumstance:
For 'tis the little gifts of grudging Chance,
Well husbanded, make victors.

                                        Long he sought
Without avail; and, crawling back, he thought
Of how the dogs were growing less afraid,
And how one might be skinned without a blade.

A flake of flint might do it: he would try.
And then he saw—or did the servile eye
Trick out a mental image like the real?
He saw a glimmering of whetted steel
Beside a heap now washed with morning light!

Scarce more of marvel and the sense of might
Moved Arthur when he reached a hand to take
The fay-wrought brand emerging from the lake,
Whereby a kingdom should be lopped of strife,
Than Hugh now, pouncing on a trader's knife
Worn hollow in the use of bounteous days!

And now behold a rich man by the blaze
Of his own hearth—a lord of steel and fire!
Not having, but the measure of desire
Determines wealth.   Who gaining more, seek most,
Are ever the pursuers of a ghost
And lend their fleetness to the fugitive.
For Hugh, long goaded by the wish to live,
What gage of mastery in fire and tool!—
That twain wherewith Time put the brute to school,
Evolving Man, the maker and the seer.

'Twixt urging hunger and restraining fear
The gaunt dogs hovered round the man; while he
Cajoled them in the language of the Ree
And simulated feeding them with sand,
Until the boldest dared to sniff his hand,
Bare-fanged and with conciliative whine.
Through bristled mane the quick blade bit the spine

[418]

Below the skull; and as a flame-struck thing
The body humped and shuddered, withering;
The lank limbs huddled, wilted.

                                    Now to skin
The carcass, dig a hole, arrange therein
And fix the pelt with stakes, the flesh-side up.
This done, he shaped the bladder to a cup
On willow withes, and filled the rawhide pot
With water from the river—made it hot
With roasted stones, and set the meat a-boil.
Those days of famine and prodigious toil
Had wrought bulimic cravings in the man,
And scarce the cooking of the flesh outran
The eating of it.   As a fed flame towers
According to the fuel it devours,
His hunger with indulgence grew, nor ceased
Until the kettle, empty of the feast,
Went dim, the sky and valley, merging, swirled
In subtle smoke that smothered out the world.
Hugh slept.

                    And then—as divers, mounting, sunder
A murmuring murk to blink in sudden wonder
Upon a dazzling upper deep of blue—
He rose again to consciousness, and knew
The low sun beating slantly on his face.

Now indolently gazing round the place,
He noted how the curs had revelled there—
The bones and entrails gone; some scattered hair
Alone remaining of the pot of hide.
How strange he had not heard them at his side!

And granting but one afternoon had passed,
What could have made the fire burn out so fast?
Had daylight waned, night fallen, morning crept,
Noon blazed, a new day dwindled while he slept?
And was the friendlike fire a Jamie too?
Across the twilit consciousness of Hugh
The old obsession like a wounded bird
Fluttered.

              He got upon his knees and stirred
The feathery ash; but not a spark was there.
Already with the failing sun the air
Went keen, betokening a frosty night.
Hugh winced with something like the clutch of fright.
How could he bear the torture, how sustain
The sting of that antiquity of pain
Rolled back upon him—face again the foe,
That yielding victor, fleet in being slow,
That huge, impersonal malevolence?

So readily the tentacles of sense
Root in the larger standard of desire,
That Hugh fell farther in the loss of fire
Than in the finding of it he arose.
And suddenly the place grew strange, as grows
A friend's house, when the friend is on his bier,
And all that was familiar there and dear
Puts on a blank, inhospitable look.

Hugh set his face against the east, and took
That dreariest of ways, the trail of flight.
He would outcrawl the shadow of the night
And have the day to blanket him in sleep.
But as he went to meet the gloom a-creep,

Bemused with life's irrational rebuffs,
A yelping of the dogs among the bluffs
Rose, hunger-whetted, stabbing; rent the pall
Of evening silence; blunted to a drawl
Amid the arid waterways, and died.
And as the echo to the sound replied,
So in the troubled mind of Hugh was wrought
A reminiscent cry of thought to thought
That, groping, found an unlocked door to life:
The dogs—keen flint to skin one—then the knife
Discovered. Why, that made a flint and steel!
No further with the subtle foe at heel
He fled; for all about him in the rock,
To waken when the needy hand might knock,
A savior slept! He found a flake of flint,
Scraped from his shirt a little wad of lint,
Spilled on it from the smitten stone a shower
Of ruddy seed; and saw the mystic flower
That genders its own summer, bloom anew!

And so capricious luck came back to Hugh;
And he was happier than he had been
Since Jamie to that unforgiven sin
Had yielded, ages back upon the Grand.
Now he would turn the cunning of his hand
To carving crutches, that he might arise,
Be manlike, lift more rapidly the skies
That crouched between his purpose and the mark.
The warm glow housed him from the frosty dark,
And there he wrought in very joyous mood
And sang by fits—whereat the solitude
Set laggard singers snatching at the tune.
The gaunter for their hunt, the dogs came soon

To haunt the shaken fringes of the glow,
And, pitching voices to the timeless woe,
Outwailed the lilting. So the Chorus sings
Of terror, pity and the tears of things
When most the doomed protagonist is gay.
The stars swarmed over, and the front of day
Whitened above a white world, and the sun
Rose on a sleeper with a task well done,
Nor roused him till its burning topped the blue.

When Hugh awoke, there 'woke a younger Hugh,
Now half a stranger; and 'twas good to feel
With ebbing sleep the old green vigor steal,
Thrilling, along his muscles and his veins,
As in a lull of winter-cleansing rains
The gray bough quickens to the sap a-creep.
It chanced the dogs lay near him, sound asleep,
Curled nose to buttock in the noonday glow.
He killed the larger with a well-aimed blow,
Skinned, dressed and set it roasting on a spit;
And when 'twas cooked, ate sparingly of it,
For need might yet make little seem a feast.

Fording the river shallows, south by east
He hobbled now along a withered rill
That issued where old floods had gashed the hill—
A cyclopean portal yawning sheer.
No storm of countless hoofs had entered here:
It seemed a place where nothing ever comes
But change of season. He could hear the plums
Plash in the frosted thicket, over-lush;
While, like a spirit lisping in the hush,

[422]

The crisp leaves whispered round him as they fell.
And ever now and then the autumn spell
Was broken by an ululating cry
From where far back with muzzle to the sky
The lone dog followed, mourning.   Darkness came,
And huddled up beside a cozy flame,
Hugh's sleep was but a momentary flight
Across a little shadow into light.

So day on day he toiled: and when, afloat
Above the sunset like a stygian boat,
The new moon bore the spectre of the old,
He saw—a dwindling strip of blue outrolled—
The valley of the tortuous Cheyenne.
And ere the half moon sailed the night again,
Those far lone leagues had sloughed their garb of blue,
And dwindled, dwindled, dwindled after Hugh,
Until he saw that Titan of the plains,
The sinewy Missouri.   Dearth of rains
Had made the Giant gaunt as he who saw.
This loud Chain-Smasher of a late March thaw
Seemed never to have bellowed at his banks;
And yet, with staring ribs and hollow flanks,
The urge of an indomitable will
Proclaimed him of the breed of giants still;
And where the current ran a boiling track,
'Twas like the muscles of a mighty back
Grown Atlantean in the wrestler's craft.
Hugh set to work and built a little raft
Of driftwood bound with grapevines.   So it fell
A gray old man who had a tale to tell
Came drifting to the gates of Kiowa.

[423]

IV

THE RETURN OF THE GHOST

Not long Hugh let the lust of vengeance gnaw
Upon him idling; though the tale he told
And what report proclaimed him, were as gold
To buy a winter's comfort at the Post.
"I can not rest; for I am but the ghost
Of someone murdered by a friend," he said,
"So long as yonder traitor thinks me dead,
Aye, buried in the bellies of the crows
And kiotes!"
                    Whereupon said one of those
Who heard him, noting how the old man shook
As with a chill: "God fend that one should look
With such a blizzard of a face for me!"
For he went grayer like a poplar tree
That shivers, ruffling to the first faint breath
Of storm, while yet the world is still as death
Save where, far off, the kenneled thunders bay.

So brooding, he grew stronger day by day,
Until at last he laid the crutches by.
And then one evening came a rousing cry
From where the year's last keelboat hove in view
Around the bend, its swarthy, sweating crew
Slant to the shouldered line.
                              Men sang that night
In Kiowa, and by the ruddy light

Of leaping fires amid the wooden walls
The cups went round; and there were merry brawls
Of bearded lads no older for the beard;
And laughing stories vied with tales of weird
By stream and prairie trail and mountain pass,
Until the tipsy Bourgeois bawled for Glass
To 'shame these with a man's tale fit to hear.'

The graybeard, sitting where the light was blear,
With little heart for revelry, began
His story, told as of another man
Who, loving late, loved much and was betrayed.
He spoke unwitting how his passion played
Upon them, how their eyes grew soft or hard
With what he told; yet something of the bard
He seemed, and his the purpose that is art's,
Whereby men make a vintage of their hearts
And with the wine of beauty deaden pain.
Low-toned, insistent as October rain,
His voice beat on; and now and then would flit
Across the melancholy gray of it
A glimmer of cold fire that, like the flare
Of soundless lightning, showed a world made bare,
Green Summer slain and all its leafage stripped.

And bronze jaws tightened, brawny hands were gripped,
As though each hearer had a fickle friend.
But when the old man might have made an end,
Rounding the story to a peaceful close
At Kiowa, songlike his voice arose,
The grinning gray mask lifted and the eyes
Burned as a bard's who sees and prophesies,

Conning the future as a time long gone.
Swaying to rhythm the dizzy tale plunged on
Even to the cutting of the traitor's throat,
And ceased—as though a bloody strangling smote
The voice of that gray chanter, drunk with doom.
And there was shuddering in the blue-smeared gloom
Of fallen fires. It seemed the deed was done
Before their eyes who heard.

                              The morrow's sun,
Low over leagues of frost-enchanted plain,
Saw Glass upon his pilgrimage again,
Northbound as hunter for the keelboat's crew.
And many times the wide autumnal blue
Burned out and darkened to a deep of stars;
And still they toiled among the snags and bars—
Those lean up-stream men, straining at the rope,
Lashed by the doubt and strengthened by the hope
Of backward winter—engines wrought of bone
And muscle, panting for the Yellowstone,
Bend after bend and yet more bends away.
Now was the river like a sandy bay
At ebb-tide, and the far-off cutbank's boom
Mocked them in shallows; now 'twas like a flume
With which the toilers, barely creeping, strove.
And bend by bend the selfsame poplar grove,
Set on the selfsame headland, so it seemed,
Confronted them, as though they merely dreamed
Of passing one drear point.

                              So on and up
Past where the tawny Titan gulps the cup
Of Cheyenne waters, past the Moreau's mouth;
And still wry league and stubborn league fell south,

Becoming haze and weary memory.
Then past the empty lodges of the Ree
That gaped at cornfields plundered by the Sioux;
And there old times came mightily on Hugh,
For much of him was born and buried there.
Some troubled glory of that wind-tossed hair
Was on the trampled corn; the lonely skies,
So haunted with the blue of Jamie's eyes,
Seemed taunting him; and through the frosted wood
Along the flat, where once their tent had stood,
A chill wind sorrowed, and·the blackbirds' brawl
Amid the funeral torches of the Fall
Ran raucously, a desecrating din.

Past where the Cannon Ball and Heart come in
They labored.   Now the Northwest 'woke at last.
The gaunt bluffs bellowed back the trumpet blast
Of charging winds that made the sandbars smoke.
To breathe now was to gulp fine sand, and choke:
The stinging air was sibilant with whips.
Leaning the more and with the firmer grips,
Still northward the embattled toilers pressed
To where the river yawns into the west.
There stood the Mandan village.
                                    Now began
The chaining of the Titan.   Drift-ice ran.
The wingéd hounds of Winter ceased to bay.
The stupor of a doom completed lay
Upon the world.   The biting darkness fell.
Out in the night, resounding as a well,
They heard the deckplanks popping in a vise
Of frost; all night the smithies of the ice

[427]

Reëchoed with the griding jar and clink
Of ghostly hammers welding link to link:
And morning found the world without a sound.
There lay the stubborn Prairie Titan bound,
To wait the far-off Heraclean thaw,
Though still in silent rage he strove to gnaw
The ragged shackles knitting at his breast.

And so the boatman won a winter's rest
Among the Mandan traders: but for Hugh
There yet remained a weary work to do.
Across the naked country west by south
His purpose called him at the Big Horn's mouth—
Three hundred miles of winging for the crow;
But by the river trail that he must go
'Twas seven hundred winding miles at least.

So now he turned his back upon the feast,
Snug ease, the pleasant tale, the merry mood,
And took the bare, foot-sounding solitude
Northwestward. Long they watched him from the Post,
Skied on a bluff-rim, fading like a ghost
At gray cock-crow; and hooded in his breath,
He seemed indeed a fugitive from Death
On whom some tatter of the shroud still clung.
Blank space engulfed him.
                              Now the moon was young
When he set forth; and day by day he strode,
His scarce healed wounds upon him like a load;
And dusk by dusk his fire outflared the moon
That waxed until it wrought a spectral noon
At nightfall. Then he came to where, awhirl
With Spring's wild rage, the snow-born Titan girl,

[428]

A skyey wonder on her virgin face,
Receives the virile Yellowstone's embrace
And bears the lusty Seeker for the Sea.
A bleak, horizon-wide serenity
Clung round the valley where the twain lay dead.
A winding sheet was on the marriage bed.

'Twas warmer now; the sky grew overcast;
And as Hugh strode southwestward, all the vast
Gray void seemed suddenly astir with wings
And multitudinary whisperings—
The muffled sibilance of tumbling snow.
It seemed no more might living waters flow,
Moon gleam, star glint, dawn smoulder through, bird
          sing,
Or ever any fair familiar thing
Be so again.   The outworn winds were furled.
Weird weavers of the twilight of a world
Wrought, thread on kissing thread, the web of doom.
Grown insubstantial in the knitted gloom,
The bluffs loomed eerie, and the scanty trees
Were dwindled to remote dream-traceries
That never might be green or shield a nest.

All day with swinging stride Hugh forged southwest
Along the Yellowstone's smooth-paven stream,
A dream-shape moving in a troubled dream.
And all day long the whispering weavers wove.
And close on dark he came to where a grove
Of cottonwoods rose tall and shadow-thin
Against the northern bluffs.   He camped therein
And with cut boughs made shelter as he might.

[429]

Close pressed the blackness of the snow-choked night
About him, and his fire of plum wood purred.
Athwart a soft penumbral drowse he heard
The tumbling snowflakes sighing all around,
Till sleep transformed it to a Summer sound
Of boyish memory—susurrant bees,
The southwind in the tousled apple trees
And slumber flowing from their leafy gloom.

He wakened to the cottonwoods' deep boom.
Black fury was the world.   The northwest's roar,
As of a surf upon a shipwreck shore,
Plunged high above him from the sheer bluff's verge;
And, like the backward sucking of the surge,
Far fled the sobbing of the wild snow-spray.

Black blindness grew white blindness—and 'twas day.
All being now seemed narrowed to a span
That held a sputtering wood fire and a man;
Beyond was tumult and a whirling maze.
The trees were but a roaring in a haze;
The sheer bluff-wall that took the blizzard's charge
Was thunder flung along the hidden marge
Of chaos, stridden by the ghost of light.
White blindness grew black blindness—and 'twas night
Wherethrough nor moon nor any star might grope.

Two days since, Hugh had killed an antelope
And what remained sufficed the time of storm.
The snow, banked round his shelter, kept him warm
And there was wood to burn for many a day.
The third dawn, oozing through a smudge of gray,

Awoke him.   It was growing colder fast.
Still from the bluff high over boomed the blast,
But now it took the void with numbing wings.
By noon the woven mystery of things
Frayed raggedly, and through a sudden rift
At length Hugh saw the beetling bluff-wall lift
A sturdy shoulder to the flying rack.
Slowly the sense of distances came back
As with the waning day the great wind fell.
The pale sun set upon a frozen hell.
The wolves howled.

        Hugh had left the Mandan town
When, heifer-horned, the maiden moon lies down
Beside the sea of evening.   Now she rose
Scar-faced and staring blankly on the snows
While yet the twilight tarried in the west;
And more and more she came a tardy guest
As Hugh pushed onward through the frozen waste
Until she stole on midnight shadow-faced,
A haggard spectre; then no more appeared.

'Twas on that time the man of hoary beard
Paused in the early twilight, looming lone
Upon a bluff-rim of the Yellowstone,
And peered across the white stream to the south
Where in the flatland at the Big Horn's mouth
The new fort stood that Henry's men had built.
What perfect peace for such a nest of guilt!
What satisfied immunity from woe!
Yon sprawling shadow, pied with candle-glow

And plumed with sparkling wood-smoke, might have
        been
A homestead with the children gathered in
To share its bounty through the holidays.
Hugh saw their faces round the gay hearth-blaze:
The hale old father in a mood for yarns
Or boastful of the plenty of his barns,
Fruitage of honest toil and grateful lands;
And, half a stranger to her folded hands,
The mother with October in her hair
And August in her face. One moment there
Hugh saw it. Then the monstrous brutal fact
Wiped out the dream and goaded him to act,
Though now to act seemed strangely like a dream.

Descending from the bluff, he crossed the stream,
The dry snow fifing to his eager stride.
Reaching the fort stockade, he paused to bide
The passing of a whimsy. Was it true?
Or was this but the fretted wraith of Hugh
Whose flesh had fed the kiotes long ago?

Still through a chink he saw the candle-glow,
So like an eye that brazened out a wrong.
And now there came a flight of muffled song,
The rhythmic thudding of a booted heel
That timed a squeaking fiddle to a reel!
How swiftly men forget! The spawning Earth
Is fat with graves; and what is one man worth
That fiddles should be muted at his fall?
He should have died and did not—that was all.
Well, let the living jig it! He would turn
Back to the night, the spacious unconcern

Of wilderness that never played the friend.
Now came the song and fiddling to an end,
And someone laughed within.   The old man winced,
Listened with bated breath, and was convinced
'Twas Jamie laughing!   Once again he heard.
Joy filled a hush 'twixt heart-beats like a bird;
Then like a famished cat his lurking hate
Pounced crushingly.

             He found the outer gate,
Beat on it with his shoulder, raised a cry.
No doubt 'twas deemed a fitful wind went by;
None stirred.   But when he did not cease to shout,
A door creaked open and a man came out
Amid the spilling candle-glimmer, raised
The wicket in the outer gate and gazed
One moment on a face as white as death,
Because the beard was thick with frosted breath
Illumined by the stars.   Then came a gasp,
The clatter of the falling wicket's hasp,
The crunch of panic feet along the snow;
And someone stammered huskily and low:
"My God! I saw the Old Man's ghost out there!"
'Twas spoken as one speaks who feels his hair
Prickle the scalp.   And then another said—
It seemed like Henry's voice—"The dead are dead:
What talk is this, Le Bon?   You saw him die!
Who's there?"

          Hugh strove to shout, to give the lie
To those within; but could not fetch a sound.
Just so he dreamed of lying under ground
Beside the Grand and hearing overhead
The talk of men.   Or was he really dead,

[433]

And all this but a maggot in the brain?
Then suddenly the clatter of a chain
Aroused him, and he saw the portal yawn
And saw a bright rectangled patch of dawn
As through a grave's mouth—no, 'twas candle-light
Poured through the open doorway on the night;
And those were men before him, bulking black
Against the glow.

              Reality flashed back;
He strode ahead and entered at the door.
A falling fiddle jangled on the floor
And left a deathly silence. On his bench
The fiddler shrank. A row of eyes, a-blench
With terror, ran about the naked hall.
And there was one who huddled by the wall
And hid his face and shivered.

                For a spell
That silence clung; and then the old man: "Well,
Is this the sort of welcome that I get?
'Twas not my time to feed the kiotes yet!
Put on the pot and stew a chunk of meat
And you shall see how much a ghost can eat!
I've journeyed far if what I hear be true!"

Now in that none might doubt the voice of Hugh,
Nor yet the face, however it might seem
A blurred reflection in a flowing stream,
A buzz of wonder broke the trance of dread.
"Good God!" the Major gasped; "We thought you dead!
Two men have testified they saw you die!"
"If they speak truth," Hugh answered, "then I lie

Both here and by the Grand.   If I be right,
Then two lie here and shall lie from this night.
Which are they?''
                    Henry answered: ''Yon is one.''

The old man set the trigger of his gun
And gazed on Jules who cowered by the wall.
Eyes blinked, expectant of the hammer's fall;
Ears strained, anticipative of the roar.
But Hugh walked leisurely across the floor
And kicked the croucher, saying: ''Come, get up
And wag your tail!   I couldn't kill a pup!''
Then turning round: ''I had a faithful friend;
No doubt he too was with me to the end!
Where's Jamie?''
                    ''Started out before the snows
For Atkinson.''

V

JAMIE

THE Country of the Crows,
Through which the Big Horn and the Rosebud run,
Sees over mountain peaks the setting sun;
And southward from the Yellowstone flung wide,
It broadens ever to the morning side
And has the Powder on its vague frontier.
About the subtle changing of the year,
Ere even favored valleys felt the stir
Of Spring, and yet expectancy of her
Was like a pleasant rumor all repeat
Yet none may prove, the sound of horses' feet
Went eastward through the silence of that land.
For then it was there rode a little band
Of trappers out of Henry's Post, to bear
Dispatches down to Atkinson, and there
To furnish out a keelboat for the Horn.
And four went lightly, but the fifth seemed worn
As with a heavy heart; for that was he
Who should have died but did not.

                 Silently
He heard the careless parley of his men,
And thought of how the Spring would come again,
That garish strumpet with her world-old lure,
To waken hope where nothing may endure,

To quicken love where loving is betrayed.
Yet now and then some dream of Jamie made
Slow music in him for a little while;
And they who rode beside him saw a smile
Glimmer upon that ruined face of gray,
As on a winter fog the groping day
Pours glory through a momentary rift.
Yet never did the gloom that bound him lift;
He seemed as one who feeds upon his heart
And finds, despite the bitter and the smart,
A little sweetness and is glad for that.

Now up the Powder, striking for the Platte
Across the bleak divide the horsemen went;
Attained that river where its course is bent
From north to east: and spurring on apace
Along the wintry valley, reached the place
Where from the west flows in the Laramie.
Thence, fearing to encounter with the Ree,
They headed eastward through the barren land
To where, fleet-footed down a track of sand,
The Niobrara races for the morn—
A gaunt-loined runner.

                    Here at length was born
Upon the southern slopes the baby Spring,
A timid, fretful, ill-begotten thing,
A-suckle at the Winter's withered paps:
Not such as when announced by thunder-claps
And ringed with swords of lightning, she would ride,
The haughty victrix and the mystic bride,
Clad splendidly as never Sheba's Queen,
Before her marching multitudes of green

In many-bannered triumph! Grudging, slow,
Amid the fraying fringes of the snow
The bunch-grass sprouted; and the air was chill.
Along the northern slopes 'twas winter still,
And no root dreamed what Triumph-over-Death
Was nurtured now in some bleak Nazareth
Beyond the crest to sunward.

                                    On they spurred
Through vacancies that waited for the bird,
And everywhere the Odic Presence dwelt.
The Southwest blew, the snow began to melt;
And when they reached the valley of the Snake,
The Niobrara's ice began to break,
And all night long and all day long it made
A sound as of a random cannonade
With rifles snarling down a skirmish line.

The geese went over. Every tree and vine
Was dotted thick with leaf-buds when they saw
The little river of Keyapaha
Grown mighty for the moment. Then they came,
One evening when all thickets were aflame
With pale green witch-fires and the windflowers blew,
To where the headlong Niobrara threw
His speed against the swoln Missouri's flank
And hurled him roaring to the further bank—
A giant staggered by a pigmy's sling.
Thence, plunging ever deeper into Spring,
Across the greening prairie east by south
They rode, and, just above the Platte's wide mouth,
Came, weary with the trail, to Atkinson.
There all the vernal wonder-work was done:

No care-free heart might find aught lacking there.
The dove's call wandered in the drowsy air;
A love-dream brooded in the lucent haze.
Priapic revellers, the shrieking jays
Held mystic worship in the secret shade.
Woodpeckers briskly plied their noisy trade
Along the tree-boles, and their scarlet hoods
Flashed flame-like in the smoky cottonwoods.
What lacked?   Not sweetness in the sun-lulled breeze;
The plum bloom, murmurous with bumblebees,
Was drifted deep in every draw and slough.
Not color; witcheries of gold and blue
The dandelion and the violet
Wove in the green.   Might not the sad forget,
The happy here have nothing more to seek?
Lo, yonder by that pleasant little creek,
How one might loll upon the grass and fish
And build the temple of one's wildest wish
'Twixt nibbles!   Surely there was quite enough
Of wizard-timber and of wonder-stuff
To rear it nobly to the blue-domed roof!

Yet there was one whose spirit stood aloof
From all this joyousness—a gray old man,
No nearer now than when the quest began
To what he sought on that long winter trail.

Aye, Jamie had been there; but when the tale
That roving trappers brought from Kiowa
Was told to him, he seemed as one who saw
A ghost, and could but stare on it, they said:
Until one day he mounted horse and fled

Into the North, a devil-ridden man.
"I've got to go and find him if I can,"
Was all he said for days before he left.

And what of Hugh?   So long of love bereft,
So long sustained and driven by his hate,
A touch of ruth now made him desolate.
No longer eager to avenge the wrong,
With not enough of pity to be strong
And just enough of love to choke and sting,
A gray old hulk amid the surge of Spring
He floundered on a lee-shore of the heart.

But when the boat was ready for the start
Up the long watery stairway to the Horn,
Hugh joined the party.   And the year was shorn
Of blooming girlhood as they forged amain
Into the North; the late green-mantled plain
Grew sallow; and the ruthless golden shower
Of Summer wrought in lust upon the flower
That withered in the endless martyrdom
To seed.   The scarlet quickened on the plum
About the Heart's mouth when they came thereto;
Among the Mandans grapes were turning blue,
And they were purple at the Yellowstone.
A frosted scrub-oak, standing out alone
Upon a barren bluff top, gazing far
Above the crossing at the Powder's bar,
Was spattered with the blood of Summer slain.
So it was Autumn in the world again,
And all those months of toil had yielded nought
To Hugh.   (How often is the seeker sought

By what he seeks—a blind, heart-breaking game!)
For always had the answer been the same
From roving trapper and at trading post:
Aye, one who seemed to stare upon a ghost
And followed willy-nilly where it led,
Had gone that way in search of Hugh, they said—
A haggard, blue-eyed, yellow-headed chap.

And often had the old man thought, 'Mayhap
He'll be at Henry's Post and we shall meet;
And to forgive and to forget were sweet;
'Tis for its nurse that Vengeance whets the tooth!
And O the golden time of Jamie's youth,
That it should darken for a graybeard's whim!'
So Hugh had brooded, till there came on him
The pity of a slow rain after drouth.

But at the crossing of the Rosebud's mouth
A shadow fell upon his growing dream.
A band of Henry's traders, bound down stream,
Who paused to traffic in the latest word—
Down-river news for matters seen and heard
In higher waters—had not met the lad,
Not yet encountered anyone who had.

Alas, the journey back to yesterwhiles!
How tangled are the trails! The stubborn miles,
How wearily they stretch! And if one win
The long way back in search for what has been,
Shall he find aught that is not strange and new?
Thus wrought the melancholy news in Hugh,

Now turning back with those who brought the news;
For more and more he dreaded now to lose
What doubtful seeking rendered doubly dear.
And in the time when keen winds stripped the year
He came with those to where the Poplar joins
The greater river.   There Assinoboines,
Rich from the Summer's hunting, had come down
And flung along the flat their ragged town,
That traders might bring goods and winter there.

So leave the heartsick graybeard.   Otherwhere
The final curtain rises on the play.
'Tis dead of Winter now.   For day on day
The blizzard wind has thundered, sweeping wide
From Mississippi to the Great Divide
Out of the North beyond Saskatchewan.
Brief evening glimmers like an inverse dawn
After a long white night.   The tempest dies;
The snow-haze lifts.   Now let the curtain rise
Upon Milk River valley, and reveal
The stars like broken glass on frosted steel
Above the Piegan lodges, huddled deep
In snowdrifts, like a freezing flock of sheep.
A crystal weight the dread cold crushes down
And no one moves about the little town
That seems to grovel as a thing that fears.

But see! a lodge-flap swings; a squaw appears,
Hunched with the sudden cold.   Her footsteps creak
Shrill in the hush.   She stares upon the bleak,
White skyline for a moment, then goes in.
We follow her, push back the flap of skin,

Enter the lodge, inhale the smoke-tanged air
And blink upon the little faggot-flare
That blossoms in the center of the room.
Unsteady shadows haunt the outer gloom
Wherein the walls are guessed at. Upward, far,
The smoke-vent now and then reveals a star
As in a well. The ancient squaw, a-stoop,
Her face light-stricken, stirs a pot of soup
That simmers with a pleasant smell and sound.
A gnarled old man, cross-legged upon the ground,
Sits brooding near. He feeds the flame with sticks;
It brightens. Lo, a leaden crucifix
Upon the wall! These heathen eyes, though dim,
Have seen the white man's God and cling to Him,
Lest on the sunset trail slow feet should err.

But look again. From yonder bed of fur
Beside the wall a white man strives to rise.
He lifts his head, with yearning sightless eyes
Gropes for the light. A mass of golden hair
Falls round the face that sickness and despair
Somehow make old, albeit he is young.
His weak voice, stumbling to the mongrel tongue
Of traders, flings a question to the squaw:
"You saw no Black Robe? Tell me what you saw!"
And she, brief-spoken as her race, replies:
"Heaped snow—sharp stars—a kiote on the rise."

The blind youth huddles moaning in the furs.
The firewood spits and pops, the boiled pot purrs
And sputters. On this little isle of sound
The sea of winter silence presses round—
One feels it like a menace.

Now the crone
Dips out a cup of soup, and having blown
Upon it, takes it to the sick man there
And bids him eat.   With wild, unseeing stare
He turns upon her: "Why are they so long?
I can not eat! I've done a mighty wrong;
It chokes me! O no, no, I must not die
Until the Black Robe comes!"   His feeble cry
Sinks to a whisper.   "Tell me, did they go—
Your kinsmen?"

          "They went south before the snow."
"And will they tell the Black Robe?"

                      "They will tell."

The crackling of the faggots for a spell
Seems very loud.   Again the sick man moans
And, struggling with the weakness in his bones,
Would gain his feet, but can not.   "Go again,
And tell me that you see the bulks of men
Dim in the distance there."

          The squaw obeys;
Returns anon to crouch beside the blaze,
Numb-fingered and a-shudder from the night.
The vacant eyes that hunger for the light
Are turned upon her: "Tell me what you saw!
Or maybe snowshoes sounded up the draw.
Quick, tell me what you saw and heard out there!"
"Heaped snow—sharp stars—big stillness everywhere."

One clutching at thin ice with numbing grip
Cries while he hopes; but when his fingers slip,
He takes the final plunge without a sound.
So sinks the youth now, hopeless.   All around

The winter silence presses in; the walls
Grow vague and vanish in the gloom that crawls
Close to the failing fire.
                              The Piegans sleep.
Night hovers midway down the morning steep.
The sick man drowses.   Nervously he starts
And listens; hears no sound except his heart's
And that weird murmur brooding stillness makes.
But stealthily upon the quiet breaks—
Vague as the coursing of the hearer's blood—
A muffled, rhythmic beating, thud on thud,
That, growing nearer, deepens to a crunch.
So, hungry for the distance, snowshoes munch
The crusted leagues of winter, stride by stride.
A camp-dog barks; the hollow world outside
Brims with the running howl of many curs.

Now wide-awake, half risen in the furs,
The youth can hear low voices and the creak
Of snowshoes near the lodge.   His thin, wild shriek
Startles the old folk from their slumberings:
"He comes!   The Black Robe!"
                                  Now the door-flap swings,
And briefly one who splutters Piegan, bars
The way, then enters.   Now the patch of stars
Is darkened with a greater bulk that bends
Beneath the lintel.   "Peace be with you, friends!
And peace with him herein who suffers pain!"
So speaks the second comer of the twain—
A white man by his voice.   And he who lies
Beside the wall, with empty, groping eyes

Turned to the speaker: "There can be no peace
For me, good Father, till this gnawing cease—
The gnawing of a great wrong I have done."

The big man leans above the youth: "My son—"
(Grown husky with the word, the deep voice breaks,
And for a little spell the whole man shakes
As with the clinging cold) "— have faith and hope!
'Tis often nearest dawn when most we grope.
Does not the Good Book say, Who seek shall find?"

"But, Father, I am broken now and blind,
And I have sought, and I have lost the way."
To which the stranger: "What would Jesus say?
Hark! In the silence of the heart 'tis said—
By their own weakness are the feeble sped;
The humblest feet are surest for the goal;
The blind shall see the City of the Soul.
Lay down your burden at His feet to-night."

Now while the fire, replenished, bathes in light
The young face scrawled with suffering and care,
Flinging ironic glories on the hair
And glinting on dull eyes that once flashed blue,
The sick one tells the story of old Hugh
To him whose face, averted from the glow,
Still lurks in gloom. The winds of battle blow
Once more along the steep. Again one sees
The rescue from the fury of the Rees,
The graybeard's fondness for the gay lad; then
The westward march with Major Henry's men
With all that happened there upon the Grand.
"And so we hit the trail of Henry's band,"

The youth continues; "for we feared to die:
And dread of shame was ready with the lie
We carried to our comrades.   Hugh was dead
And buried there beside the Grand, we said.
Could any doubt that what we said was true?
They even praised our courage!   But I knew!
The nights were hell because I heard his cries
And saw the crows a-pecking at his eyes,
The kiotes tearing at him.   O my God!
I tried and tried to think him under sod;
But every time I slept it was the same.
And then one night—I lay awake—he came!
I say he came—I know I hadn't slept!
Amid a light like rainy dawn, he crept
Out of the dark upon his hands and knees.
The wound he got that day among the Rees
Was like red fire.   A snarl of bloody hair
Hung round the eyes that had a pleading stare,
And down the ruined face and gory beard
Big tear-drops rolled.   He went as he appeared,
Trailing a fog of light that died away.
And I grew old before I saw the day.
O Father, I had paid too much for breath!
The Devil traffics in the fear of death,
And may God pity anyone who buys
What I have bought with treachery and lies—
This rat-like gnawing in my breast!

                                        "I knew
I couldn't rest until I buried Hugh;
And so I told the Major I would go
To Atkinson with letters, ere the snow

Had choked the trails.   Jules wouldn't come along;
He didn't seem to realize the wrong;
He called me foolish, couldn't understand.
I rode alone—not south, but to the Grand.
Daylong my horse beat thunder from the sod,
Accusing me; and all my prayers to God
Seemed flung in vain at bolted gates of brass.
And in the night the wind among the grass
Hissed endlessly the story of my shame.

"I do not know how long I rode: I came
Upon the Grand at last, and found the place,
And it was empty.   Not a sign or trace
Was left to show what end had come to Hugh.
And O that grave!   It gaped upon the blue,
A death-wound pleading dumbly for the slain.
I filled it up and fled across the plain,
And somehow came to Atkinson at last.
And there I heard the living Hugh had passed
Along the river northward in the Fall!
O Father, he had found the strength to crawl
That long, heart-breaking distance back to life,
Though Jules had taken blanket, steel and knife,
And I, his trusted comrade, had his gun!

"They said I'd better stay at Atkinson,
Because old Hugh was surely hunting me,
White-hot to kill.   I did not want to flee
Or hide from him.   I even wished to die,
If so this aching cancer of a lie
Might be torn out forever.   So I went,
As eager as the homesick homeward bent,
In search of him and peace.

                                        But I was cursed.
For even when his stolen rifle burst
And spewed upon me this eternal night,
I might not die as any other might;
But God so willed that friendly Piegans came
To spare me yet a little unto shame.
O Father, is there any hope for me?"

"Great hope indeed, my son!" so huskily
The other answers.   "I recall a case
Like yours—no matter what the time and place—
'Twas somewhat like the story that you tell;
Each seeking and each sought, and both in hell;
But in the tale I mind, they met at last."

The youth sits up, white-faced and breathing fast:
"They met, you say?   What happened?   Quick!   O
        quick!"

"The old man found the dear lad blind and sick
And both forgave—'twas easy to forgive—
For O we have so short a time to live—"
Whereat the youth: "Who's here?   The Black Robe's
        gone!
Whose voice is this?"

                        The gray of winter dawn
Now creeping round the door-flap, lights the place
And shows thin fingers groping for a face
Deep-scarred and hoary with the frost of years
Whereover runs a new springtide of tears.

"O Jamie, Jamie, Jamie—I am Hugh!
There was no Black Robe yonder—Will I do?"